POWER

Ȑevised Edition

VS.

FORCE

Also by Dr. David R. Hawkins

Orthomolecular Psychiatry (with Linus Pauling)

*Qualitative and Quantitative Calibration of the
Levels of Human Consciousness*

The Eye of the I

Please visit the Hay House Website at: **hayhouse.com**

POWER vs. FORCE

The Hidden Determinants of Human Behavior

David R. Hawkins, M.D., Ph.D.

Hay House, Inc.
Carlsbad, California • Sydney, Australia • London, U.K.
Canada • Hong Kong

Published and distributed in the United States by: Hay House, Inc., P.O. Box 5100, Carlsbad, CA 92018-5100 • *Phone:* (760) 431-7695 or (800) 654-5126 • *Fax:* (760) 431-6948 or (800) 650-5115 • www.hayhouse.com • *Published and distributed in Australia by:* Hay House Australia Ltd., 18/36 Ralph St., Alexandria NSW 2015 • *Phone:* 612-9669-4299 • *Fax:* 612-9669-4144 • www.hayhouse.com.au • *Published and Distributed in the United Kingdom by:* Hay House UK, Ltd. • Unit 202, Canalot Studios • 222 Kensal Rd., London W10 5BN • *Phone:* 44-20-8962-1230 • *Fax:* 44-20-8962-1239 • www.hayhouse.co.uk • *Distributed in Canada by:* Raincoast • 9050 Shaughnessy St., Vancouver, B.C. V6P 6E5 • *Phone:* (604) 323-7100 • *Fax:* (604) 323-2600

Editorial supervision: Jill Kramer • *Design:* Summer McStravick

Library of Congress Cataloging-in-Publication Data

Hawkins, David R., 1927–
    Power vs. force : the hidden determinants of human behavior / David R. Hawkins.
        p. cm.
    Originally published: Sedona, Ariz. : Veritas Pub., © 1995
    Includes bibliographical references and index.
    ISBN 1-56170-933-6 (trade paper)
    1. Consciousness. 2. Kinesiology. 3. Human behavior. I. Title: Power versus force. II. Title.
BF311 .H385 2002
155.2'34—dc21

2001039310

ISBN 1-56170-933-6

06 05 04 03   11 10 9 8
1st printing, February 2002
8th printing, June 2003

Printed in the United States of America

◎ ◎ ◎

The skillful are not obvious
They appear to be simple-minded
Those who know this know the patterns of the Absolute
To know the patterns is the Subtle Power
The Subtle Power moves all things and has no name

◎ ◎ ◎

CONTENTS

Foreword 1
Preface 9
Introduction 25

PART I: TOOLS

Chapter 1:   Critical Advances
in Knowledge 41

Chapter 2:   History and
Methodology 55

Chapter 3:   Test Results and
Interpretation 67

Chapter 4:   Levels of Human
Consciousness..................75

Chapter 5:   Social Distribution of
Consciousness Levels 95

Chapter 6:   New Horizons in
Research 103

Chapter 7:   Everyday Critical
Point Analysis 115

Chapter 8:   The Source of Power......131

PART II: WORK

Chapter 9:   Power Patterns in
Human Attitudes 145

Chapter 10:   Power in Politics 151

Chapter 11:   Power in the
Marketplace 161

Chapter 12:   Power and Sports 171
Chapter 13:   Social Power and the
              Human Spirit 179
Chapter 14:   Power in the Arts 189
Chapter 15:   Genius and the Power
              of Creativity 195
Chapter 16:   Surviving Success 203
Chapter 17:   Physical Health
              and Power 209
Chapter 18:   Wellness and the
              Disease Process 215

PART III: MEANING

Chapter 19:   The Database of
              Consciousness 227
Chapter 20:   The Evolution of
              Consciousness 235
Chapter 21:   The Study of
              Pure Consciousness 249
Chapter 22:   Spiritual Struggle 261
Chapter 23:   The Search for Truth 271
Chapter 24:   Resolution 285

APPENDIX A: Calibrated Levels of
              Truth of the Chapters 293
APPENDIX B: Details of Kinesiological
              Testing...........................295

Notes 301
Glossary 313
Bibliography 321
Index 331
About the Author 340

FOREWORD

I magine—what if you had access to a simple yes-or-no (Y/N) answer to any question you wished to ask? A demonstrably true answer to *any* question. Think about it. . . .

There's the obvious: "Jane is seeing another guy?" (Y/N?); "Johnny is telling the truth about school?" (Y/N?) But it's only a short step to: "This is a safe investment?" (Y/N?), or "This career is worthy of my pursuit?" (Y/N?)

What if *everyone* had such access? Staggering implications suggest themselves immediately. Think again: What would happen to our ponderous and all-too-often flawed judicial system if there was a clear, confirmable answer to the proposition, "John Doe is guilty as charged?" (Y/N?)

What would happen to politics as we know it if all of us could ask the question, "Candidate X honestly intends to fulfill this campaign

promise?" (Y/N?)—and all of us got the same answer?
And what would happen to advertising, period?
You get the idea. But the idea gets bigger, fast. What
happens to nationalism ("Nation X is *really* dedicated to
the overthrow of Democracy?")? To government ("This
bill does in fact protect the rights of citizens?")?
What happens to "The check is in the mail"?

If, as has been said, man learned to lie an hour after he
learned to talk, then a phenomenon such as the one we're
discussing would be the genesis of the most fundamental
change in human knowledge since the beginning of society;
the transformations it would wreak—in fields from communications to ethics, in our most basic concepts, in every
detail of daily existence—would be so profound that it's difficult to even conceive what life would be like in a subsequent new era of truth. The world as we know it would be
irrevocably changed, right down to its very roots.

✝ ✝ ✝

kinesiology: —n. The study of muscles and their movements, esp. as applied to physical conditioning. [Gk. Kinesis,
movement (kinein, to move) + -logy.][1]

The study of kinesiology first received scientific attention in the second half of the last century through the
work of Dr. George Goodheart, who pioneered the specialty he called *applied kinesiology* after finding that benign physical stimuli—for instance, beneficial nutritional
supplements—would increase the strength of certain indicator muscles, whereas hostile stimuli would cause those

muscles to suddenly weaken. The implication was that at a level far below conceptual consciousness, the body "knew," and through muscle testing was able to signal, what was good and bad for it. The classic example, cited later in this work, is a universally observed weakening of indicator muscles in the presence of a chemical sweetener; the same muscles strengthen in the presence of a healthful and natural supplement.

In the late '70s, Dr. John Diamond refined this specialty into a new discipline he called *behavioral kinesiology*. Dr. Diamond's startling discovery was that indicator muscles would strengthen or weaken in the presence of positive or negative *emotional and intellectual stimuli*, as well as physical stimuli.[2] A smile will make you test strong, while the statement, "I hate you" will make you test weak.

Before we go any further, let us explain in detail exactly how one "tests," especially as readers will certainly wish to try this themselves. Here is Dr. Diamond's outline, from his 1979 book, *Your Body Doesn't Lie*,[3] of the procedure adapted by him from the classic description in H. O. Kendall's *Muscles: Testing and Function* (Baltimore: Williams & Wilkins, 2nd ed., 1971).

It takes two people to perform a kinesiological test. Choose a friend or a family member for testing. We'll call him or her your subject.

1. Have the subject stand erect, right arm relaxed at his side, left arm held out parallel to the floor, elbow straight. (You may use the other arm if you wish.)

2. Face your subject and place your left hand on his right shoulder to steady him. Then place your right hand on the subject's extended left arm just above the wrist.

3. Tell the subject to resist when you try to push his arm down.

4. Now push down on his arm fairly quickly, firmly, and evenly. The idea is to push just hard enough to test the spring and bounce in the arm, not so hard that the muscle becomes fatigued. It is not a question of who is stronger, but of whether the muscle can "lock" the shoulder joint against the push.

Assuming there is no physical problem with the muscle and the subject is in a normal, relaxed state of mind, receiving no extraneous stimuli (for this reason it's important that the tester not smile or otherwise interact with the subject), the muscle will "test strong"—the arm will remain locked. If the test is repeated in the presence of a negative stimulus (for instance, artificial sweetener), "although you are pushing down no harder than before, the muscle will not be able to resist the pressure and the subject's arm will fall to his side."[4]

A striking aspect of Diamond's research was the uniformity of response among his subjects. Diamond's results were predictable, repeatable, and universal. This was so even where no rational link existed between stimulus and response. For totally undetermined reasons, certain abstract symbols caused all subjects to test weak; others, the opposite.

Some results were perplexing: Certain pictures, with no overtly positive or negative content would cause all subjects to test weak, while other "neutral" pictures caused all subjects to test strong. And some results were food for considerable surmise: Whereas virtually all classical music and most pop music (including "classic" rock and roll) caused a universally strong response, the "hard" or "metal" rock that first gained acceptance in the late '70s produced a universally weak response.

There was one other phenomenon that Diamond noted in passing, although he devoted no deeper analysis to its extraordinary implications. Subjects listening to tapes of known deceits—even though the speakers seemed to be telling the truth and sounded convincing—tested weak. While listening to recordings of demonstrable, true statements, they universally tested strong.[5] This was the starting point of the work of the author of this volume, the well-known psychiatrist and physician, David R. Hawkins. In 1975, Dr. Hawkins began research on the kinesiological response to truth and falsehood.

It had been established that test subjects didn't need any conscious acquaintance with the substance (or issue) being tested. In double-blind studies—and in mass demonstrations involving entire lecture audiences—subjects universally tested weak in response to unmarked envelopes containing artificial sweetener, and strong to identical placebo envelopes. The same naïve response appeared in testing intellectual values.

What seems to be at work is a form of communal consciousness, *spiritus mundi*, or as Hawkins calls it, following Jung, a "database of consciousness." The phenomenon seen so commonly in other social animals —whereby a fish swimming at one edge of a school will turn instantaneously when its fellows a quarter mile away flee a predator—also pertains in some subconscious way to our species. There are simply too many documented instances of individuals having intimate acquaintance with information experienced firsthand by remote strangers for us to deny that there are forms of shared knowledge other than those achieved by rational consciousness. Or perhaps, more simply, the same spark of inner subrational wisdom that can discriminate healthy from unhealthy can discriminate true from false.

One highly suggestive element of this phenomenon is the binary nature of the response. Hawkins found that questions must be phrased so that the answer is very clearly yes or no, like a nerve synapse that's on or off; like the most basic cellular forms of "knowledge"; like so much of what our cutting-edge physicists tell us is the essential nature of universal energy. Is the human brain, at some primal level, a wondrous computer linked with a universal energy field, that knows far more than it knows it knows?

Be that as it may. As Dr. Hawkins's research continued, his most fertile discovery was a means of calibrating a scale of relative truth by which intellectual positions, statements, or ideologies could be rated on a range of 1 to 1,000. One can ask, "This item (book, philosophy, teacher) calibrates at 200 (Y/N?): at 250 (Y/N?)," and so on, until the point of common weak response determines the calibration. The enormous implication of these calibrations was that for the first time in human history, ideological validity could be appraised as an innate quality in *any* subject. Through 20 years of similar calibrations, Hawkins was able to analyze the full spectrum of the levels of human consciousness, developing a fascinating map of the geography of man's experience. This "anatomy of consciousness" produces a profile of the entire human condition, allowing a comprehensive analysis of the emotional and spiritual development of individuals, societies, and the race in general. So profound and far-reaching a view provides not only a new understanding of man's journey in the universe, but also a guide to all of us as to where we and our neighbors are on the ladder of spiritual enlightenment, and on our own personal journeys to become who we could be.

In this volume, Dr. Hawkins brings these fruits of decades of research and insight into the penetrating illumination of revolutionary discoveries in advanced particle physics and nonlinear dynamics. For the first time in our Western intellectual record, he shows that the cold light of science is confirming what mystics and saints have always said about the self, God, and the very nature of reality. This vision of being, essence, and divinity presents a picture of man's relation to the universe that is unique in its capacity to satisfy both soul and reason. There is a rich intellectual and spiritual harvest here . . . much that you can take, and much more than you can give yourself.

Turn the page. The future starts now.

E. Whalen, Editor
Bard Press
Arizona, 1995

◉ ◉ ◉

PREFACE

While the truths reported in this book were scientifically derived and objectively organized, like all truths, they were first experienced personally. Beginning at a very young age, a lifelong sequence of intense states of awareness first inspired, and then gave direction to, the process of subjective realization that has finally taken form in this book.

When I was three years old, a sudden, full consciousness of existence occurred, a subverbal but complete understanding of the meaning of *I am*—followed immediately by the frightening realization that "I" might not have come into existence at all. This was an instant awakening from oblivion into a conscious awareness of being itself. In that moment, the personal self was born, and the duality of *Is* and *Is not* entered my subjective awareness.

Throughout childhood and early adolescence, the paradox of existence and the question of the reality of the self remained a repeated concern. The personal self would sometimes begin slipping back into a greater, *im*personal Self, and the initial fear of non-existence, the fundamental fear of Nothingness, would recur.

Awakening the Presence

In 1939, I was a paperboy in rural Wisconsin and had a 17-mile route. One dark winter's night, I was caught miles from home in a blizzard. The temperature was 20 degrees below zero, and my bicycle toppled over on an icy, snow-covered field. A fierce wind ripped out the newspapers that I carried in my handlebar basket, strewing them across the terrain. I broke into tears of frustration and exhaustion; my clothes were frozen stiff, and I was far from home. To get out of the wind, I broke through the icy crust of a high snowbank and dug out a place to burrow into. The shivering stopped and was replaced by a delicious warmth . . . and then a state of peace beyond all description. This was accompanied by a suffusion of light and a Presence of infinite love, which had no beginning and no end, and which was indistinguishable from my own essence. I became oblivious of the physical body and surroundings as my awareness fused with this all-present illuminated state. The mind grew silent; all thought stopped. An infinite Presence was all that was or could be, and it was beyond time or description.

After what seemed like eons, I was drawn back to an awareness of someone shaking my knee—my father's anxious face subsequently appeared. There was great reluctance to return to the body and all that it entailed . . . but I loved my father dearly, and because of his anguish, I chose to do so. In a detached way, I sympathized with his fear of my death, but at the same time, the concept of "death" seemed absurd.

This experience was never discussed with anyone. There was no context available with which to comprehend it; I had never heard of spiritual experiences (other than those reported in the lives of the saints). But after this experience, the accepted reality of the world began to seem only provisional; traditional religious teaching lost significance, and, paradoxically, I became an agnostic. Compared to the light of Divinity that I had felt bathing all existence, the god of traditional religion shone dully indeed. I had lost religion . . . but discovered spirituality.

During World War II, I was assigned to hazardous duty on a minesweeper, and often brushed close to death—but unlike my fellow crew members, I had no fear of it. It was as though death had lost its authenticity. After the war, I worked my way through medical school, as I was fascinated by the complexities of the mind and wanted to study psychiatry. My training psychoanalyst, a professor at Columbia University, was also an agnostic—both of us took a dim view of religion. The analysis went well, as did my career, and I became quite successful.

However, I didn't settle quietly into professional life: I succumbed to a progressive and fatal illness that did not respond to any available treatment. By the time I was 38,

I knew I was about to die. I didn't care about my body, but my spirit was in a state of extreme anguish and despair. As my final moment approached, the thought flashed through my mind, *What if there is a God?* So I called out in prayer, "If there is a God, I ask Him to help me now." I surrendered to whatever God there might be, and went unconscious. When I awoke, a transformation of such enormity had taken place that I was struck dumb with awe.

The person I had been no longer existed. There was no personal self or ego left—just an Infinite Presence of such unlimited power that it was all that was. This Presence had replaced what had been "me," and the body and its actions were controlled solely by the Presence's infinite will. The world was illuminated by the clarity of an Infinite Oneness, which expressed itself as all things revealed in their immeasurable beauty and perfection.

For nine months, this stillness persisted. I had no will of my own; unbidden, the physical entity went about its business under the direction of the infinitely powerful, but exquisitely gentle, will of the Presence. In that state, there was no need to think about anything. All truth was self-evident; no conceptualization was necessary or even possible. At the same time, the nervous system felt extremely overtaxed, as though it were carrying far more energy than its circuits had been designed for.

It was not possible to function effectively in the world. Along with fear and anxiety, all ordinary motivations had disappeared. There was nothing to seek, as all was perfect. Fame, success, and money were meaningless. Friends urged me to be pragmatic and return to my practice, but there was no incentive to do so. However, I discovered that I could perceive the reality that underlay personalities; I saw how the origin of emotional sickness lay in people's belief that they *were* their personalities. And so, of its own, my practice resumed and eventually became huge. People came from all over the United States—I treated 1,000 new patients a year. I eventually had 50 therapists and other employees working for me; 2,000 outpatients; a suite of 25 offices; and research and electroencephalic laboratories. I was invited to appear on radio and network television shows—including *The MacNeil/Lehrer News Hour,* the *Today* show, and *The Barbara Walters Show.* In 1973, I reported on the work I was doing in the book *Orthomolecular Psychiatry* (with Nobelist Linus Pauling as co-author), and it seemed to strike a nerve with many people.

Love, Radiance, and Miracles

The overall condition of my nerves improved slowly, and then another phenomenon began—a sweet, delicious band of energy started to flow continuously up the spine and into the brain, where it created an intense sensation of continuous pleasure. Everything in life happened by synchronicity, evolving in perfect harmony, and the miraculous was commonplace. The origin of what the world would call *miracles* was the Presence, not a personal self. What remained of the personal "me" was only a witness to these phenomena. The greater "I," deeper than my self or its former thoughts, determined all that happened.

The state had been reported by others, which led to my investigating spiritual teachings—including those of the Buddha, Huang Po, and other enlightened sages; and

more recent teachers such as Ramana Maharshi and Nisargadatta Maharaja—and thus confirmed that these experiences weren't unique. Suddenly, the Bhagavad Gita
made complete sense; eventually the same spiritual ecstasy reported by Sri Ramakrishna and the Christian saints
occurred.

Everything and everyone in the world was luminous
and exquisitely beautiful. All living things became radiant,
and expressed this radiance in stillness and splendor. It was
apparent that all of mankind is actually motivated by
inner love, but has simply become unaware; most people
live their lives as though they're sleepers unawakened to
the perception of who they really are. Everyone looked as
if they were asleep, but they were incredibly beautiful—I
was in love with everyone.

It was necessary to stop the habitual practice of med-
itating for an hour in the morning and then again before
dinner because it would intensify the bliss to such an ex-
tent that functioning was not possible. An experience similar to the one I had as a boy in the snowbank would recur,
but it became increasingly difficult to leave that state and
return to ordinary life. The incredible beauty of all things
shone forth in all its perfection, and where the world saw
ugliness, I saw only timeless beauty. This spiritual love per-
meated all of my perception; all boundaries between here
and there, then and now, or me and you disappeared.

The years were spent in inner silence, and the strength
of the Presence grew. I had no personal life—my personal
will no longer existed. I was an instrument of the Infinite
Presence, and I went about and did as it willed. People felt
an extraordinary peace in the aura of that Presence; seekers sought answers from me, but as there was no such

individual as "David" any longer. What these people were doing was finessing answers from their own selves, which were no different from mine. As I looked at each person, my self shone forth from their eyes. *How did I get into all these bodies?* I wondered.

The miraculous happened, beyond ordinary comprehension. Many chronic maladies from which I had suffered for years disappeared; my eyesight spontaneously normalized, and I no longer needed the bifocals I had worn for much of my life. Occasionally I would feel an exquisitely blissful energy—an infinite love—that would suddenly begin to radiate from my heart toward the scene of some calamity. For instance, I was once driving on a highway when this amazing energy began to beam out of my chest. As I rounded a bend, I saw that an auto accident had just occurred; in fact, the wheels of the upturned car were still spinning. The energy passed, with great intensity, from me to the occupants of the car, and then it stopped of its own accord. Another time, I was walking down the streets of a strange city, when the energy started to flow down the block ahead of me. I happened to arrive at the scene of an incipient gang fight, and the combatants fell back and began to laugh. Then the energy stopped again.

Profound changes of perception came, without warning, in improbable circumstances. While dining alone at a restaurant on Long Island, the Presence suddenly intensified until every person and thing, which had appeared separate in ordinary perception, melted into a timeless universality and oneness. In the motionless silence, I saw that there are no "events" or "things" and that nothing actually "happens" because past, present, and future are merely artifacts of perception, as is the illusion of a separate "I," subject to birth and death. As my limited, false self dissolved into the universal Self of its true origin, there was an ineffable sense of having returned home, a state of absolute peace and relief from all suffering. For it's only the illusion of individuality that is the origin of all suffering—when one realizes that one *is* the universe, complete and at one with all that is, forever without end, then no further suffering is possible.

Using the Presence to Heal

Patients came to see me from every country in the world, and some were the most hopeless of the hopeless. Grotesque, writhing, and wrapped in wet sheets for transport from faraway hospitals, they came to me, hoping for treatment for advanced psychoses and grave, incurable mental disorders. Some were catatonic; many had been mute for years. But in each patient, beneath the crippled appearance, I clearly saw the shining essence of love and beauty, perhaps so obscured to ordinary vision that he or she had become totally unloved in this world.

One day, a mute catatonic was brought into the hospital in a straitjacket. She had a severe neurologic disorder and was unable to stand—she squirmed on the floor in spasms, and her eyes were rolling back in her head. Her hair was matted and she'd torn all of her clothes and could only utter guttural sounds. Her family was fairly wealthy; therefore, she'd been seen by innumerable physicians over the years, including famous specialists from all over the world. Every treatment had been tried on her, until the medical profession had finally given up, calling her situation "hopeless."

I looked at her and asked nonverbally, "What do you want me to do with her, God?" I then realized that I was just to love her; that was all. Her inner self shone through her eyes, and I connected with that loving essence. In that second, she was healed by her own recognition of who she really was; what happened to her mind or body didn't matter to her any longer.

This, in essence, happened with countless patients. Some recovered in the eyes of the world, and some did not, but whether or not a clinical recovery had occurred no longer mattered to the patients. Their inner agony was over; as they felt loved and at peace within, their pain stopped. This phenomenon can only be explained by saying that the compassion of the Presence recontextualized each patient's reality so that he or she experienced healing on a level that transcended the world and its appearances. The inner peace in which I existed encompassed us both, beyond time and identity.

I saw that *all pain and suffering arises solely from the ego and not from God.* This was a truth that I silently communicated to the minds of my patients. When I intuited this mental block in another mute catatonic who had not spoken in many years, through my mind, I said to him, "You're blaming God for what your ego has done to you." He then jumped off the floor and began to talk, much to the shock of the nurse who witnessed the incident.

But this work became increasingly taxing, eventually overwhelming. Patients were backed up and waiting for beds to open—although the hospital with which I was affiliated had built an extra ward to house my patients. I felt an enormous frustration in the face of the tide of human suffering because I could only encounter one patient at a time. It was like trying to bail out the sea with a small cup. I felt that there must be some way to address the causes of the common malaise and the endless stream of spiritual distress and human suffering.

When I first encountered kinesiology, I was instantly amazed by the potential I saw. It was the "wormhole" between two universes—the physical, and the mind and spirit—an interface between dimensions. In a world full of sleepers lost from their source, here was a tool to recover that lost connection with the higher reality and demonstrate it for all to see. I proceeded to test every substance, thought, and concept I could think of, and had my students and research assistants do the same. Then I noticed a strange thing: Whereas all subjects went weak from negative stimuli (such as fluorescent lights, pesticides, and artificial sweeteners), students of spiritual disciplines who had advanced their level of awareness did not go weak as ordinary people did. Something important and decisive had shifted in the subjects' consciousness—apparently as they realized that they weren't at the mercy of the world, but rather were affected only by what their minds believed. Perhaps the very process of progress toward enlightenment could be shown to increase man's ability to resist the mutability of existence.

I was more and more powerfully struck by the capacity to change things in the world by merely envisioning them; I saw how love changed the world each time it replaced "unlove." The entire scheme of civilization could be profoundly altered by focusing this power of love at a very specific point. Whenever this happened, history branched out to new roads.

It now appeared that these crucial insights could not only be communicated with the world, but could also be visibly and irrefutably demonstrated. It seemed that the great tragedy of human life had always been that the psyche is so easily deceived; discord and strife have been the inevitable consequence of mankind's inability to distinguish the false from the true. But here was an answer to this fundamental dilemma, a way to recontextualize the nature of consciousness itself and make explicable that which otherwise could only be inferred.

A Journey of the Spirit

It was time to leave my life in New York, where I had an apartment on Fifth Avenue and an estate on Long Island; after all, I had discovered something more important. I left that world and everything in it and took up a reclusive life in a small town, where the next seven years of my life were spent in meditation and study. Before I could make my ideas concrete, I needed to perfect this state of consciousness as an instrument.

But overpowering states of bliss would return, unsought, and eventually I realized that I had to teach myself to be in the Divine Presence and still function in society. I had lost track of what was happening in the world at large, so in order to do research and writing, it was necessary to stop all spiritual practice and focus on the world of form. I started reading the paper and watching TV to catch up on world events—who was who, and the nature of the current social dialogue. I didn't know who was running for office or who Princess Di was . . . but I found it a pleasure to become reacquainted with the news of the day.

Exceptional, subjective experiences of truth—the providence of the mystic, who affects all mankind by sending forth energy of his level into the collective consciousness—simply are not understandable to the majority of human beings, and therefore are of limited meaning except to other spiritual seekers. I sought now to be ordinary, because just being ordinary in and of itself is an expression of divinity; the truth of one's real self can be discovered through the pathway of everyday life. The commonplace and God aren't distinct. To live with care and kindness is all that is necessary; the test reveals itself in due time.

And so, after a long, circular journey of the spirit, I returned to the most important work, which is to bring the Presence that has moved my life perhaps at least a little closer to the grasp of as many of my fellow beings as I can reach.

The Presence is silent and conveys a state of peace. It's infinitely gentle and yet like a rock. With it, all fear disappears, and spiritual joy occurs on a quiet level of inexplicable ecstasy. Because the experience of time stops, there's no apprehension, regret, pain, or anticipation; the source of joy is unending and ever-present. With no beginning or ending, there can be no loss, grief, or desire—

and nothing needs to be done, for everything is already perfect and complete.

When time stops, all problems disappear, for they are merely artifacts of a point of perception. As the Presence prevails, there is no further identification with the body or mind. When the mind grows silent, the thought *I am* also disappears, and Pure Awareness shines forth to illuminate what one is, was, and always will be, beyond all worlds and all universes—infinite and beyond time.

People wonder, *How does one reach this state of awareness?* I can only share my own experience with you, and note that few follow the steps *because they're so simple.* First, the desire to reach that state was intense. Then came the discipline to act with constant and universal forgiveness and gentleness, *without exception.* One has to be compassionate toward *everything*, including one's own self and thoughts. Next came a willingness to hold desires in abeyance and surrender personal will at every moment. As each thought, feeling, longing, or deed was surrendered to God, the mind became increasingly silent. At first, I turned over entire stories and paragraphs in my mind, then ideas and concepts. As one lets go of the desire to own these thoughts, they no longer reach such elaboration, and begin to fragment while only half-formed. Finally, it was possible to turn over the energy behind thought itself, before it even became thought.

The task of constant and unrelenting fixity of focus—allowing not even a moment of distraction from meditation—continued while doing ordinary activities. At first, this seemed very difficult, but as time went on, it became habitual, automatic, and effortless. The process is like a rocket leaving Earth: At first, it requires enormous power, then less and less as it leaves the earth's gravitational field; and finally, it moves through space under its own momentum.

Suddenly, without warning, a shift in awareness occurred, and the Presence was there, unmistakable, all-encompassing. There were a few moments of apprehension as the self died, and then the absoluteness of the Presence inspired a flash of awe. This breakthrough was spectacular, more intense than anything previously known—it has no counterpart in ordinary experience. The profound shock entailed is cushioned by the Love of the Presence. Without the support and protection of that Love, one would be annihilated.

A moment of terror followed as the ego clung to its existence, fearing it would become nothingness. Instead, as it died, it was replaced by the Self as Everything-ness, the All in which everything is known and obvious in its perfect expression of its own essence. With nonlocality came the awareness that one is all that ever was or can be. One is total and complete, beyond all identities, gender, or even humanness itself. One need never again fear suffering and death.

What happens to the body, from this point, is immaterial. At certain levels of spiritual awareness, ailments of the body heal, or spontaneously disappear. But in the absolute state, such considerations are irrelevant. The body will run its predicted course and then return from whence it came. It's a matter of no importance; one is unaffected. The body appears to be an "it," rather than a "me," another object like the furniture in the room. It may seem comical that people still address the body as though it was the individual person, but there's no way to explain this state of awareness to the unaware. It's best to just go about one's business, and allow Providence to handle the social adjustment. However, as one reaches bliss, it becomes very difficult to conceal that state of intense ecstasy. There's a common desire at this point to share this state with others and to use it for the benefit of all. The world may be dazzled as well, and people come from far and wide to be in the accompanying aura. Metaphysical seekers and the spiritually curious may be drawn (as the very ill may be), seeking miracles; one may become a magnet and a source of joy to them.

The ecstasy that accompanies this condition isn't absolutely stable; keep in mind that there are also moments of great agony. The most intense moments occur when the state fluctuates and suddenly ceases for no apparent reason. These times bring on periods of intense despair, a fear that one has been forsaken by the Presence. These falls make the path arduous, and to surmount these reversals requires great will. It finally becomes obvious that one must transcend this level or constantly suffer excruciating "descents from grace." The glory of ecstasy, then, has to be relinquished, as one enters upon the demanding task of transcending duality, until one is beyond all oppositions and their conflicting pulls. But while it's one thing to happily give up the iron restraints of ego, it's quite another to abandon the golden chains of ecstatic joy. It feels as though one is giving up God, and a new level of fear arises, never before anticipated; this is the final terror of absolute aloneness.

In my own case, the fear of nonexistence was formidable, and I drew back from it repeatedly. The purpose of the agonies, of the dark nights of the soul, then became apparent—they're so intolerable that their exquisite pain spurs one on to the extreme effort required to surmount them. When vacillation between heaven and hell becomes unendurable, the desire for existence itself has to be surrendered. Only once this is done may one finally move beyond allness or nothingness, beyond existence or nonexistence. This culmination of the inner work is the most difficult phase, the ultimate watershed, where one is starkly aware that the illusion of existence one transcends here is irrecoverable. There's no returning from this step, and this specter of irreversibility makes this last barrier appear the most formidable choice of all.

But, in fact, in this final apocalypse of the self, the dissolution of the sole remaining duality—that of existence and non-existence, identity itself—dissolves in universal divinity, and no individual consciousness is left to choose. The last step, then, is taken by God alone.

Follow this fascinating journey and you'll see how easy it can be to raise your consciousness to the levels of power, rather than force, so that you can become one of those who is awake and aware in this world. Your life will certainly never be the same.

INTRODUCTION

All human endeavor has the common goal of understanding or influencing our experience. To this end, man has developed numerous descriptive and analytical disciplines: morality, philosophy, psychology, and so on. Spectacular amounts of time and money are invested in data collection and analysis in the attempt to predict human trends. Implicit in this frenetic search is the expectation of finding some ultimate "answer." The "answer," we seem to perennially believe, will, once found, allow us to solve the problems of the economy, crime, national health, or politics. But so far, we haven't solved any of these problems at all.

It isn't that we lack information—we're virtually drowning in it. The obstacle is that we don't have the proper tools to interpret the significance of our data. We haven't yet asked the right questions because we haven't had an adequate gauge of our questions' relevance or accuracy.

Man's dilemma—now and always—has been that he misidentifies his own intellectual artifacts as reality.[1] But these artificial suppositions are merely the products of an arbitrary point of perception. The inadequacy of the answers we receive is a direct consequence of the limitations implicit in the viewpoints of the questioner. Slight errors in the formation of questions result in gross errors in the answers that follow.

Understanding doesn't proceed simply from examining data; it comes from examining data in a particular context. Information is useless until we know what it *means*. To understand its meaning, we don't only need to ask the right question; we also need the appropriate instruments with which to measure the data in a meaningful process of sorting and description.

The fatal faults of all thought systems have been, primarily: (1) failure to differentiate between subjective and objective; (2) disregard of the limitation of context inherent in basic design and terminology; (3) ignorance of the nature of consciousness itself; and (4) misunderstanding of the nature of causality. The consequences of these shortcomings will become obvious as we explore the major areas of human experience from a new perspective, with new tools.

Society constantly expends its efforts to correct *effects* instead of *causes,* which is one reason why the development of human consciousness proceeds so slowly. Human beings are barely on the first rung of the evolutionary ladder; we haven't yet solved even such primitive problems as world hunger. In fact, the accomplishments of mankind thus far are most impressive for having been achieved—almost blindly—through trial and error. While this random search for solutions has resulted in a maze of baffling complexity, true answers always have the hallmark of simplicity. The basic law of the universe is *economy*. The universe doesn't waste a single quark; everything serves a purpose and fits into a balance—there are no extraneous events.

Man is stuck with his lack of knowledge about himself until he can learn to look beyond apparent causes. From the human record, we may note that answers never arise from identifying "causes" in the world. Instead, it's necessary to identify the conditions that underlie ostensible causes; and these conditions exist only within man's consciousness itself. No definitive answer to any problem can be found by isolating sequences of events and projecting upon them a mental notion of "causality." *There are no causes within the observable world.* As we shall demonstrate, *the observable world is a world of effects.*

The difference in finding effective means reduces itself, on examination, to our inability to discriminate the essential from the nonessential. Thus far, there has been no system affording a method by which to distinguish powerful and effective solutions from weak, ineffective ones. Our means of evaluation themselves have been inherently incapable of performing realistic appraisal.

Societal choices, more often than not, are the result of expediency, statistical fallacy, sentiment, political or media pressure, or personal prejudice and vested interest. Crucial decisions affecting the lives of everyone on the planet are made under conditions that virtually guarantee failure. Because societies lack the necessary reality base for formulation of effective problem resolutions, they fall back, over and over, on a resort of *force* (in its various expressions—such as war, law, taxation, rules, and regulations), which is extremely costly, instead of employing *power,* which is very economical.

Man's two basic types of operational faculties, reason and feeling, are both inherently unreliable, as our history of precarious individual and collective survival attests. Although we ascribe our actions to reason, man in fact operates primarily out of pattern recognition; the logical arrangement of data serves mainly to enhance a pattern-recognition system that then becomes "truth."[2] But nothing is ever "true," except under certain circumstances, and then only from a particular viewpoint, characteristically unstated.

As a result, thoughtful man deduces that all of his problems arise from the difficulty of "knowing." Ultimately, the mind arrives at *epistemology,* the branch of philosophy that examines the question of how—and to what degree—man really knows anything. Such philosophical discourse may seem either erudite or irrelevant, but the questions they pose are at the very core of human experience. No matter where we start in an examination of human knowledge, we always end up looking at the phenomena of *awareness* and the nature of human consciousness. And we eventually come to the same realization: Any further advance in man's condition requires a verifiable basis for knowing, upon which we may place our trust.

The main obstacle to man's development, then, is his lack of knowledge about the nature of consciousness itself. If we look within ourselves at the instant-by-instant processes of our minds, we'll soon notice that the mind acts much more rapidly than it would acknowledge. It becomes apparent that the notion that our actions are based on thoughtful decisions is a grand illusion. The decision-making process is a function of consciousness itself; the mind makes choices based on millions of pieces of data and their correlations and projections, far beyond conscious comprehension, and with enormous rapidity. This is a global function dominated by the energy patterns that the new science of nonlinear dynamics terms *attractors*.[3] Consciousness automatically chooses what it deems best from moment to moment because that ultimately is the only function of which it is capable. The relative weight and merit given to certain data are determined by a predominant attractor pattern operating in the individual or in a collective group of minds. These patterns can be identified, described, and calibrated; out of that information arises a totally new understanding of human behavior, history, and the destiny of mankind. And as we explore the nature of man's problems, it becomes clear that there has never been a reliable experimental yardstick with which to measure and interpret man's motivations and experiences over the course of his history.

✣ ✣ ✣

Kinesiology is now a well-established science, based on the testing of an all-or-none muscle response stimulus. A positive stimulus provokes a strong muscle response; a negative stimulus results in a demonstrable weakening of the test muscle. Clinical kinesiological muscle testing as a diagnostic technique has found widespread verification over the last 25 years. Dr. George Goodheart's original research on the subject was given wider application by Dr. John Diamond. Diamond determined that this positive or negative response occurs with stimuli both physical *and* mental, and his books brought the subject to the general public.

The research reflected in this volume has taken Diamond's technique several steps further, through the discovery that this kinesiologic response reflects the human organism's capacity to differentiate not only positive from negative stimuli, but also anabolic (life-threatening) from catabolic (life-consuming), and, most dramatically, truth from falsity.

The test itself is simple, rapid, and relatively foolproof: A positive muscle reaction occurs in response to a statement that is obviously true; a negative response occurs if the test subject is presented with a false statement. This phenomenon occurs independently of the test subject's own opinion or knowledge of the topic, and the response has proven cross-culturally valid in any population and consistent over time. This technique provides, for the first time in human history, an objective basis for distinguishing truth from falsehood, which is totally verifiable across time with randomly selected, naïve test subjects.

Moreover, we found that this testable phenomenon can be used to calibrate human levels of consciousness so that an arbitrary logarithmic scale of whole numbers emerges, stratifying the relative power of levels of consciousness in all areas of human experience. Exhaustive investigation has resulted in a calibrated scale of consciousness, in which the log of whole numbers from 1 to 1,000 calibrates the degree of power of all possible levels of human awareness.

The millions of calibrations that confirmed this discovery further disclosed a stratification of levels of power in human affairs, revealing a remarkable distinction between power and force and their respective qualities. This, in turn, led to a comprehensive reinterpretation of human behavior in order to identify the invisible energy fields that control it. The calibrated scale was found to coincide with sublevels of the hierarchy of the *perennial philosophy;* correlations with emotional and intellectual phenomena in sociology, clinical psychology, and traditional spirituality immediately suggested themselves.

The calibrated scale has been examined here in light of current discoveries in advanced theoretical physics and the nonlinear dynamics of *chaos theory.* Calibrated levels, we suggest, represent powerful *attractor fields* within the domain of consciousness itself, that dominate human existence and therefore define content, meaning, and value, and serve as organizing energies for widespread patterns of human behavior.

This stratification of attractor fields, according to corresponding levels of consciousness, provides a new paradigm for recontextualizing the human experience throughout all time. In practical terms, by accessing data to which there has heretofore been no avenue of approach, our method promises both great value in researching history and enormous possible benefit for mankind's future. In attempting to emphasize the value of this technique as a research tool, examples have been given of its potential uses in a wide range of human activities: speculatively, in art, history, commerce, politics, medicine, sociology, and the natural sciences; pragmatically, in marketing, advertising, research and development; and empirically, in psychological, philosophic, and religious inquiry. Specific applications have been suggested in such diverse fields as criminology, intelligence, addictionology, and self-improvement.

✝ ✝ ✝

To explain that which is "simple" can sometimes be almost impossible; yet if we can understand even one simple thing in depth, we'll have greatly expanded our capacity for comprehending the nature of the universe and of life itself. Much of this book is devoted to the process of making the simple obvious. But because the subject matter presented here is, in fact, extraordinarily simple, it's difficult to present in a world enamored of complexity. Despite our mistrust of ease and clarity, we may see two general classes of people in the world: believers and nonbelievers. To the nonbelievers, everything is false until proven true; to the believers, everything said in good faith is probably true unless it's proven otherwise. The pessimistic position of cynical skepticism stems from fear, while the more optimistic manner of accepting information arises from self-confidence. Either style works, and each has its pros and cons. I've been faced, therefore, with the problem of presenting my data in a manner that will satisfy both approaches.

This book is, therefore, oxymoronic in style, as it's written to facilitate both so-called left- and right-brain comprehension. In actuality, human beings come to know things by pattern-recognition—the easiest way to grasp an entirely new concept is by familiarity. This kind of understanding is encouraged by a style of writing characterized by "closure." Instead of using only sparse adjectives or examples to express thoughts, concepts are instead run out and completed by use of repetition. The idea is then "done," and the mind is left at ease.

Such an approach is desirable because the mind that reads Chapter 3 won't be the same as the mind that reads

Chapter 1. For that matter, the idea of having to start from Chapter 1 and read progressively to the end is merely a fixed left-brain concept. This is the pedestrian path of Newtonian physics, based on a limited and limiting view of the world in which all events supposedly happen in an A→B→C sequence. This form of myopia arises from an outdated paradigm of reality. Our wider and far more comprehensive view draws not only upon the essence of the most advanced physics, mathematics, and nonlinear theory, but also upon intuitions that can be experientially validated by anyone.

In general, the challenge in presenting this material lies in the paradox of comprehending nonlinear concepts in a linear, sentence-by-sentence structure. The fields of science from which the data emerged are of themselves complex and difficult enough: advanced theoretical physics and the mathematics thereof; nonlinear dynamics; chaos theory and its mathematics; advanced behavioral kinesiology; neurobiology; turbulence theory; as well as the philosophical considerations of epistemology and ontology. Beyond this, it was necessary to address the nature of human consciousness itself, an uncharted area at the perimeter of which the sciences have all drawn back. To conclusively comprehend such subjects from a purely intellectual viewpoint would be a staggering enterprise, requiring a lifetime of study. Instead of undertaking so formidable a task, I've tried to extract (and work only with) the essence of each subject.

Even a rudimentary attempt to explain the workings of the testing technique fundamental to this book, which seems initially to transcend known laws of the universe, inevitably leads us into the intellectual territories of advanced theoretical physics, nonlinear dynamics, and chaos theory. Therefore, I've attempted, as much as possible, to present these subjects in nontechnical terms. There's no need to worry that some erudite intellectual capacity is required to digest this material—it isn't. We'll circle around the same concepts over and over until they're obvious to you. Each time we return to comment on an example, greater comprehension will occur. This kind of learning is like surveying new terrain in an airplane: On the first pass, it all looks unfamiliar; the second time around, we spot some points of reference; the third time, it starts to make sense, and we finally gain familiarity through simple exposure. The inborn pattern-recognition mechanism of the mind takes care of the rest.

✜ ✜ ✜

To quell my own fear that perhaps, despite my best efforts, the reader might not get the essential message of this book, I'm going to spell it out in advance:

> The individual human mind is like a computer terminal connected to a giant database. The database is human consciousness itself, of which our own cognizance is merely an individual expression, but with its roots in the common consciousness of all mankind. This database is the realm of genius; because to be human is to participate in the database, everyone, by virtue of his birth, has access to genius. The unlimited information contained in the database has now been shown to be readily available to anyone in a few seconds, at any time and in any place. This is

indeed an astonishing discovery, bearing the power to change lives, both individually and collectively, to a degree never yet anticipated.

The database transcends time, space, and all limitations of individual consciousness. This distinguishes it as a unique tool for future research, and opens as yet undreamed-of areas for possible investigation. It holds forth the prospect of the establishment of an objective basis for human values, behaviors, and belief systems. The information obtained by this method reveals a new context for understanding human behavior and a new paradigm for validating objective truth. Because the technique itself can be used by anyone, anywhere, at any time, it has the capacity to initiate a new era of human experience based on observable and verifiable truth.

Although the subject matter has proved easy to teach in lecture or videotape (see page 300) my challenge has been to work it into readable form. The proofs can be complex; the demonstrations, however, are ultra-simple—children get it right away and follow with delight, for there's nothing here that's surprising to them. They have always known that they were connected to the database; we adults have merely forgotten it. The inherent genius of children is close to the surface, which is why it was children who saw that the emperor wasn't wearing any clothes. Genius is like that.

We have at our fingertips a means of accurately distinguishing truth from falsehood, workable from unworkable, benevolent from malign. We can illuminate the hidden forces, hitherto overlooked, that determine human behavior. We have a means of finding answers to previously unresolved personal and social problems at our disposal. Falsehood needn't hold sway over our lives any longer.

✛ ✛ ✛

This book makes a huge promise, perhaps the biggest promise that has ever been made to you: It can provide you the means by which you may detect if you're being misled. (You never need to read a book or buy into any major teaching again without testing it first—it's too dangerous and too costly.) The level of truth of this edition of the work itself has been calibrated at 810 (see Appendix A), which is unusually high for this time in our culture. I pray that it's already a partial fulfillment of the promise.

In fact, our research teams used the testing method the book describes to calibrate the levels of truth in every chapter, paragraph, and sentence. (For instance, testing revealed an error in a list of celebrities who had destroyed themselves as a consequence of fame. When we checked each word, the name "John Lennon" was found to be in error—for he didn't self-destruct, he was shot by an assassin. When his name was deleted, the level of truth of the sentence, and therefore the paragraph and the page, rose to match the rest of the chapter.)

One interesting fact observed was that the scores of tested individuals increased after encountering the material in this book; it appears that mere exposure to the data "raised" the subjects' level of consciousness. Because the implications and practical applications of the work are so varied, and any aspect of the material can be expanded and focused to suit the interests of a given audience, portions of it have lent themselves clinically to presentations for various special-interest groups. But further uses and extrapolations of the research method detailed herein have been barely hinted at. Although the results described here are the product of 20 years of investigation and millions of calibrations on thousands of subjects by teams of investigators, *Power vs. Force* represents only a beginning exploration of the method's potential to enhance our knowledge in all of the arts and sciences. Perhaps most important is its promise as an aid in spiritual growth and maturation to the most advanced levels of consciousness, even enlightenment itself. This book can make such understanding available to anyone. That this revelation proceeds from a fortuitous connection between the physiology of consciousness, the function of the human nervous system, and the physics of the universe isn't surprising when we remind ourselves that we are, after all, part of a universe in which everything is connected to everything; all its secrets are thus, theoretically, at least, available to us if we know where (and how) to look.

Can man lift himself by his bootstraps? Why not? All he has to do is increase his buoyancy and he'll effortlessly rise to a higher state. Force cannot accomplish that feat; power not only can, but constantly does.

Man thinks he lives by virtue of the forces he can control, but in fact, he's governed by power from unrevealed sources, power over which he has *no* control. Because power is effortless, it goes unseen and unsuspected. Force is experienced through the senses; power can be recognized only through inner awareness. Man is immobilized in his present condition by his alignment with enormously powerful attractor energy patterns, which he himself unconsciously sets in motion. Moment by moment, he is suspended at this state of evolution, restrained by the energies of force, impelled by the energies of power.

The individual is like a cork in the sea of consciousness—he doesn't know where he is, where he came from, or where he's going, and he doesn't know why. Human beings wander about in their endless conundrums, asking the same questions century after century, and, failing a quantum leap in consciousness, we will continue to do so. One mark of such a sudden expansion of context and understanding is an inner experience of relief, joy, and awe. All who have had such an experience feel afterwards that the universe has granted them a precious gift. Facts are accumulated by effort, but truth reveals itself effortlessly.[4]

This book will have been successful if by the end of it you exclaim, "I always knew that!" What is contained herein is only a reflection of that which you already know, but don't know that you know. All that is attempted here is a connecting of the dots so that the hidden picture emerges. The hope is that this work might undo the very sources of pain, suffering, and failure, and assist the evolution of human consciousness in each of us to rise to the level of joy that should be the essence of each and every human being's experience. Hopefully, through this book, you'll be able to comprehend, and then prepare the conditions for, such a personal revelation. To do so is the ultimate adventure.

David R. Hawkins, M.D., Ph.D.
The Institute for Advanced Spiritual Research
Sedona, Arizona, 2002

PART I
TOOLS

CHAPTER ONE

Critical Advances in Knowledge

The evolution of this work, which began in 1965, was fostered by developments in numerous scientific fields—but a few of them were of special importance. Clinical research on the physiology of the nervous system and the holistic functioning of the human organism resulted in the development in the 1970s of the new science of *kinesiology*.[1] Meanwhile, in the technological arena, computers were being designed that were capable of millions of calculations in milliseconds, making the new tools of artificial intelligence possible.[2] This abrupt access to formerly inconceivable masses of data fostered a revolutionary perspective on natural phenomena: *chaos theory*. Simultaneously, in the theoretical sciences, quantum mechanics led to advanced theoretical physics; through associated mathematics, a whole new study of *nonlinear dynamics* emerged—this was one of the most far-reaching developments of modern science, the long-term impact of which has yet to be realized.[3]

Kinesiology exposed, for the first time, the intimate connection between mind and body, revealing that the mind "thinks" with the body itself. Therefore, it provided an avenue for the exploration of the ways consciousness reveals itself in the subtle mechanisms behind the disease process.[4]

Advanced computers, permitting the depiction of vast amounts of data through graphics, disclosed unsuspected systems within what had been ignored by Newtonian physics as indecipherable or meaningless data (chaos).[5] Theoreticians in diverse fields were suddenly able to intimate coherent ways of understanding data that had been considered incoherent or nonlinear—it was diffuse, or chaotic, and therefore inaccessible through conventional probabilistic logical theory and mathematics.

Analysis of this "incoherent" data identified hidden energy patterns, or *attractors* (which had been postulated by the advanced mathematics of nonlinear equations) behind apparently random natural phenomena.[6] Computer graphics clearly demonstrated the designs of these attractor fields. The implicit potential for analyzing supposedly unpredictable systems in such disparate areas as fluid mechanics, human biology, and stellar astronomy appeared to be limitless. (But the public has remained generally unaware of the field of nonlinear dynamics, except for the appearance in the marketplace of some intriguing new computer graphics patterns generated by "fractal" geometry.)

During the era preceding these revelations, linear science had grown progressively divorced from concern with the basis of life itself—all life processes are, in fact, nonlinear. This isolation was also characteristic of medicine, which, when presented with the amazing discoveries of kinesiology, merely ignored the information because it had no context, no paradigm of reality, with which to comprehend it. Medicine had forgotten that it was an *art*, and that science was merely a tool of that art.

Within medicine, psychiatry had always been held at a distance by traditionalists because in dealing with the immeasurables of human life it appeared less "scientific"— that is, from the Newtonian viewpoint. Academic psychiatry, in fact, has made major scientific breakthroughs in psychopharmacology since the 1950s. However, it remains the most nonlinear area of medicine, examining such subjects as intuition, decision-making, and the whole phenomenon of life as *process*. Although in the academic psychiatric literature there is little mention of such things as love, meaning, value, or will, the psychiatric discipline at least essays a somewhat larger view of man than other traditional medical fields do.

✣ ✣ ✣

Regardless of what branch of inquiry one starts from— philosophy, political theory, theology—all avenues of investigation eventually converge at a common meeting point: the quest for an organized understanding of the nature of pure consciousness. But all of the major enterprises in human knowledge discussed above—even kinesiology and nonlinear dynamics—halted at this last great barrier to human knowledge, the investigation of the nature of consciousness itself. It's true that some advanced thinkers did go beyond the parameters of their respective fields and began to ask questions about the relationship between the universe, science, and consciousness in its experience as mind.[7] We'll refer to their theories and their impact on the advance of human understanding as we proceed. The thesis of the present work derives from combining these several scientific disciplines into a methodology both elegantly simple and rewarding. We have thereby found that consciousness can indeed be investigated. Although no road maps for such a study have thus far been available, research into the subject has produced its own design, and with it, the context needed to comprehend its findings.

Inasmuch as everything in the universe is connected with everything else,[8] it isn't surprising that one of the primary objectives of this study—a map of the energy fields of consciousness—would correlate with, and be corroborated by, all other avenues of investigation, uniting the diversity of human experience and its expressions in an all-encompassing paradigm.[9] Such an insight can bypass the artificial dichotomy between subject and object, transcending the limited viewpoint that creates the illusion of duality. The subjective and objective are, in fact, one and the same,[10] as can be demonstrated without resorting to nonlinear equations or computer graphics.

By identifying subjective and objective as the same, we are able to transcend the constraints of the concept of time, which by its very definition is a major hindrance to comprehension of the nature of life, especially in its expression as human experience. If, in actuality, the subjective and objective are one and the same, then we can find the answers to all questions by merely looking within man himself. By simply recording observations, we can see a grand picture emerge, one that sees no limitations with respect to further investigation.

Each of us possesses a computer far more advanced than the most elaborate artificial intelligence machine available, one that's available at any time—the human mind itself. The basic function of any measuring device is simply to give a signal indicating the detection by the instrument of slight change. In the experiments to be described in this book, the reactions of the human body provide such a signal of change in conditions. As will be seen, the body can discern, to the finest degree, the difference between that which is supportive of life and that which is not.

This isn't surprising: After all, living things react positively to what is life-supportive and negatively to what is not; this is a fundamental mechanism of survival. Inherent in all life forms is the capacity to detect change and react correctively—thus, trees become smaller at higher elevations as the oxygen in the atmosphere becomes scarcer. Human protoplasm is far more sensitive than that of a tree.

The methodology, proceeding from the study of nonlinear dynamics, which we employed in this work of developing a map of the fields of human consciousness, is known as *attractor research*. It's concerned with the identification of power ranges of energy fields utilizing *critical point analysis*.[11] (Critical point analysis is a technique derived from the fact that in any highly complex system there is a specific, critical point at which the smallest input will result in the greatest change. For instance, the great gears of a windmill can be halted by lightly touching the right escape mechanism, and it's possible to paralyze a giant locomotive if you know exactly where to put your finger.)

Nonlinear dynamics enables these significant patterns to be identified in complex presentations, even when they're obscured by incoherence or sheer mass of indecipherable data. It discovers the relevance in what the world discards as irrelevant, using an entirely different approach and totally different methods of problem resolution from the ones with which the world is familiar.[12]

The world conventionally assumes that the processing of problems requires starting from the known (the question or conditions) and moving on to the unknown (the answer) in a time sequence following definite steps and logical progression. Nonlinear dynamics moves in the opposite direction: From the unknown (the nondeterministic data of the question) to the known (the answer)! It operates within a different paradigm of causality. The problem is seen as one of definition and access rather than of logical sequence (as in solving a problem by differential equations).[13]

But before we attempt to define the questions of this study further, let's examine some of the material we have introduced in greater detail.

Attractors

Attractor is the name given to an identifiable pattern that emerges from a seemingly unmeaningful mass of data. There is a hidden coherence in all that appears incoherent, which was first demonstrated in nature by Edward Lorenz. Lorenz studied computer graphics derived from weather patterns over long courses of time, and the attractor pattern he identified is now quite famously known as "Lorenz's Butterfly" (see Figure 1).

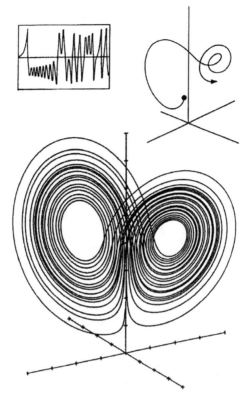

Figure 1
Lorenz's Butterfly.

Different types of attractors are denoted by different names, for instance, *strange attractors*. But most important to our research is the discovery that some patterns are very powerful and others are much weaker. There's a critical point that differentiates the two distinct classes— this phenomenon is parallel and corollary to the high and low energy bonds in the mathematics of the chemical bond.

Fields of Dominance

A *field of dominance* is exhibited by high energy patterns in their influence over weaker ones.

This may be likened to the coexistence of a small magnetic field within the much larger field of a giant electromagnet. The phenomenological universe is the expression of the interaction of endless attractor patterns of varying strengths. The unending complexities of life are the reflections of the endless reverberations of the augmentations and diminutions of these fields, compounded by their harmonics and other interactions.

Critical Point Analysis

The traditional Newtonian concept of causality (see the next page) had excluded all such "nondeterministic" data because such information didn't fit into its paradigm. With the discoveries of Einstein, Heisenberg, Bell, Bohr, and other great innovators, however, our model of the universe expanded rapidly. Advanced theoretical physics demonstrated that everything in the universe is subtly dependent upon everything else.[14]

The classic Newtonian four-dimensional universe is often described as a giant clockworks with the three dimensions of space manifesting linear processes in time. If we look at an even simpler clockworks, we'll then notice that some gears move slowly and ponderously, while others move very rapidly, with tiny balances twirling about as escape mechanisms seesaw back and forth. To place pressure on one of the large moving gears would have no effect on the mechanism; however, somewhere there is a delicate balance mechanism at which the slightest touch stops the entire device. This is identified as the "critical point," where the least force exerts the greatest effort.

Causality

Within the observable world, causality has conventionally been presumed to work in the following manner:

$$A \rightarrow B \rightarrow C$$

This is called a deterministic linear sequence—like billiard balls sequentially striking each other. The implicit presumption is that A causes B causes C.

But our own research indicates that causality operates in a completely different manner:

From this diagram we see that cause (ABC), which is unobservable, results in the sequence $A \rightarrow B \rightarrow C$, which is an observable phenomenon within the measurable three-dimensional world. The typical problems the world attempts to deal with exist on the observable level of

A→B→C. But our work is to find the inherent attractor pattern, the ABC out of which the A→B→C arises.

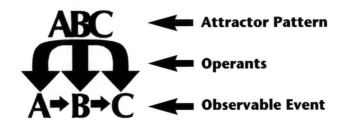

In this simple diagram, the operants transcend both the observable and the nonobservable; we might picture them as a rainbow bridging the deterministic and the nondeterministic realms. (The existence of operants can be inferred by asking the question, "What encompasses both the possible and the impossible, the known and the unknown?"—that is, what is the matrix of all possibility?)

This description of how the universe works is in accord with the theories of physicist David Bohm, who has described a holographic universe with an invisible *implicate* ("enfolded") and a manifest *explicate* ("unfolded") order.[15] It's important to note that this scientific insight corresponds with the view of reality experienced through history by enlightened sages who have evolved beyond consciousness to a state of pure awareness.[16] Bohm postulates a source that is beyond both the explicate and implicate realms, very much like the state of pure awareness described by the sages.[17]

✛ ✛ ✛

The advent of artificial intelligence supercomputers has allowed the application of the theories of nonlinear dynamics to be applied to the study of brain function through the technique of *neurophysiologic modeling.*[18] The function of memory is especially being studied by means of neural models, among which attractor networks have been identified. Conclusions of current research are that the brain's neural networks act as attractors, so that the system does not behave in a random fashion overall, although each individual neuron may behave randomly.[19]

Neuron models of consciousness disclose a class of neural networks called *constraint satisfaction systems.*[20] In these systems, a network of interconnected neuron units operates within a series of limits and thus sets up attractor patterns, some of which are now being identified with psychopathology.[21] This kind of modeling correlates behavior with physiology and parallels the results of our kinesiologic muscle testing, demonstrating the connection between mind and body.

In terms derived from chaos theory, the clinical study described in the following pages has identified a *phase space,* encompassing the full range of the evolution of human consciousness. Within this range, numerous attractor patterns of increasing power have been designated. These patterns represent energy fields that are qualities of consciousness itself rather than of any particular individual, as is shown by their occurrence across large populations over long periods of time, independent of testers or subjects.

The evolution of consciousness and the development of human society can be depicted in the mathematical terms of nonlinear dynamics. Our study concerned itself with a limited set of parameters of consciousness that we calibrated from 1 to 1,000. The numbers represent the logarithm (to the base 10) of the power of the respective fields. The entire field or phase space of consciousness itself is unlimited, going on to infinity. The range of 1 to 600, representing the domain of the vast majority of human experience, is the primary scope of this study; the levels from 600 to 1,000, which is the realm of non-ordinary evolution—of enlightenment, sages, and the highest spiritual states—will also be described.

Within the total field studied, sequential patterns emerged identifying the progressive powers of attractor fields in which there were local variations, but global consistency. Strange attractors can be of either high or low energy, and the critical point in our data appeared to be the calibration range of 200, below which the power of attractors could be described as weak or negative, above which as strong or positive. By the time we reached the calibration of 600, the attractors were enormously powerful.

An important element of chaos theory, which is helpful in understanding this evolution of consciousness, is the law of *sensitive dependence on initial conditions.*[22] This refers to the fact that an extremely minute variation over a course of time can have the effect of producing a profound change,[23] much as a ship whose bearing is one degree off compass will eventually find itself hundreds of miles off course. This phenomenon, which we'll refer to in more detail later, is an essential mechanism of all evolution and also underlies the potential of the creative process.

✝ ✝ ✝

In overview, we can see that from time immemorial, man has tried to make sense of the enormous complexity and frequent unpredictability of human behavior. A multitude of systems has been constructed to try to make that which is incomprehensible comprehensible. To "make sense" has ordinarily meant to be definable in terms that are linear—logical and rational. But the process, and therefore the experience, of life itself, is organic—that is to say, nonlinear by definition. This is the source of man's inescapable intellectual frustration.

In this study, however, test responses were independent of our subjects' belief systems or intellectual content. What emerged were patterns of energy fields that were aspects of consciousness itself, irrespective of individual identities. In common left-brain/right-brain parlance, we could say that the test subjects reacted globally to an attractor field, regardless of the individual variation of their left-brain logic, reason, or sequential thought systems. The results of the study indicated that profoundly powerful patterns organize human behavior.

We can intuit, then, an infinite domain of infinite potential—consciousness itself—within which there is an enormously powerful attractor field organizing all of human behavior into what is innate to "humanness." Within the giant attractor field are sequential fields of progressively less energy and power. These fields, in turn, dominate behavior, so that definable patterns are consistent across cultures and time, throughout human history. The interactions of these variations within attractor fields make up the history of civilization and mankind. (A side study not herein reported indicated that the animal and vegetable kingdoms are also controlled by attractor fields of hierarchic power as well.)

Our study correlates well with Rupert Sheldrake's "morphogenetic fields" hypothesis, as well as with Karl Pribram's holographic model of brain-mind function.[24] (Note that in a holographic universe, the achievements of every individual contribute to the advancement and well-being of the whole.) Our study also correlates with the conclusions reached by Nobelist Sir John Eccles that the brain acts as a receiving set for energy patterns residing in the mind itself, which exist as consciousness expressed in the form of thought.[25] It's the vanity of the ego that claims thoughts as "mine." Genius, on the other hand, commonly attributes the source of creative leaps of awareness to that basis of all consciousness—which has traditionally been called divinity.

CHAPTER TWO

History and Methodology

The basis of this work is research done over a 20-year period, involving millions of calibrations on thousands of test subjects of all ages and personality types, and from all walks of life. By design, the study is clinical in method and thus has widespread, pragmatic implications. Because the testing method is valid in application to all forms of human expression, calibrations have successfully been taken for literature, architecture, art, science, world events, and the complexities of human relationships. The test space for the determination of the data is the totality of the human experience throughout all time.

Mentally, test subjects ranged from what the world calls "normal" to severely ill psychiatric patients. Subjects were tested in Canada, the United States, Mexico, and throughout South America, Northern Europe, and the Far East.

55

They were of all nationalities, ethnic backgrounds, and religions, ranging in age from children to elders in their 90s, and covered a wide spectrum of physical and emotional health. Subjects were tested individually and in groups by many different testers and groups of testers. But in all cases, *without exception,* the results were identical and entirely reproducible, fulfilling the fundamental requirement of the scientific method: perfect experimental replicability.[1]

Subjects were selected at random and tested in a wide array of physical and behavioral settings: On top of mountains and at the seashore, at holiday parties and during the course of everyday work, in moments of joy and of sorrow. None of these circumstances had any effect on test results, which were found to be universally consistent irrespective of any extraneous factor, with the singular exception of the methodology of the testing procedure itself. Because of the significance of this factor, the testing method will be described in detail below.

Historical Background

In 1971, three physiotherapists published a definitive study on muscle testing.[2] Dr. George Goodheart, of Detroit, Michigan, had studied muscle testing techniques extensively in his clinical practice and made the breakthrough discovery that the strength or weakness of every muscle was connected to the health or pathology of a specific corresponding body organ.[3] He further determined that each individual muscle was associated with an acupuncture meridian and correlated his work with that of the physician

Felix Mann on the medical significance of the acupuncture meridians.[4]

By 1976, Goodheart's book on applied kinesiology had reached its 12th edition; he began to teach the technique to his colleagues and also published monthly research tapes. His work was rapidly picked up by others, which led to the formation of the International College of Applied Kinesiology; in addition, many members also belonged to the Academy of Preventive Medicine. A thorough exposition of the development of the field was detailed by David Walther in his extensive volume on applied kinesiology, also published in 1976.[5]

Initially, the most striking finding of kinesiology was a clear demonstration that muscles instantly become weak when the body is exposed to harmful stimuli. For instance, if a patient with functional hypoglycemia put sugar on his tongue, upon muscle-testing, the deltoid muscle (the one usually used as an indicator) instantly went weak. Accordingly, it was discovered that substances that were therapeutic to the body made the muscles instantly become strong.

Since the weakness of any particular muscle indicated the presence of a pathologic process in its corresponding organ (corroborated by diagnosis through acupuncture and physical or laboratory examination), it was a highly useful clinical tool to detect disease. Thousands of practitioners began to use the method, and data rapidly accumulated showing kinesiology to be an important and reliable diagnostic technique that could accurately monitor a patient's response to treatment.

The technique found widespread acceptance among professionals from many disciplines, and although it never caught on in mainstream medicine, it was used extensively by holistically oriented physicians. One of these was Dr. John Diamond, a psychiatrist who began to use kinesiology in diagnosing and treating psychiatric patients, which he labeled "behavioral kinesiology."[6]

While other investigators were researching the usefulness of the method in detecting allergies, nutritional disorders, and responses to medications, Dr. Diamond used the technique to research the beneficial or adverse effects of a great variety of psychological stimuli, such as art forms, music, facial expression, voice modulation, and emotional stress. He was an excellent teacher, and his seminars attracted thousands of professionals who returned to their own practices with renewed interest and curiosity as they explored applications of the technique.

In addition to its inclusive applicability, the test was quick, simple, easy to perform, and highly decisive; all researchers confirmed the absolute replicability of test results. For example, an artificial sweetener made every subject test weak, whether placed on the tongue, held in its package adjacent to the solar plexus, or hidden in a plain envelope (the contents of which neither the tester nor the subject knew).

That the body responded even when the mind was naïve was quite impressive. Most practitioners did their own verification research, placing various substances in plain, numbered envelopes and having a naïve second person test a third. The overwhelming conclusion was that the body would indeed respond accurately, even when the conscious mind was unaware.

The reliability of the testing experience never ceased to amaze the public and patients—and, for that matter, the practitioners themselves. When I was on the lecture circuit, in audiences of 1,000 people, 500 envelopes containing artificial sweetener would be passed out to the audience, along with 500 identical envelopes containing organic vitamin C. The audience would then be divided up and would alternate testing each other. When the envelopes were opened, the audience reaction was always one of amazement and delight when they saw that everybody had gone weak in response to the artificial sweetener and strong in response to the vitamin C. The nutritional habits of countless families across the country were changed due to this simple demonstration.

In the early 1970s, the medical profession in general, and psychiatry in particular, was highly resistant—if not outwardly hostile—to the idea that nutrition had much to do with health at all, let alone emotional health or brain function. Publication of the book *Orthomolecular Psychiatry*, by myself and Nobelist Linus Pauling, received a favorable reception from a wide variety of audiences, but not from the medical establishment.[7] (Interestingly enough, more than 20 years later, the concepts presented in the book are fundamental to the current treatment of mental illness.)

The thrust of this book was that serious mental illnesses, such as psychosis, as well as lesser ones, such as emotional disorder, had a genetic basis involving an abnormal biochemical pathway in the brain, a molecular basis that could be corrected on the molecular level. Manic-depressive illness, schizophrenia, alcoholism, and depression, therefore, could be affected by nutrition as well as medication. In 1973, when *Orthomolecular Psychiatry* was published, the psychiatric establishment was still psychoanalytically oriented; the work was primarily accepted by holistic practitioners. The suggested treatment methods and results were frequently verified with kinesiology.

However, it was Dr. Diamond's demonstration that the body instantly went weak in response to unhealthy emotional attitudes or mental stresses that had the greatest ongoing clinical influence. His refinement of the muscle-testing technique, the one used by most practitioners, was used in this study over a period of 15 years. It was universally observed by practitioners and researchers that test responses were completely independent of the test subjects' belief systems, intellectual opinions, reason, or logic. It was also observed that a test response where the subject went weak was accompanied by desynchronization of the cerebral hemispheres.[8]

The Testing Technique

To begin the testing procedure, two people are required. One acts as test subject by holding out one arm laterally, parallel to the ground. The second person then presses down with two fingers on the wrist of the extended arm and says, "Resist." The subject then resists the downward pressure with all his strength. That's all there is to it.

A statement may be made by either party. While the subject holds it in mind, his arm's strength is tested by the tester's downward pressure. If the statement is negative, false, or reflects a calibration below 200 (see "Map of Consciousness," Chapter 3), the test subject will "go weak."

If the answer is yes or calibrates over 200, he will "go strong."

To demonstrate the procedure, one might have the subject hold an image of Abraham Lincoln in mind while being tested, and then, for contrast, an image of Adolf Hitler. The same effect can be demonstrated by holding in mind someone who is loved in contrast to someone who is feared, hated, or about whom there is some strong regret.

Once a numeric scale is elicited (see below) calibrations can be arrived at by stating, "This item" (such as this book, organization, this person's motive, and so on) is "over 100," then "over 200," then "over 300," until a negative response is obtained. The calibration can then be refined: "It is over 220? 225? 230?," and so on. Tester and testee can trade places, and the same results will be obtained. Once one is familiar with the technique, it can be used to evaluate companies, movies, individuals, or events in history; it can also be used to diagnose current life problems.

Please note that the procedure is to use the muscle test to verify the truth or falsity of a *declarative statement*. If the question has not been put into this form, unreliable responses will be obtained. Nor can any reliable result be obtained from inquiry into the future; only statements regarding existent conditions or events will produce consistent answers.

It's necessary to be impersonal during the procedure to avoid transmitting positive or negative feelings. Accuracy is increased by having the test subject close his eyes, and there should be no music in the background.

Because the test is so deceptively simple, an inquirer should first verify its accuracy to his own satisfaction. Responses can be checked by cross-questioning, and everyone who becomes acquainted with the technique thinks of tricks to satisfy himself that it's reliable.[9] It will soon be found that the same response is observed in all subjects, that it isn't necessary for the subject to have any knowledge of the matter in question, and that the response will always be independent of the test subject's personal opinions about the question.

Before presenting an inquiry, we have found it instrumental to first test the statement, "I may ask this question." This is analogous to an entry on a computer terminal, and will occasionally return a "no" answer. This indicates that one should leave that question alone or inquire into the reason for the "no." Perhaps the questioner might have experienced psychological distress from the answer or its implications at that time.[10]

In this study, test subjects were asked to focus on a specified thought, feeling, attitude, memory, relationship, or life circumstance. The test was frequently done in large groups of people; for demonstration purposes, we first established a baseline by asking the subjects, eyes closed, to hold in mind the memory of a time when they were angry, upset, jealous, depressed, guilty, or fearful—at that point, everyone universally went weak. We would then ask them to hold in mind a loving person or life situation, and all would go strong—as a murmur of surprise typically would ripple through the audience at the implications of what they had just discovered.

The next phenomenon demonstrated was that a mere image of a substance held in the mind produced the same response as if the substance were in physical contact with the body. As an example, we would hold up an apple grown with pesticides and ask the audience to look directly at it while being tested; all would go weak. We would then hold up an organically grown apple, free of contaminants, and as the audience focused on it, they would instantly go strong. Inasmuch as no one in the audience knew which apple was which, nor, for that matter, had any anticipation of the test, the reliability of the method was demonstrated to everyone's satisfaction.[11]

Keep in mind that people process experience differently—some primarily adopt a feeling mode, others are more auditory, and still others are more visual. Therefore, test questions should avoid such phrasing as "How do you feel?" about a person, situation, or experience; or "How does it look?"or "How does it sound?" Customarily, if one says, "Hold the situation (or person, place, thing, or feeling) in mind," the subject will instinctively select his appropriate mode.[12]

Occasionally, in an effort, perhaps even unconscious, to disguise their response, subjects will select a mode that is not their customary mode of processing and give a false response. When the tester elicits such a response, the question should be rephrased. For example, a patient who feels guilty about his anger toward his mother may hold in mind a photograph of her and test strong. However, if the tester were to rephrase the question by asking this subject to hold in mind his present attitude toward his mother, the subject would instantly go weak.

Other precautions to maintain the accuracy of the test include removing eyeglasses, especially if they have metal frames, and hats (synthetic materials on top of the head make everyone go weak). The testing arm should also be free of jewelry, especially quartz wristwatches. When an irregular response does occur, further investigation should eventually reveal the cause—the tester, for instance, might be wearing a perfume to which the patient has an adverse reaction, producing false negative responses. If a tester experiences repeated failures while attempting to elicit an accurate response, the effect of his voice on other subjects should be evaluated, for some testers, at least at certain times, may express sufficient negative emotion in their voices to affect test results.[13]

Another factor to be considered in the face of a paradoxical response is the time frame of the memory or image involved. If a test subject is holding in mind a given person and their relationship, the response will depend on the period the memory or image represents. If he's remembering his relationship with his brother from childhood, he may have a different response than if he's holding in mind an image of the relationship as it is today. Questioning always has to be narrowed down quite specifically.[14]

One other cause for paradoxical test results is a physical condition of the test subject resulting from stress, or depression of the thymus gland function from encountering a very negative energy field. The thymus gland is located directly behind the top of the breastbone and is the central controller of the body's acupuncture energy system. When its energy is low, test results are unpredictable; this can be easily remedied in a few seconds by a simple technique discovered by Dr. John Diamond, which he called the "thymus thump." With clenched fist, pound over this area rhythmically several times while smiling and thinking of someone you love. At each thump, say, "Ha-ha-ha." Retesting will now show the resumption of thymic dominance, and test results will return to normal.[15]

Use of the Testing Procedure in This Study

The testing technique just described is that recommended by Dr. Diamond in *Behavioral Kinesiology.* The only variation introduced in our study was the correlation of responses with a logarithmic scale to calibrate the relative power of the energy of different attitudes, thoughts, feelings, situations, and relationships. Since the test is rapid, actually taking less than ten seconds, it's possible to process an enormous amount of information about these matters in a short time.

The numerical scale elicited spontaneously from test subjects—it ranges from the value of mere physical existence at 1, to 600, which is the apex of ordinary consciousness, and then on to 1,000, comprehending advanced states of enlightenment. Responses in the form of simple yes-or-no answers determine the calibration of the subject. For example, "If just being alive is one, then the power of love is over 200?" (Subject goes strong, indicating a yes.) "Love is over 300?" (Subject still goes strong.) "Love is over 400?" (Subject stays strong.) "Love is 500 or over?" (Subject still strong.) In this case, love calibrated at 500, and this figure proved reproducible regardless of how many subjects were tested. With repeated testing—using individuals or groups of testers with individuals or groups of subjects—a consistent scale emerged, which correlates well with human experience, history, and common opinion, as well as the findings of psychology, sociology, psychoanalysis, philosophy, and medicine. It also correlates quite precisely with the perennial philosophy's strata of consciousness.[16]

The tester must be cautious, realizing that the answers

to some questions may be quite disturbing to the subject. The technique must not be used irresponsibly and should always respect the subject's willingness to participate; it should never be used as a confrontational technique. In clinical situations, a personal question is never posed to the test subject unless it's pertinent to a therapeutic purpose. It's possible, though, to pose a question that precludes personal involvement on the part of the test subject, who then functions merely as an indicator for the purposes of calibration.

The test response is independent of the subject's physical strength. It's frequently dumbfounding to well-muscled athletes when they go just as weak as anyone else in response to a noxious stimulus. The tester may well be a frail woman who weighs less than 100 pounds, and the subject may be a professional football player who weighs more than 200, but the test results will be the same, as she puts down his powerful arm with a mere two fingers.

For accurate results, both persons doing the kinesiologic testing must themselves calibrate at level 200 (integrity) or above, and the motivation should be integrous. For numeric calibrations, it's also necessary to refer to the specific scale described in this research; for example, "On a scale of 1 to 1,000, where 200 is the level of integrity or truth, this _____ calibrates at _____." Or, one can merely refer to the scale, or look at or imagine it; that is, "According to the reference scale, this _____ calibrates at _____." Unless a specific scale is alluded to, one might get wildly erroneous responses.

◎ ◎ ◎

CHAPTER THREE

Test Results and Interpretation

One of the goals of this study is to generate a practical map of the energy fields of consciousness so as to delineate the range and general geography of an uncharted area of human investigation. In order to make this more easily understandable for the reader, the numerical designations arrived at for the various energy fields have been rounded to comparative figures.

As we look at the Map of Consciousness (following page), it becomes clear that the calibrated levels correlate with specific processes of consciousness—emotions, perceptions, or attitudes, worldviews and spiritual beliefs. If space permitted, the chart could be extended to include all areas of human behavior. Throughout, the research results were mutually corroborating; the more detailed and extensive the investigation, the greater their corroboration was.

MAP OF CONSCIOUSNESS

God-view	Life-View	Level	Log	Emotion	Process
Self	Is	Enlightenment	700-1,000	Ineffable	Pure Consciousness
All-Being	Perfect	Peace	600	Bliss	Illumination
One	Complete	Joy	540	Serenity	Transfiguration
Loving	Benign	Love	500	Reverence	Revelation
Wise	Meaningful	Reason	400	Understanding	Abstraction
Merciful	Harmonious	Acceptance	350	Forgiveness	Transcendence
Inspiring	Hopeful	Willingness	310	Optimism	Intention
Enabling	Satisfactory	Neutrality	250	Trust	Release

God-View	Life-View	Level	Log	Emotion	Process
Permitting	Feasible	**Courage**	200	Affirmation	Empowerment
Indifferent	Demanding	**Pride**	175	Scorn	Inflation
Vengeful	Antagonistic	**Anger**	150	Hate	Aggression
Denying	Disappointing	**Desire**	125	Craving	Enslavement
Punitive	Frightening	**Fear**	100	Anxiety	Withdrawal
Disdainful	Tragic	**Grief**	75	Regret	Despondency
Condemning	Hopeless	**Apathy**	50	Despair	Abdication
Vindictive	Evil	**Guilt**	30	Blame	Destruction
Despising	Miserable	**Shame**	20	Humiliation	Elimination

The critical response point in the scale of consciousness calibrates at level 200, which is the level associated with integrity and courage. All attitudes, thoughts, feelings, associations, entities, or historical figures below that level of calibration make a person go weak—those that calibrate higher make subjects go strong. This is the balance point between weak and strong attractors, between negative and positive influence.

At the levels below 200, the primary impetus is personal survival, although at the very bottom of the scale—the zone of hopelessness and depression—even this motive is lacking. The higher levels of Fear and Anger are characterized by egocentric impulses arising from this drive for personal survival. At the level of Pride, the survival motive may expand to comprehend the survival of others as well. As one crosses the demarcation between negative and positive influence into Courage, the well-being of others becomes increasingly important. By the 500 level, the happiness of others emerges as the essential motivating force. The high 500s are characterized by interest in spiritual awareness for both oneself and others, and by the 600s, the good of mankind and the search for enlightenment are the primary goals. From 700 to 1,000, life is dedicated to the salvation of all of humanity.

Discussion

Reflection on this map can bring about a profound expansion of one's empathy for life in its variety of expressions. If we examine ostensibly less "virtuous" emotional attitudes, we realize they're neither good nor bad; moralistic judgments are merely a function of the viewpoint from which they proceed.

We see, for instance, that a person in Grief, which calibrates at the low energy level of 75, will be in much better condition if he rises to Anger, which calibrates at 150. Anger, itself a destructive emotion, is still a low state of consciousness, but as social history shows, Apathy can imprison entire subcultures as well as individuals. If the hopeless can come to want something better (Desire—125) and then use the energy of Anger at 150 to develop Pride (175), they may then be able to take the step to Courage, which calibrates at 200, and proceed to improve their individual or collective conditions.

Conversely, the person who has arrived at a habitual state of unconditional Love will find anything less to be unacceptable. As one advances in the evolution of his individual consciousness, the process starts to perpetuate and correct itself so that self-improvement becomes a way of life. This phenomenon can be commonly observed among members of 12-step groups who constantly work at trying to overcome such negative attitudes as self-pity or intolerance. Even people further down on the scale of consciousness may find these same attitudes acceptable and will quite righteously defend them.

Throughout history, all of the world's great spiritual disciplines have been concerned with techniques to ascend through these levels of consciousness. Most have also implied, or even specifically stated, that to move up this ladder is an arduous task—success depends on having a teacher (or at least teachings) to give specific instruction and inspiration to the aspirant, who might otherwise despair over his inability to achieve the goal unaided. Hopefully, this chart will help to facilitate this ultimate human endeavor.

The epistemological effect of awareness of this schema is subtle, but can be far-reaching; implications of these findings have pragmatic applications to sports, medicine, psychiatry, psychology, personal relationships, and the general quest for happiness. Contemplation of the Map of Consciousness can, for instance, transform one's understanding of causality. As perception itself evolves with one's level of consciousness, it becomes apparent that what the world calls *the domain of causes* is in fact *the domain of effects*. By taking responsibility for the consequences of his own perceptions, the observer can transcend the role of victim to an understanding that "nothing out there has power over you." It isn't life's events, but how one reacts to them and the attitude that one has about them, that determines whether such events have a positive or negative effect on one's life, whether they're experienced as opportunity or as stress.

Psychological stress is the net effect of a condition that is being resisted . . . but the condition does not have any power in itself. Nothing has the power to "create" stress. The loud music that raises the blood pressure of one person can be a source of delight to another. A divorce may be traumatic if it's unwanted, or a release into freedom if it's desired.

The Map of Consciousness also casts a new light on the progress of history. The distinction between force and true power is most important for the purposes of this study. We can, for example, investigate a historical epoch such as the end of British colonialism in India. If we calibrate the position of the British Empire at the time, which was one of self-interest and exploitation, we find that it was well below the critical level of 200 on the scale of consciousness. The motivation of Mahatma Gandhi (calibrated at 700) was very near the top of the range of normal human consciousness. Gandhi won in this struggle because his position was one of far greater power. The British Empire represented force (calibrated at 175), and whenever force meets power, force is eventually defeated.

We may observe how throughout history, society has tried to "treat" social problems by legislative action, warfare, market manipulation, laws, and prohibitions—all manifestations of force—only to see these problems persist or recur despite the treatment. Although governments (or individuals) proceeding from positions of force are myopic, to the sensitive observer it eventually becomes obvious that conditions of social conflict won't disappear until the underlying origins have been exposed and "healed."

The difference between *treating* and *healing* is that in the former, the context remains the same, whereas in the latter, the clinical response is elicited by a change of context so as to bring about an absolute removal of the cause of the condition rather than mere recovery from its symptoms. It's one thing to prescribe an anti-hypertensive medication for high blood pressure; it's quite another to expand the patient's context of life so that he stops being angry and repressive.

The empathy derived from contemplating this Map of Consciousness will hopefully make the path to Joy a shorter one. The key to Joy is unconditional kindness to all life, including one's own, which we refer to as *compassion*.[1] Without compassion, little of any significance is

ever accomplished in human endeavor. We may general-
ize to the greater social context from individual therapies,
wherein the patient can't be truly cured or fundamentally
healed until he invokes the power of compassion, both for
himself and others. At that point, the healed may become
a healer.

CHAPTER FOUR

Levels of Human Consciousness

Over the years of this study, millions of calibrations have defined a range of values accurately corresponding to well-recognized sets of attitudes and emotions, localized by specific attractor energy fields, much as electromagnetic fields gather iron fillings. We have adapted the following classification of these energy fields so as to be easily comprehensible, as well as clinically accurate.

It's very important to remember that the calibration figures do not represent an arithmetic, but a *logarithmic,* progression. Thus, the level 300 is *not* twice the amplitude of 150; it is 10 to the 300th power (10^{300}). An increase of even a few points represents a major advance in power; the rate of increase in power as we move up the scale is enormous.

The ways the various levels of human consciousness express themselves are profound and far-reaching; their effects are both gross and subtle. All levels below 200 are destructive of life in both the individual and society at large; all levels above 200 are constructive expressions of power. The decisive level of 200 is the fulcrum that divides the general areas of force and power.

In describing the emotional correlates of the energy fields of consciousness, keep in mind that they're rarely manifested as pure states in an individual. Levels of consciousness are always mixed; a person may operate on one level in a given area of life and on quite another level in another area. An individual's overall level of consciousness is the sum total effect of these various levels.

Energy Level 20: Shame

The level of Shame is perilously proximate to death, which may be chosen out of Shame as conscious suicide or more subtly elected by failure to take steps to prolong life. Death by avoidable accident is common here. We all have some awareness of the pain of "losing face," becoming discredited, or feeling like a "nonperson." In Shame, we hang our heads and slink away, wishing we were invisible. Banishment is a traditional accompaniment of shame, and in the primitive societies from which we all originate, banishment is equivalent to death.

Early life experiences that lead to Shame—such as sexual abuse—warp the personality for a lifetime unless these issues are resolved by therapy. Shame, as Freud determined, produces neurosis. It's destructive to emotional and psychological health and, as a consequence of low self-esteem, makes one prone to the development of physical illness. The Shame-based personality is shy, withdrawn, and introverted.

Shame is used as a tool of cruelty, and its victims often become cruel themselves. Shamed children are brutal to animals and to each other. The behavior of people whose consciousness is only in the 20s is dangerous: They're prone to hallucinations of an accusatory nature, as well as paranoia; some become psychotic or commit bizarre crimes.

Some Shame-based individuals compensate with perfectionism and rigidity, becoming driven and intolerant. Notorious examples are the moral extremists who form vigilante groups, projecting their own unconscious shame onto others whom they then feel justified in righteously attacking. Serial killers have often acted out of sexual moralism, with the justification of punishing "bad" women.

Since it pulls down the whole level of personality, Shame results in a vulnerability to the other negative emotions, and, therefore often produces false pride, anger, and guilt.

Energy Level 30: Guilt

Guilt, so commonly used in our society to manipulate and punish, manifests itself in a variety of expressions, such as remorse, self-recrimination, masochism, and the whole gamut of symptoms of victimhood. Unconscious Guilt results in psychosomatic disease, accident-proneness, and suicidal behaviors. Many people struggle with Guilt their entire lives, while others desperately attempt escape by amorally denying it altogether.

Guilt-domination results in a preoccupation with "sin," an unforgiving emotional attitude frequently exploited by religious demagogues, who use it for coercion and control. Such "sin-and-salvation" merchants, obsessed with punishment, are likely either acting out their own guilt, or projecting it on to others.

Subcultures displaying the aberration of self-flagellation often manifest other regional forms of cruelty, such as the public, ritual killing of animals. Guilt provokes rage, and killing frequently is its expression. Capital punishment is an example of how killing gratifies a Guilt-ridden populace. Our unforgiving American society, for instance, scorns its victims in the press and metes out punishments that have never been demonstrated to have any deterrent or corrective value.

Energy Level 50: Apathy

This level is characterized by poverty, despair, and hopelessness. The world and the future look bleak; pathos is the theme of life. Apathy is a state of helplessness; its victims, needy in every way, lack not only resources, but the energy to avail themselves of what may be available. Unless external energy is supplied by caregivers, death through passive suicide can result. Without the will to live, the hopeless stare blankly, unresponsive to stimuli, until their eyes stop tracking and there isn't enough energy left to even swallow proffered food.

This is the level of the homeless and the derelicts of society; it's also the fate of many of the aged and others who become isolated by chronic or progressive diseases. The apathetic are dependent; people in Apathy are "heavy" and are felt as a burden by those around them. Too often, society lacks sufficient motivation to be of any real help to cultures (as well as individuals) at this level, because they're seen as drains of resources. This is the level of the streets of Calcutta, where only the saintly, such as Mother Teresa and her followers, dare to tread. Apathy is the level of the abandonment of hope, and few have the courage to really look in its face.

Energy Level 75: Grief

This is the level of sadness, loss, and dependency. Most of us have experienced it for periods of time, but those who remain at this level live a life of constant regret and depression. This is the level of mourning, bereavement, and remorse about the past; it's also the level of habitual losers and those chronic gamblers who accept failure as part of their lifestyle, often resulting in loss of jobs, friends, family, and opportunity, as well as money and health.

Major losses early in life make one vulnerable to passive acceptance of grief later on, as though sorrow were the price of life. In Grief, one sees sadness everywhere—in little children, in life itself. This level colors one's entire vision of existence. Part of the syndrome of Grief is the notion of the irreplaceability of what's been lost or that which it symbolized. There is a generalization from the particular so that the loss of a loved one is equated with the loss of love itself. At this level, such emotional losses may trigger a serious depression or death.

Although Grief is the cemetery of life, it still has more

energy to it than Apathy does. Thus, when a traumatized, apathetic patient begins to cry, we know they're getting better. Once they start to cry, they will eat again.

Energy Level 100: Fear

At the level of 100, a lot more life energy is available—fear of danger is healthy. Fear runs much of the world, spurring on endless activity. Fear of enemies, of old age or death, of rejection, and a multitude of social fears are basic motivators in most people's lives.

From the viewpoint of this level, the world looks hazardous, full of traps and threats. Fear is the favored official tool for control by oppressive totalitarian agencies, and insecurity is the stock-in-trade of major manipulators of the marketplace. The media and advertising play to Fear to increase market shares.

The proliferation of fears is as limitless as the human imagination; once Fear is one's focus, the endless worrisome events of the world feed it. Fear becomes obsessive and may take any form—trepidation of losing a relationship leads to jealousy and a chronically high stress level. Fearful thinking can balloon into paranoia or generate neurotic defensive structures and, because it's contagious, become a dominant social trend.

Fear limits growth of the personality and leads to inhibition. Because it takes energy to rise above Fear, the oppressed are unable to reach a higher level unaided. Thus, the fearful seek strong leaders who appear to have conquered their own Fears to lead them out of its slavery.

Energy Level 125: Desire

Even more energy is available at this level; Desire motivates vast areas of human activity, including the economy. Advertisers play on our Desire to program us with needs linked to instinctual drives. Desire moves us to expend great effort to achieve goals or obtain rewards. The desire for money, prestige, or power runs the lives of many of those who have risen above Fear as their predominant life motif.

Desire is also the level of addiction, wherein it becomes a craving more important than life itself. The victim of Desire may actually be unaware of the basis of his motives. Some people become addicted to the hunger for attention and drive others away by their constant demands. The yearning for sexual approval has produced an entire cosmetics and fashion industry.

Desire has to do with accumulation and greed. But Desire is insatiable because it's an ongoing energy field, so that satisfaction of one itch is merely replaced by unsatisfied craving for something else. For instance, multimillionaires tend to remain obsessed with acquiring more and more money.

Desire is obviously a much higher state than Apathy or Grief, for in order to "get," you have to first have the energy to "want." TV has had a major influence on many oppressed people, inculcating wants and energizing their longings to the degree that they move out of Apathy and begin to seek a better life. Want can start us on the road to achievement. Desire can, therefore, become a springboard to yet higher levels of awareness.

Energy Level 150: Anger

Although Anger may lead to homicide and war, as an energy level it's much further removed from death than those below it. Anger can lead to either *con*structive or *de*structive action. As people move out of Apathy and Grief to overcome Fear as a way of life, they begin to want; Desire leads to frustration, which in turn leads to Anger. Thus, Anger can be a fulcrum by which the oppressed are eventually catapulted to freedom. Fury over social injustice, victimization, and inequality has created great movements that led to major changes in the structure of society.

But Anger expresses itself most often as resentment and revenge and is, therefore, volatile and dangerous. Anger as a lifestyle is exemplified by irritable, explosive people who are oversensitive to slights and become "injustice collectors," quarrelsome, belligerent, or litigious.

Since Anger stems from frustrated want, it's based on the energy field below it. Frustration results from exaggerating the importance of desires. The angry person may go into rage, just like a frustrated infant. Anger leads easily to hatred, which has an erosive effect on all areas of a person's life.

Energy Level 175: Pride

Pride, which calibrates at 175, has enough energy to run the United States Marine Corps. It's the level aspired to by the majority of our kind today. In contrast to the lower energy fields, people feel positive as they reach this level. This rise in self-esteem is a balm to all the pain experienced at lower levels of consciousness. Pride looks good and knows it; it struts its stuff in the parade of life. Pride is far enough removed from Shame, Guilt, or Fear that to rise, for instance, out of the despair of the ghetto to the self-respect of being a Marine is an enormous jump. Pride generally has a good reputation and is socially encouraged, yet as we see from the chart of the levels of consciousness, it's sufficiently negative to remain below the critical level of 200. This is why Pride feels good *only* in contrast to the lower levels.

The problem, as we all know, is that "Pride goeth before a fall." Pride is defensive and vulnerable because it's dependent upon external conditions, without which it can suddenly revert to a lower level. The inflated ego is vulnerable to attack. Pride remains weak because it can be knocked off its pedestal back to Shame, which is the threat that fires the fear of loss and pride.

Pride is divisive and gives rise to factionalism; the consequences are costly. Man has habitually died for Pride—armies still regularly slaughter each other for that aspect of it called *nationalism*. Religious wars, political terrorism and zealotry, the ghastly history of the Middle East and Central Europe—these are all the price of Pride, which all of society pays.

The downside of Pride is arrogance and denial. These characteristics block growth; in Pride, recovery from addictions is impossible because emotional problems or character defects are denied. The whole problem of denial is one of Pride. Thus Pride is a very sizable block to the acquisition of real power, which displaces Pride with true stature and prestige.

Energy Level 200: Courage

At the 200 level, power first appears. When we test subjects at all the energy levels below 200, we find, as can be readily verified, that all go weak. Everyone goes strong in response to the life-supportive fields above 200. This is the critical line that distinguishes the positive and negative influences of life. At the level of Courage, an attainment of true power occurs; therefore, it's also the level of empowerment. This is the zone of exploration, accomplishment, fortitude, and determination. At the lower levels, the world is seen as hopeless, sad, frightening, or frustrating; but at the level of Courage, life is seen to be exciting, challenging, and stimulating.

Courage implies the willingness to try new things and deal with the changes and challenges of life. At this level of empowerment, one is able to cope with and effectively handle the opportunities of life. At 200, for instance, the energy to learn new job skills is available. Growth and education become attainable goals. There's the capacity to face fears or character defects and to grow despite them; anxiety also does not cripple endeavor as it would at lower stages of evolution. Obstacles that defeat people whose consciousness is below 200 act as stimulants to those who have evolved into the first level of true power.

People at this level put back into the world as much energy as they take; at lower levels, populations as well as individuals drain energy from society without reciprocating. Because accomplishments result in positive feedback, self-reward and esteem become progressively self-reinforcing. This is where productivity begins.

The collective level of consciousness of mankind remained at 190 for many centuries and, curiously, only jumped to its current level of 207 within the last decade.

Energy Level 250: Neutrality

Energy becomes very positive as we get to the level we have termed *Neutral*, because it's epitomized by release from the positionality that typifies lower levels. Below 250, consciousness tends to see dichotomies and take on rigid positions, an impediment in a world that's complex and multifactorial rather than black and white.

Taking such positions creates polarization, which in turn creates opposition and division. As in the martial arts, a rigid position becomes a point of vulnerability; that which doesn't bend is liable to break. Rising above barriers or oppositions that dissipate one's energies, the Neutral condition allows for flexibility and nonjudgmental, realistic appraisal of problems. To be Neutral means to be relatively unattached to outcomes; not getting one's way is no longer experienced as defeating, frightening, or frustrating.

At the Neutral level, a person can say, "Well, if I don't get this job, then I'll get another." This is the beginning of inner confidence; sensing one's power, one isn't easily intimidated or driven to prove anything. The expectation that life, with its ups and downs, will be basically okay if one can roll with the punches in a 250-level attitude.

People of Neutrality have a sense of well-being; the mark of this level is a confident capability to live in the world. This is the level of safety—people at this level are easy to get along with and safe to be around and associate with because they're not interested in conflict, competition, or guilt. They're comfortable and basically undisturbed emotionally. This attitude is nonjudgmental and doesn't lead to any need to control other people's behaviors. Correspondingly, due to Neutral people's value of freedom, they're difficult to control.

Energy Level 310: Willingness

This very positive level of energy may be seen as the gateway to the higher levels. For instance, at the Neutral level, jobs are done adequately, but at the level of Willingness, work is done *well* and success in all endeavors is common. Growth is rapid here; these are people chosen for advancement. Willingness implies that one has overcome inner resistance to life and is committed to participation. Below the 200 calibration, people tend to be close-minded, but by level 310, a great opening occurs. At this level, people become genuinely friendly, and social and economic success seem to follow automatically. The Willing aren't troubled by unemployment; they'll take any job when they have to, or create a career or self-employment for themselves; they don't feel demeaned by service jobs or by starting at the bottom. They're helpful to others and contribute to the good of society. They're also willing to face inner issues and don't have major learning blocks.

At this level, self-esteem is high and is reinforced by positive feedback from society in the forms of recognition, appreciation, and reward. Willingness is sympathetic and responsive to the needs of others. Willing people are builders of, and contributors to, society. With their capacity to bounce back from adversity and learn from experience, they tend to become self-correcting. Having let go of Pride, they're willing to look at their defects and learn from others. At the level of Willingness, people become excellent students. They're easily trainable and represent a considerable source of power for society.

Energy Level 350: Acceptance

At this level of awareness, a major transformation takes place, with the understanding that one is oneself the source *and* creator of the experience of one's life. Taking such responsibility is distinctive of this degree of evolution, characterized by the capacity to live harmoniously with the forces of life.

All people at levels below 200 tend to be powerless and see themselves as victims, at the mercy of life. This stems from a belief that the source of one's happiness or the cause of one's problems is "out there." An enormous jump—taking back one's own power—is completed at this level, with the realization that the source of happiness is within oneself. At this more evolved stage, nothing "out there" has the capacity to make one happy, and love isn't something that's given or taken away by another, but is created from within.

This level is not to be confused with passivity, which is a symptom of apathy. Acceptance allows engagement in life on life's own terms, without trying to make it conform to an agenda. There's emotional calm with Acceptance, and perception is widened as denial is transcended. One now sees things without distortion or misinterpretation; the context of experience is expanded so that one is capable of "seeing the whole picture." Acceptance has to do essentially with balance, proportion, and appropriateness. The individual at the level of Acceptance isn't interested in determining right or wrong, but instead is dedicated to resolving issues and finding out what to do about problems. Tough jobs don't cause discomfort or dismay. Long-term goals take precedence over short-term ones; self-discipline and mastery are prominent.

At the level of Acceptance, we're not polarized by conflict or opposition; we see that other people have the same rights as we do, and we honor equality. While lower levels are characterized by rigidity, at this level, social plurality begins to emerge as a form of resolution of problems. Therefore, this level is free of discrimination or intolerance; there's an awareness that equality doesn't exclude diversity; Acceptance includes rather than rejects.

Energy Level 400: Reason

Intelligence and rationality rise to the forefront when the emotionalism of the lower levels is transcended. Reason is capable of handling large, complex amounts of data and making rapid, correct decisions; of understanding the intricacies of relationships, gradations, and fine distinctions; and expert manipulation of symbols as abstract concepts becomes increasingly important. This is the level of science, medicine, and of generally increased capacity for conceptualization and comprehension. Knowledge and education are here sought as capital. Understanding and information are the main tools of accomplishment, which is the hallmark of the 400 level. This is the level of Nobel Prize winners, great statesmen, and Supreme Court justices. Einstein, Freud, and many of the other great thinkers of history also calibrate here.

The shortcomings of this level involve the failure to clearly distinguish the difference between symbols and what they represent, and confusion between the objective and subjective worlds that limits the understanding of causality. At this level, it's easy to lose sight of the forest for the trees, to become infatuated with concepts and theories and end up missing the essential point. Intellectualizing can become an end in itself. Reason is limited in that it doesn't afford the capacity for the discernment of essence or of the critical point of a complex issue.

Reason does not of itself provide a guide to truth. It produces massive amounts of information and documentation, but lacks the capability to resolve discrepancies in data and conclusions. All philosophical arguments sound convincing on their own. Although Reason is highly effective in a technical world where the methodologies of logic dominate, Reason itself, paradoxically, is the major block to reaching higher levels of consciousness. Transcending this level is relatively uncommon in our society.

Energy Level 500: Love

Love as depicted in the mass media is not what this level is about. What the world generally refers to as *love* is an intense emotional condition, combining physical attraction, possessiveness, control, addiction, eroticism, and novelty. It's usually fragile and fluctuating, waxing and waning with varying conditions. When frustrated, this emotion often reveals an underlying anger and dependency that it had masked. That love can turn to hate is a common perception, but here, an addictive sentimentality is likely what's being spoken about, rather than Love; there probably never was actual love in such a relationship, for Hate stems from Pride, not Love.

The 500 level is characterized by the development of a Love that is unconditional, unchanging, and permanent. It doesn't fluctuate—its source isn't dependent on external factors. Loving is a state of being. It's a forgiving, nurturing, and supportive way of relating to the world. Love isn't intellectual and doesn't proceed from the mind; Love emanates from the heart. It has the capacity to lift others and accomplish great feats because of its purity of motive.

As this level of development, the capacity to discern essence becomes predominant; the core of an issue becomes the center of focus. As reason is bypassed, there arises the capacity for instantaneous recognition of the totality of a problem and a major expansion of context, especially regarding time and process. Reason deals only with particulars, whereas Love deals with entireties. This ability, often ascribed to intuition, is the capacity for instantaneous understanding without resorting to sequential symbol processing. This apparently abstract phenomenon is, in fact, quite concrete; it's accompanied by a measurable release of endorphins in the brain.

Love takes no position, and thus is global, rising above separation. It's then possible to be "one with another," for there are no longer any barriers. Love is therefore inclusive and expands the sense of self progressively. Love focuses on the goodness of life in all its expressions and augments that which is positive—it dissolves negativity by recontextualizing it, rather than by attacking it. This is the level of true happiness, but although the world is fascinated with the subject of Love, and all viable religions calibrate at 500 or over, it's interesting to note that only 0.4 percent of the world's population ever reaches this level of evolution of consciousness.

Energy Level 540: Joy

As Love becomes more and more unconditional, it begins to be experienced as inner Joy. This isn't the sudden joy of a pleasurable turn of events; it's a constant accompaniment to all activities. Joy arises from within each moment of existence, rather than from any other source; 540 is also the level of healing and of spiritually based self-help groups.

From level 540 up is the domain of saints, and advanced spiritual students and healers. A capacity for enormous patience and the persistence of a positive attitude in the face of prolonged adversity is characteristic of this energy field; the hallmark of this state is compassion. People who have attained this level have a notable effect on others. They're capable of a prolonged, open visual gaze, which induces a state of love and peace.

At the high 500s, the world one sees is illuminated by the exquisite beauty and perfection of creation. Everything happens effortlessly, by synchronicity, and the world and everything in it is seen to be an expression of love and divinity. Individual will merges into divine will. A Presence is felt whose power facilitates phenomena outside conventional expectations of reality, termed *miraculous* by the ordinary observer. These phenomena represent the power of the energy field, not of the individual.

One's sense of responsibility for others at this level is of a different quality from that shown at the lower levels: There's a desire to use one's state of consciousness for the benefit of life itself rather than for particular individuals. This capacity to love many people simultaneously is accompanied by the discovery that the more one loves, the more one can love.

Near-death experiences, characteristically transformative in their effect, have frequently allowed people to experience the energy level between 540 and 600.

Energy Level 600: Peace

This energy field is associated with the experience designated by such terms as *transcendence, self-realization,* and *God-consciousness.* It's extremely rare, attained by only 1 in 10 million people. When this state is reached, the distinction between subject and object disappears, and there's no specific focal point of perception. Not uncommonly, individuals at this level remove themselves from the world, as the state of bliss that ensues precludes ordinary activity. Some become spiritual teachers; others work anonymously for the betterment of mankind. A few become great geniuses in their respective fields and make major contributions to society. These people are saintly and may eventually be officially designated as such, although at this level, formal religion is commonly transcended, to be replaced by the pure spirituality out of which all religion originates.

Perception at the level of 600 and above is sometimes reported as occurring in slow motion, suspended in time and space—nothing is stationary, and all is alive and radiant. Although this world is the same as the one seen by others, it has become continuously flowing, evolving in an exquisitely coordinated evolutionary dance in which significance and source are overwhelming. This awesome revelation takes place nonrationally, so that there is an infinite silence in the mind, which has stopped conceptualizing. That which is witnessing and that which is witnessed take on the same identity; the observer dissolves into the landscape and becomes equally the observed. Everything is connected to everything else by a Presence whose power is infinite, exquisitely gentle, yet rock-solid.

Great works of art, music, and architecture that calibrate between 600 and 700 can transport us temporarily to higher levels of consciousness and are universally recognized as inspirational and timeless.

Energy Levels 700–1,000: Enlightenment

This is the level of the Great Ones of history who originated the spiritual patterns that countless people have followed throughout the ages. All are associated with divinity, with which they're often identified. This is the level of powerful inspiration; these beings set in place attractor energy fields that influence all of mankind. At this level, there is no longer the experience of an individual personal self separate from others; rather, there is an identification of Self with Consciousness and Divinity. The Unmanifest is experienced as Self beyond mind. This transcendence of the ego also serves by example to teach others how it can eventually be accomplished. This is the peak of the evolution of consciousness in the human realm.

Great teachings uplift the masses and raise the level of awareness of all of humanity. To have such vision is called *grace,* and the gift it brings is infinite peace, described as indefinable, beyond words.[1] At this level of realization, the sense of one's existence transcends all time and individuality. There's no longer any identification with the physical body as "me," and therefore, its fate is of no concern. The body is seen as merely a tool of consciousness through the intervention of mind, its prime value that of communication. The self merges back into the Self. This is the level of nonduality, or complete Oneness. There is no localization of consciousness; awareness is equally present everywhere.[2]

Great works of art depicting individuals who have reached the level of Enlightenment characteristically show the teacher with a specific hand position, called *mudra*—wherein the palm of the hand radiates benediction—this is the act of transmitting this energy field to the consciousness of mankind. This level of divine grace calibrates up to 1,000, the highest level attained by anybody who has lived in recorded history—to wit, the Great Avatars for whom the title "Lord" is appropriate: Lord Krishna, Lord Buddha, and Lord Jesus Christ.

◉ ◉ ◉

CHAPTER FIVE

Social Distribution
of Consciousness
Levels

A graphic representation of the distribution of the respective energy levels among the world's population would resemble the shape of a pagoda roof, in that 85 percent of the human race calibrates below the critical level of 200, while the overall average level of human consciousness today is approximately 207.[1] The power of the relatively few individuals near the top counterbalances the weakness of the masses toward the bottom to achieve this overall average. As mentioned, only 4 percent of the world's population calibrates at an energy field of 500 or above; only 0.4 percent reach 540; and a level of consciousness calibrating at 600 or above is reached by only 1 in 10 million.

At first glance, these figures may seem improbable, but if we examine world conditions, we'll quickly be reminded that the populations of entire subcontinents live at a barely existing

level. Famine and disease are commonplace, frequently accompanied by political oppression and scant social resources. Many of these people live in a state of hopelessness calibrating at the level of Apathy, in resignation to
their abject poverty. We must also realize that much of the
remainder of the world's population—civilized as well as
primitive—lives primarily in Fear; the majority of humans
spend their lives in a quest for one form of security or another. Those whose lifestyles transcend the imperative of
survival to allow discretionary options become grist for the
Desire-driven world economic mill, and success in attaining these desires leads at best to Pride.

Any meaningful human satisfaction cannot even com-
mence until the level of 250, where some degree of self-
confidence begins to emerge as a basis for positive life
experiences in the evolution of consciousness.

Cultural Correlations

- The energy fields **below 200** are most common in **extremely primitive conditions** where
  people eke out bare survival. Clothing is
  meager, illiteracy is the rule, infant mortality
  is high, disease and malnutrition are widespread, and there is a vacuum of social
  power. Skills are rudimentary and center
  around gathering fuel and food and preparing shelter, and there is total dependance on
  the vagaries of the immediate environment.
  This is the Stone Age cultural level, little
  more than animal existence.

- Populations characterized by the **low 200s** are typified by unskilled labor, rudimentary trade, and the building of simple artifacts, such as dugout canoes and temporary housing. Mobility begins to express itself in the **nomadic lifestyle,** and in populations that average a somewhat higher consciousness, agriculture appears and barter evolves into the use of token currency.

- The **mid-200s** are associated with **semiskilled labor.** Simple but life-sustaining housing and food economy become dependably available; clothing is adequate, and elementary education begins.

- The **high 200s** are represented by skilled labor, blue-collar workers, tradesmen, retail commerce, and industries. At lower levels, for example, fishing is an individual or a tribal activity, but above the mid-200s, it becomes an **industry.**

- At the level of **300,** we find technicians, skilled and advanced craftsmen, routine managers, and a **more sophisticated business structure.** Completion of secondary education becomes customary. An interest in style, sport, and public entertainment appears; TV is the great pastime at this level.

- In the mid-300s, we find upper management,
  artisans, and educators with an informed
  awareness of public events and a worldview
  that extends beyond the tribe, neighborhood,
  or city to the nation at large and its welfare.
  Social dialogue becomes a meaningful matter
  of interest. Survival has been assured by the
  acquisition of skills and information adequate to function as a civilized society.
  There's social mobility and flexibility, and
  resources that enable a limited amount of
  travel and other stimulating recreation.

- The 400s are the level of the awakening of
  the intellect, where true literacy, higher education, the professional class, executives, and
  scientists can be found. The home, which is
  devoid of reading materials at the lower levels, here exhibits magazines, periodicals, and
  full bookcases. There's an interest in educational broadcast channels on TV, and a more
  sophisticated political awareness. Great communication adeptness, intellectual preoccupation, and artistic creativity are common.
  Recreational activities take the form of chess,
  travel, theater, and concerts. Civic enterprises intended to enhance the social milieu
  receive serious attention. Supreme Court justices, presidents, statesmen, inventors, and
  leaders of industry occupy this general range.
     Because education is the underpinning of
  this level, individuals tend to gather in met-

ropolitan areas where they have access to
sources of information and instruction, such
as at universities. Some aspire to faculty status, while others become lawyers or members of other professional classes. The welfare of one's fellow man is a common
concern, but not yet a driving force. The
high 400s are associated with leaders in their
respective fields; and with high social prestige, accomplishment, and corresponding social trappings. Both Einstein and Freud calibrate at 499. But while the 400s are the level
of universities and doctorates, they're also
the source of limited and limiting Newtonian
visions of the universe and of the Cartesian
split between mind and body (Newton and
Descartes also calibrate at 499).

• Just as the level 200 demarcates a critical
change of consciousness, 500 is a point at
which awareness makes another giant leap.*
Although survival of the individual is still
important, the motivation of Love begins to
color all activities, and creativity comes into
full expression, accompanied by commitment, dedication, and expressions of
charisma. Here, **excellence is common in
every field of human endeavor,** from sport to
scientific investigation. Altruism becomes a
motivating factor, along with dedication to
principles. Leadership is accepted rather than

---

*Due to change of not just power, but of *quality*.

sought. From this level, great music, art, and architecture emerge, as does the capacity to uplift others by one's mere presence.

In the upper 500s, inspirational leaders who set an example for the rest of society are found and, in their respective fields, create new paradigms with their far-reaching implications for all mankind. Although well aware themselves that they still have defects and limitations, people on this level are often seen by the general public as out of the ordinary and may be recognized with emblems of distinction. Many people in the mid-500s begin to have spiritual experiences of profound import and become immersed in spiritual pursuit. Some astonish their friends and families with sudden breakthroughs into new, subjective contexts of reality. Consciousness at this level can be described as *vision* and may focus on uplifting society as a whole. A few even make the great leap to the region that calibrates at 600. At this point, an individual's life may become legendary. The signature of the 600s is *compassion,* pervading all motivation and activity.

Progression of Consciousness

Although the levels we have described span a great variation, it's uncommon for people to move from one level to another during their lifetimes. The energy field that is calibrated for an individual at birth only increases, on the average, by about five points. That an individual's level of consciousness is already in effect at birth is a sobering idea with profound implications. And consciousness itself, in its expression as human civilization, evolves slowly indeed, through innumerable generations.

The majority of people utilize their life experiences to elaborate and express the variations of their native energy field; it's the rare individual who manages to move beyond it, although many may make considerable internal improvement. The reason for this is more easily understandable when we see that what defines one's level is *motivation*. Motivation proceeds from meaning, and meaning, in turn, is an expression in context. Thus, achievement is bounded by context, which, when correspondingly aligned with motivation, determines the individual's relative power.

The average advance of a mere five points in a lifetime is, of course, a statistical figure, produced by, among other things, the unfortunate fact that people's cumulative life choices many times result in a net *lowering* of their level of consciousness. As will be enumerated in detail later (see Chapter 23), the influence of a very few individuals of advanced consciousness counterbalances entire populations at the lower levels. But, conversely, the extreme negativity of a few perverse individuals can sway entire cultures and produce a global drag on the general level of consciousness, as history illustrates too well. Kinesiological testing indicates that a mere 2.6 percent of the human population, identifiable by an abnormal kinesiological polarity (testing strong to negative attractors and weak to positive attractors), accounts for 72 percent of society's problems.

Nonetheless, it's possible to make sudden positive jumps, leaping up even hundreds of points. If one can truly escape the egocentric draw of sub-200 attractor fields, consciously choosing a friendly, earnest, kind, and forgiving approach to life, and eventually making charity toward others one's primary focus, higher levels can certainly be attained. In practice, great will is required.

Thus, although it is not ordinary to move out of one energy field into another during one's lifetime, the opportunity still exists. It remains for motivation to activate that potential; without the exercise of choice, no progression will occur. It's important to keep in mind that the progression of the calibrated power levels is logarithmic; thus, individual choice can have a mighty effect. What's significant is power level—for instance, the difference between 361.0 and 361.1 is very meaningful and capable of transforming both one's life and one's effect on the world at large.

◎ ◎ ◎

CHAPTER SIX

New Horizons in Research

Our concern thus far has been primarily to clarify the structure of the anatomy of consciousness, with some reference to the mechanisms of force and power. But in no sense is this a purely theoretical subject. The unique nature of the research method described herein allows exploration of hitherto inaccessible areas of potential knowledge. It's as applicable to the most everyday practical questions as to the most advanced theoretical explorations. Let's investigate a few general examples.

Social Problems

Drug and alcohol addiction is a crucial social concern that feeds the parallel problems of crime, poverty, and welfare. Addiction has proved an obstinate social and clinical problem, thus far not understood beyond the most basic description. By the term *addiction,* we mean clinical addiction in the classical sense of continued dependence on alcohol or drugs despite serious consequences, a condition exceeding the capacity of the user to discontinue use of the substance unaided, because the will itself has been rendered ineffective. But what is the essential nature of addiction, and what is the addict really hooked on?

The common belief is that it's the substance itself to which the victim has become addicted, due to that substance's power to create a "high" state of euphoria. But if we reexamine the nature of addiction through the methodology outlined herein, a different formulation of the process emerges. Alcohol or drugs do not have the power to create a "high" at all; they calibrate at only 100 (the level of vegetables). The so-called high that the drug or alcohol user experiences, however, can calibrate from 350 to 600. The actual effect of drugs is merely to suppress the lower energy fields, thereby allowing the user to exclusively experience the higher ones. It's as though a filter screened out all the lower tones coming from an orchestra so that all that could be heard were the high notes. The suppression of the low notes doesn't create the high ones; it merely reveals them.

Within the levels of consciousness, the higher frequencies are extremely powerful, and few people routinely experience these as pure states because they're masked by lower energy fields of anxiety, fear, anger, resentment, and so on. Rarely does the average person get to experience, for instance, love without fear, or pure joy, much less ecstasy. But these higher states are so powerful that once they have been experienced, they are never forgotten, and therefore, are sought ever after.

It is to this experience of higher states that people become addicted.[1] A good illustration is presented in the classic movie, *Lost Horizon*. As a concept, Shangri-La (the movie's metaphor for unconditional love and beauty) calibrates at 600—once experienced, it reprograms the experiencer so that he's never content with ordinary consciousness again. The hero of the movie discovers this fact when, after returning from Shangri-La, he's unable to find happiness in the ordinary world again. He then gives up everything in order to seek out and return to that state of consciousness—spending years in a struggle, which almost costs him his life, to find Shangri-La again.

This same reprogramming process occurs in people who have reached high states of consciousness by other means, such as near-death experiences, or experiencing *samadhi* through intense meditation. Such individuals are frequently observed to have changed forever. It isn't uncommon for them to leave all that the material world represents and become seekers of truth; many who had transcendental experiences with LSD in the 1960s did the same thing. Such higher states are also attained through the experiences of love and religion, classical music or art, or through the practice of spiritual disciplines.

The high state that people seek, by whatever means, is in fact the experience field of their own consciousness (Self). If they're spiritually unsophisticated and lack a context with which to comprehend the experience, they believe it's created for something "out there" (such as a guru, music, drugs, lovers, and so forth)—but all that has actually happened is that, under special circumstances, they have experienced what is, in reality, "in here." The majority of people are so divorced from their own states of pure consciousness that they don't recognize them when they experience them, because they identify with their own lower ego states, or their own lowest common denominator. A negative self-image blots out the joyous brilliance that is the true essence of their identities, which therefore goes unrecognized. That this joyous, peaceful, fulfilling state is really one's own essence has been a basic tenet of every great spiritual leader (for example, "the kingdom of God is within you").[2]

A "high" is any state of consciousness above one's customary level of awareness. Therefore, to a person who lives in Fear, moving up to Anger (for instance, rioters in third-world ghettos) is a "high." Fear at least feels better than Despair, and Pride feels far better than Fear. Acceptance is much more comfortable than Courage; Love makes any lower state feel comparatively unattractive. While Joy surpasses all lesser human emotions, ecstasy is a rarely felt emotion in a class by itself. The most sublime experience of all is the state of infinite peace so exquisite that it belies all attempts at description.

The higher the attainment of each of these states, the greater its power to reprogram the subject's entire life. Just one instant in a very high state can completely change a person's orientation to life, as well as his goals and values. It can be said that the individual who was is no more, and a new person is born out of the experience. Through hard-won progress on a dedicated spiritual path, this is the very mechanism of spiritual evolution.

The permanent high-state experience that may be legitimately attained only through a lifetime of dedicated inner work can be reached by artificial means . . .

temporarily. But the balance of nature dictates that to artificially acquire that state without having earned it creates a debt, and the negative imbalance results in negative consequences. The cost of such stolen pleasure is the desperation of addiction, and finally, both the addict and society pay the price.

Ours is a society that idealizes the pleasureless—hard work, stoicism, self-sacrifice, restraint—and condemns pleasure in most of its simpler forms, frequently even declaring these illegal. (Politicians, whether secular or ecclesiastic, understand this phenomenon well. Part of the standard repertoire of local politicians to gain headlines these days is to publicly announce their intent to prohibit erotic magazine in prisons, for instance, or deny the inmates tobacco or TV.)[3] In our society, unfulfilled promises and enticement are legitimized, but satisfaction is denied. Commercialized sexual allure, for instance, is used to sell products endlessly, but the enjoyment of actual commercial sex is forbidden as immoral.

Historically, all ruling classes have achieved status and wealth by controlling society through some form of puritanical ethic. The harder the underlings work, and the more meager their pleasures, the richer the ruling system will be, whether it be a theocracy, aristocracy, oligarchy, or corporate industrial barony. Such power is built upon the forfeited pleasure of workers. Experientially, as we've seen, pleasure is merely high energy. The energies of the masses have been co-opted over the centuries to produce for the overclasses the very wealth of pleasures denied the underclasses.

In truth, the pleasures of life energy are mankind's basic capital; robbing man of this has resulted in the wide division between "haves" and multitudes of "have-nots." What working classes envy in the lives of upper classes is, appropriately, their pleasures, from the joys of exercising power in its varied forms to the beautiful trophies of self-indulgence. The realization that the delights one is denied are being enjoyed by others begets the outrage of revolution or, sublimated, the repression of restrictive laws against the pleasures of one's peers.

The moral code thus functions as a rationalized exploitation of the life energy of the masses, through a calculated distortion of values. The illusion proffered is that the more hellish one's life is, the more heavenly the reward will be. This distorted coupling of pleasure with suffering has produced a morally perverse social milieu, in which pain becomes associated with pleasure. In this atmosphere, the insane alternation of suffering and euphoria that typifies addiction becomes at least provisionally defensible in a deadly antisocial game of winning and losing the forbidden high.

From the same lifeview, society's current method of "treating the problem" by playing the other half of the game arises—denying the nature of substance abuse. By doing so, we've created a marketplace that is so highly lucrative and easily entered into that an entire criminal industry flourishes as a result, corrupting life on multiple levels. The arrest of a drug kingpin, for instance, has no effect at all on the problem; before he's even jailed, he will have been replaced by a new "top dog." For example, when South American drug lord Pablo Escobar died, he was instantly supplanted by three new kingpins, so the hydra now had three heads instead of one.[4]

Society's drug problem requires a social approach

calibrating at 350, and our current anti-drug program calibrates at only 150. Therefore, it's ineffective, and the money spent on it is wasted.

Industrial and Scientific Research

The diagnostic method we've described quickly tracks fruitful areas for research and development in science and industry. Historical examples illustrate how the use of this method could save years of effort and millions of dollars.

Materials Research

Thomas Edison tested more than 1,600 substances before he arrived at tungsten as the most suitable element to be used for his historic development of the incandescent lightbulb.[5] An easier way to detect the best material would be to divide the possible alternatives into two groups and ask, "The material is in this group." (Y/N?) After this determination, the group is again subdivided, and so on. By this method, an answer can be derived in a matter of minutes rather than years.

Product Development

RJR Nabisco Holdings Corporation wasted approximately $350 million to research and produce a smokeless cigarette,[6] on the mistaken assumption that smoking is primarily an oral habit. (In fact, it's since been discovered that when people go blind, they tend to quit. Smoking has multiple bases, of which oral gratification is only one.)[7] A kinesiological test of the market viability of any potential product can arrive at clear conclusions regarding public acceptance and feasibility of marketing in less than a minute. Product acceptability and profitability can be ascertained very accurately if questions are phrased with precision and all contingencies are investigated, including timing, markets, advertising, and subpopulations to be addressed.

Scientific Inquiry

Science provides a field of kinesiological exploration that offers a group of inquirers excitement eclipsing any parlor game. (It's also fascinating for a group to compare what they have discovered with the findings of other groups using the same method.) In a more general application, avenues for fruitful research can be identified quickly, and it will be discovered that often the most valuable insights to be obtained have to do with the range and dimension of research. Since this method bypasses limitations of context, one of its most valuable uses is as a check on the process itself—whether or not it's a correct direction to take. We may thus confirm that basic premises from which inquiries originate have validity.

For instance, our current search for life elsewhere in the universe takes the form of broadcasting the mathematical symbol π (pi) into space. Implicit herein is the assumption that no civilization could develop radio reception unless it could understand that mathematical concept. But it's enormously presumptuous to assume that life elsewhere is even three-dimensional or detectable by human senses at all, let alone composed of distinct life units that solve problems by use of an intellect and employ symbols to communicate across space and time.

Medical Science

Kinesiological diagnosis is a science in its own right, governed by the International College of Applied Kinesiology. Each organ of the body has its corresponding detector muscle, whose weakness signals pathology in the corresponding organ. Kinesiology is already widely used to confirm both diagnosis and the efficacy of a probable therapy. The right dose of the right medicine can also be determined by the patient's kinesiologic response. Similarly, allergies can be detected, and the need for nutritional supplements may be determined.

Research in Theology, Epistemology, and Philosophy

Although the validity of its application may vary with the observer's capacity for awareness, the technique of using kinesiology to ascertain truth itself calibrates at a level of 600. This means that the method described has a degree of reliability that's beyond duality or the realm of ordinary consciousness as we know it in daily life. The level of truth of this book as a whole is approximately 810. To maintain that level throughout, the truth of every chapter, page, paragraph, and sentence has been examined by use of the method described, and all statements and conclusions have been similarly verified.

The confusion surrounding the nature of truth can be mitigated if we calibrate the level of truth of our questions as well as our answers. Paradoxes and ambiguities arise from confusing levels of consciousness; an answer is true only at its own level of consciousness. Thus, we may find that an answer is "correct" but simultaneously "invalid," like a musical note that's correctly played but at the wrong place in the score. All observations are reflections of specific levels of consciousness and are valid only on their own level. Therefore, every means of approaching a subject has its own built-in limitations.

A statement may be true at a high level of understanding, but be incomprehensible to the average mind. Its value may therefore be corrupted when the statement is distorted by the limitations of the listener. This has been the fate of religions throughout the ages, when pronouncements originating from high levels of awareness were later misinterpreted by followers vested with authority.

Such distortion can be seen in the fundamentalist sects of any religion. The fundamentalist's interpretation of religious teachings stresses negativity, and is removed from this negativity only by truth. The lowest depictions of deity are of a god who is jealous, vengeful, and angry, a god of death far removed from the God of mercy and love. The god of righteous negativity represents a glorification of the negative, and provides for his followers a disavowal of responsibility through justification of human cruelty and mayhem. In general, pain and suffering increase as one nears the bottom levels of consciousness.

The truth of each level of consciousness is self-verifying in that each level has its native range of perception, which

confirms what's already believed to be true. Thus, everyone feels justified in the viewpoints that underlie his actions
and beliefs. That's the inherent danger of all "righteousness": *Anyone* can be righteous, from the killer who justifies his rage, to ecclesiastic demagogues and political
extremists of all persuasions. By distorting context, it's possible to rationalize and justify almost any human behavior. All wars are stated to be "righteous" by their perpetrators.

The human dialogue is awesome in its enormity and
subtlety, reflecting the kaleidoscopic interactions of the
powerful attractor energy fields constituting man's consciousness. The brilliance of the world's great philoso-
phers through 25 centuries has been staggering in its
scope and complexity. Yet, overall there are few areas of
agreement with respect to the nature of truth. Without
an objective yardstick, every individual who has ever
lived has had to sift through the changing reflections of
life to discern his own truth; this seems a never-ending
struggle to which man is condemned by virtue of his
own mental design.

This design predicates that any statement will be true
only within a given context, despite the fact that the def-
initions and derivations of that context are invisible and
unstated. It's as though every individual is exploring life
with a compass that has a unique setting. That any meaningful dialogue at all is possible bespeaks man's enormous compassion for his own condition and attests that
giving cohesion to the whole is an all-inclusive, overarching

attractor field that facilitates the manifestation of the possible into the actual.

Concordance emerges from the organizing patterns hidden behind apparent chaos; thus, the evolution of mankind progresses despite the apparently aberrant signals of individuals at any given moment. Chaos is only a limited perception. Everything is a part of a larger whole; everyone is involved in the evolution of the all-inclusive attractor field of consciousness itself. It's the evolution, innate to the overall field of consciousness, which guarantees the salvation of mankind, and with it, all of life. The nobility of man is in his constant struggle with his own unasked-for existence in a world that is a house of mirrors—his sole support, and his faith in the process of life itself.

CHAPTER SEVEN

Everyday Critical Point Analysis

The potential applications for research we've described thus far offer some suggestions about the limitless uses for which this method is applicable. As the interaction of attractor fields of energy with human consciousness reveals itself in an interaction of mind and body, the basic level of available energy in any enterprise can be calibrated by anyone, anywhere, anytime. All that's required is two people, one of whom is familiar with the muscle-testing technique described in this study. The practical implications are staggering; this tool can be as important to the continuing evolution of society as any of the major discoveries of the physical sciences to date. Let's spell out in more pragmatic detail what this could mean in everyday life.

Inasmuch as the calibrated power of an identified attractor pattern is directly related to its level of truth, it's possible to cleanly distinguish true from false, constructive from destructive, the practical and efficient from the unworkable and wasteful. We can identify motive, agenda, and goal in any project or in individuals themselves. Sheep's clothing needs to hide the wolf no longer.

As we've seen, consciousness reacts decisively to the difference between truth and falsehood. You may instantly reconfirm this by stating your true age (let's say that you're 43 years old), "I am 43 years old," and having someone press down on your extended arm. You'll stay strong. Now say, "I am 45 years old," and you'll instantly go weak. Like a computer, consciousness simply answers 0 or 1, true or false. (Any ambiguities in the process are introduced by the questioning method, not the answering mechanism. See Chapter 2, Appendix B, and below.)

We can identify the level of truth of any statement, belief system, or body of knowledge. We may accurately measure the truth of any sentence, paragraph, chapter, or entire book, including this one.[1] We can reliably identify our own level of consciousness or motive in any enterprise. We now have available a perspective on social movements and history never before possible. Political research isn't confined to the present—we can look back into history to make calibrations, for instance, to compare Gorbachev with Stalin, Trotsky with Lenin, and so on.

In all of these exercises, kinesiology reveals the hidden implicit order by making it explicit, disclosing its true nature. The use of the system is self-educative and self-directing. Each answer, it will be discovered, leads to the next question—happily, in an upward and beneficial direction. We discover the truth about ourselves because our questions are themselves merely the reflections of our own motives, goals, and levels of awareness. It's always informative to calibrate not the answer, *but the question*. In discussing the process, we must emphasize again, more specifically, some aspects of the form of questioning. *Precision in working is of paramount importance.* The question might be posed, for instance, "Is this decision a good one?" But what do we mean by "good"? Good for whom, and in what time frame? Questions have to be very carefully defined: What we think is good or bad is merely subjective; what the universe "thinks" about it may be something else entirely.

Motive in questioning is highly significant. Always ask first, "I may ask this question?" Never ask a question unless you're prepared for the answer; the facts may be quite different from what you currently believe. Although there is a potential for emotional upset through the unwise use of this method, experience has shown that continuing the line of inquiry will enlarge the context and heal the disturbance. Let's say a young woman asks, "My boyfriend is honest?" or "He is good for my life?" and the answers are negative; consequently, she becomes disappointed to find that his love is selfish and his interest exploitative. But further questions provide a resolution: "I am saving myself a lot of misery now by knowing this?" (Yes.) "I can learn from the experience?" (Yes.)

On a more mundane level, the same technique can determine whether an investment is an honest one or not, or whether or not an institution can be trusted. We can accurately predict the potential of new developments, not only in marketing, but in medical research or engineering. We can check the safety precautions being used on great oil tankers. We can judge in advance the advisability of military strategy. We can ascertain who is fit to govern, and distinguish the statesman from the mere politician. In the case of a media event, we can instantly tell whether the interviewer or the interviewee is telling the truth, and, if he is, what level of truth is being expressed. (If you try this during a network news hour, you may have a shocking revelation; on many occasions, *all* the public figures shown are lying.)

Want to tell if that used car is a good one to buy? Easy. If a salesman is telling the truth? Simple. If your new romantic interest is a good bet? Is this is a reliable product? Is that employee trustworthy? What's the degree of safety of a new device? What's the integrity, skill, and competence level of a particular doctor or lawyer? Who's the best available therapist, teacher, coach, repairman, mechanic, or dentist? What levels of consciousness are required to properly discharge the duties of specific public offices, and what are the levels of the incumbents?

This capacity to instantly differentiate truth from falsehood is of such extraordinary potential value to society that we've felt it appropriate in our research to document and verify some explicit practical applications.

Current and Historic Events

Because the technique immediately distinguishes true evidence from false, it can resolve factual disputes—the identity of perpetrators, for instance, or the whereabouts of missing persons. The truth underlying major news events can be revealed, whether it's the guilt or innocence of contemporary victims and accusers, or the validity of historic conspiracy theories or unsolved mysteries, such as the Amelia Earhart disappearance, the Lindbergh kidnaping, and so on. Testimony before Senate hearings and media reports of events are verifiable in a matter of seconds.

Health Research

The failure to eradicate certain diseases or find their cure is often due to the fact that reason is its own limitation. False answers often preclude searching for true causes. For instance, it's currently dogma that tobacco causes cancer; our research, however, revealed that organically grown tobacco tests kinesiologically strong, whereas commercial tobacco tests weak. Tobacco wasn't noted as a carcinogen before 1957, but it does so now as the result of chemicals introduced into its manufacture at that time. There are other solutions to smokers' lung cancer. Research reported in *Science* in 1995 indicates that one gram per day of vitamin C prevents cell damage from smoking. Another solution is to identify and remove the carcinogenic chemicals from the manufacturing process.

Criminal Justice and Police Work

To know whether or not a witness is lying is of obvious importance in any case under investigation. But it's equally significant to discover whether the prosecution is withholding evidence or if a jury has been tampered with (or, for that matter, is even capable of understanding the evidence).

One of the most interesting applications of the technique is in crimes where there are no witnesses, and it's the word of the accuser against that of the accused. Allegations of sexual crimes against prominent people is an obvious example. Public figures are easy targets for politically motivated character assassination, and in a society where defendants are treated by the media as if proven guilty merely by virtue of having been accused, they need public protection as much as the accusers.

Statistics and Methodology: Time Saving

Great amounts of money and time are spent gathering data to document what could easily be discerned in minutes. For instance, to "prove" the validity of the kinesiological method itself to the skeptical, the following procedures had to be followed: (1) 15 different small groups totaling 360 subjects were tested with both positive and negative stimuli (statistical analysis revealed that $p \leq .001$); (2) 7 large groups totaling 3,293 volunteers were similarly tested ($p \leq .001$); (3) 325 subjects were tested individually ($p \leq .001$); (4) 616 psychiatric patients were tested in groups and individually ($p \leq .01$). The conclusion from all the above was that the null hypothesis was rejected. Traditional methodologies are indifferent.

Politics and Government

Are our leaders telling us the truth? Is a political figure upholding the Constitution of the United States or subverting it for personal gain? Does a particular candidate have the unique capacity to rise to the demands of the office he or she seeks? Are facts being misrepresented by a government agency or spokesperson? Will a proposed policy actually solve the problem that it's been designed for? Such practical issues can now be addressed with more certainty. Political debates and public addresses can be analyzed for factuality, and proposed legislation can be assessed from a clearer perspective. Programs that are worthwhile can be definitely identified, and ineffective programs can be dropped.

Commerce

It's possible to diagnose an ailing business or industry and solve its problems without risking financial resources on experiments. Complete analysis of a business starts with calibrating the current and past levels of collective motivation and the abilities of all concerned in its operation. Next, one may calibrate what level needs to be reached by the various departments to succeed. Then policies, personnel, products, supplies, advertising, marketing, and hiring procedures can be similarly assessed. Various market strategies can then be investigated without investment in expensive market analysis, preserving capital while saving enormous amounts of time and energy.

Keep in mind that in the conventions of commerce, like those of politics, truth has an ambiguous status. There's a universally accepted, implicit understanding that things said to gain advantage aren't held to any standard of personal honesty. A convenient conscience regarding the exaggerated claim, the bluff, the white lie, is as much a part of the garb of the marketplace as the business suit and tie. (In fact, intriguingly, kinesiological analysis commonly tells us to no longer believe an erstwhile trustworthy person once he's donned a suit and tie!) Therefore, numerous applications arise in everyday business—for instance, to determine whether a bill or invoice is accurate. A padded account will make any investigator's arm go weak, as will inferior quality or workmanship. Fraud and bogus imitations are easily detectable; the technique can quickly differentiate a bad check from a good one, a false diamond from a true gem, and genuine art from a fake.

Science and Research

The level of truth of any scientific paper, experiment, or theory is easily determinable, a great potential asset to the scientific community and the public at large. The benefits to be derived from a given direction of investigation can be ascertained in advance, as can the value of alternate avenues of research. Examination of the economics of research projects and the capabilities of investigators and equipment is also of practical value.

Critical factor analysis can detect the point in a system at which the least effort is capable of producing the greatest result. Computer simulation, with all its complex and uncertain variables, is the present state-of-the-art technique for predicting developments and exploring alternative proposals. The built-in limitations of logic circuits, however, can be transcended by the kinesiologic use of the world's most advanced computer, the human nervous system. Quantum nonlocality guarantees that the answers to each question are present everywhere, but this in itself can be confusing to a conventional computer.

Clinical Work

In medicine, the accuracy of diagnoses, as well as the efficacy of a prescribed treatment, can be tested. The technique is also valuable in psychological issues, where the cause of a disorder can be quickly ascertained. One currently controversial subject of investigation that obviously suggests itself is the area of so-called repressed childhood memories of alleged sexual abuse. Facts can be quickly differentiated from false "memories" elicited in response to suggestion. Freud concluded that most reports of childhood incest he encountered were of hysterical origin, and he finally stopped believing them altogether.

Kinesiologic testing is used to back up clinical judgments, as well as scientifically controlled investigation, because it can transcend the built-in design limitation of double-blind research, which can of itself create the very error it's supposed to prevent. Statistics are no substitute for truth, and in the complexity of bio-behavioral phenomena, proximal antecedents can too easily become classified as apparent causes. The real "cause" may well be the pull of the future through a hidden attractor field.

Education

A profoundly telling exercise may be performed by evaluating the books in one's library. Simply hold them over your solar plexus, and have somebody test your muscle strength. As you do so, your books will end up in two piles; reflection on the differences between the two can produce a revelation—many testers have found it one of the most valuable experiences of their lives. (Some left the two piles there for a period of time to let the lesson sink in.)

It's equally informative to try the same procedure with one's music collection. The negative group will include violent, sexist rap and heavy metal rock. The positive pile will contain classical, classic rock (including The Beatles), much country music (surprisingly, it calibrates generally at 520—the problems of the heart), reggae, popular ballads, and the like.

Spirituality

Although this chapter has dealt primarily with secular uses of this tool, it should be pointed out that applications of the technique can be profoundly spiritual. We may, for instance, test the contrasting statements: "I *am* a body," and "I *have* a body." Appropriate questions proceeding from this point can resolve one's most basic fears. All limiting self-definitions create fear because they create vulnerability. Our perceptions are essentially distorted by our own self-definition, which in turn is qualified by identifying with our limitations. Error occurs when we cling to the belief that I *am* "that." Truth is unveiled when we see that one *has* "that" or *does* "that," instead of *is* "that."

There is great freedom in the realization that I "have" a body and a mind, rather than I "am" my mind or body. Once the fear of death is transcended, life becomes a transformed experience because that particular fear underlies all others. Few people know what it is to live without fear—but beyond fear lies joy, as the meaning and purpose of existence become transparent. Once this realization occurs, life becomes effortless and the sources of suffering dissolve; suffering is only the price we pay for our attachments.

Empirical issues, however, are involved even in spiritual quests. In the matter of spiritual teachers, Americans are extremely naïve, partly because such pursuit doesn't have a long tradition here as it does in older cultures. That the world abounds with false gurus is well known in India, but such cynicism doesn't come readily to Americans. Impostors repeatedly come out of India with impressive presentations and hoodwink naïve Western spiritual aspirants who, in childlike trust, leave home and hearth, sell their belongings, and follow the charismatic spiritual con man down a path to eventual disillusionment. The shrewdness of some of these "gurus" can be dazzling, and their capacity to mimic a convincing sincerity is amazing; they often take in even sophisticated spiritual seekers. This is spiritual seduction. A mixture of truth and falsehood blended in a slick package, the teachings sound valid if one can't see that their truth has been distorted by a false context.

Such spiritual exploitation is routinely exposed in India, where these media-hungry frauds are held in low regard and often confined to their quarters by the government should they return home. Such "teachers" can inflict terrible suffering and tragedy. In clinical practice, the most catastrophic depressions occur in people who have discovered that they've been spiritually deceived. Such disillusionment and pain is far more severe than that which results from other losses in life, and recovery hasn't always been possible.

The charm of all false prophets is persuasiveness. But use of the testing method described herein provides a foolproof safeguard against such deception. It's informative to watch TV evangelists with the sound turned off and have somebody test you. False gurus also make people go weak in a dramatic fashion. It's as though the universe considers spiritual rape an especially grave error.

What of a true teacher? In the first place, a universal hallmark is that the true teacher never controls anyone's life in any way—instead, they merely explain how to advance consciousness. But if we do test, we'll find that Mother Teresa, recognized by the world through the Nobel Prize, calibrates at 700, as does the acknowledged Indian spiritual saint, Ramana Maharshi, who died in 1950. (He went into a state of enlightenment at age 16, never left the mountain where he lived, and led a life of humble simplicity, eschewing money, prestige, and followers, and would have remained anonymous had not a well-known British writer's description of Maharshi's enlightened state brought seekers to him from all over the world.)[2]

Nowhere is spiritual fraud more prevalent than in the world of channelers and psychics. It's informative to check out the level of truth these mediums express, as well as the level of the "source" on the "other side." Sometimes a surprisingly high level of truth is in fact being taught. A level of truth which calibrates at 500 is worth listening to—regardless of its origin—because the inability to love is what's at the root of most human problems. Beyond the level of 500, possessions and worldly needs become irrelevant, which is why true teachers neither seek nor desire material gain.

Appropriate use of the system will always lead to self-discovery and growth. Eventually, it can lead us to have compassion for everyone, when we see how we all must struggle with the downside of human nature. Everybody is crippled in some area, and each one of us is somewhere on the path of evolution—some people are ahead of us, and some are behind. In the steps we've walked are the old lessons of life, and before us are new teachings.

There's nothing to feel guilty about and nothing to blame. There's no one to hate, but there are those things that are better avoided, and such blind alleys will become increasingly apparent. Everyone has chosen his own level of consciousness, yet nobody could have done otherwise at any given point in time. We can only get "there" from "here." Every leap has to have a platform to originate from. Pain exists to promote evolution; its cumulative effect finally forces us in a new direction, although the mechanism may be very slow. How many times is it necessary to hit bottom before a lesson is learned? Perhaps thousands, which may account for the sheer quantity of human suffering, so vast as to be incomprehensible. Slowly, by inches, does civilization advance.

It's an interesting exercise to use the technique to reassess our society's scapegoats—for example, to calibrate the current power level of the United Nations, and then ask what level would be required to successfully do the job for which it was designed. When we see such discrepancies spelled out in plain numbers, we may stop berating individuals and institutions, realizing that they often simply do not have the requisite power to accomplish their tasks. Condemnation disappears with understanding, as does guilt. All judgment reveals itself to be self-judgment in the end, and when this is understood, a larger comprehension of the nature of life takes its place.

That which is injurious loses its capacity to harm when it's brought into the light. And now nothing need remain hidden. Every thought, action, decision, or feeling creates an eddy in the interlocking, interbalancing, ever-moving energy fields of life, leaving a permanent record for all of time. This realization can be intimidating when it first dawns on us, but it becomes a springboard for rapid evolution.

In this interconnected universe, every improvement we make in our private world improves the world at large for everyone. We all float on the collective level of consciousness of mankind so that any increment we add comes back to us. We all add to our common buoyancy by our efforts to benefit life. What we do to serve life automatically benefits all of us because we're all included in that which is life. We *are* life. It's a scientific fact that "what is good for you is good for me."

Simple kindness to one's self and all that lives is the most powerful transformational force of all. It produces no backlash, has no downside, and never leads to loss or despair. It increases one's own true power without exacting any toll. But to reach maximum power, such kindness can permit *no* exceptions, nor can it be practiced with the expectation of some selfish reward. And its effect is as far-reaching as it is subtle.

In a universe where "like goes to like" and "birds of a feather flock together," we attract to us what we emanate. Consequences may come in an unsuspected way: We're kind to the elevator man, and a year later, a helpful stranger gives us a hand on a deserted highway. An observable "this" doesn't *cause* an observable "that." Instead, in reality, a shift in motive or behavior acts on a field that then produces an increased likelihood of responding in a positive way. Our inner work is like building up a bank account, but one that we can't draw from at will. The disposition of the funds is determined by a subtle energy field, which awaits a trigger to release this power back into our own lives.

Dickens's *A Christmas Carol* is the story of all of our lives. We're all Scrooge; but we're all Tiny Tim, as well. All of us are both selfish and lame in some areas. We're all victims like Bob Cratchit, and we're all as indignantly moralistic as Mrs. Cratchit refusing to toast Scrooge. The Ghost of Christmas Past haunts all of our lives; the Spirit of Christmases to Come beckons us all to make the choices that will enhance both our own existence and that of others. (If we calibrate the energy level of Christmas, by the way—535—it then becomes obvious that its power resides within the human heart itself.)

All avenues of questioning lead to the same ultimate answer: The discovery that nothing is hidden and truth stands everywhere revealed is the key to enlightenment about the simplest practical affairs and the destiny of mankind. In the process of examining our everyday lives, we can find that all of our fears have been based on false-hood. The displacement of the false by the true is the essence of the healing of all things visible and invisible.

And always a final question will eventually arise for every questioner—the biggest question of all: "Who am I?"

◉ ◉ ◉

CHAPTER EIGHT

The Source of Power

The ultimate object of our investigation is a practical understanding (rather than an academic or philosophic one), although certain philosophical conclusions can immediately be drawn from even a brief analysis of power and force. From a practical viewpoint, before proceeding we need to know what the intrinsic source of power is and how it operates. What accounts for its greater strengths? Why is it that force always eventually succumbs to power?

In this respect, the Constitution of the United States can provide a rewarding study. This document calibrates at about 700. If one goes through it sentence by sentence, the source of its power appears: It's the concept that all men are created equal by virtue of the divinity of their creation, and human rights are intrinsic to human creation and therefore inalienable. Interestingly enough, this is the very concept that was the source of power for Mahatma Gandhi.

Power vs. Force

On examination, we'll see that power arises from *meaning*. It has to do with motive, and it has to do with principle. Power is always associated with that which supports the significance of life itself. It appeals to that part of human nature that we call *noble*—in contrast to force, which appeals to that which we call *crass*. Power appeals to what uplifts, dignifies, and ennobles. Force must always be justified, whereas power requires no justification. Force is associated with the partial, power with the whole.

If we analyze the nature of force, it becomes readily apparent why it must always succumb to power; this is in accordance with one of the basic laws of physics. Because force automatically creates counter-force, its effect is limited by definition. We could say that force is a movement—it goes from here to there (or tries to) against opposition. Power, on the other hand, is still. It's like a standing field that doesn't move. Gravity itself, for instance, doesn't move against anything. Its power moves all objects within its field, but the gravity field itself does not move.

Force always moves against something, whereas power doesn't move against anything at all. Force is incomplete and therefore has to be fed energy constantly. Power is total and complete in itself and requires nothing from outside. It makes no demands; it has no needs. Because force has an insatiable appetite, it constantly consumes. Power, in contrast, energizes, gives forth, supplies, and supports.

Power gives life and energy—force takes these away. We notice that power is associated with compassion and makes us feel positively about ourselves. Force is associated with judgment and makes us feel poorly about ourselves. Force always creates counterforce; its effect is to polarize rather than unify. Polarization always implies conflict; its cost, therefore, is always high. Because force incites polarization, it inevitably produces a win/lose dichotomy; and because somebody always loses, enemies are created. Constantly faced with enemies, force requires constant defense. Defensiveness is invariably costly, whether in the marketplace, politics, or international affairs.

In looking for the source of power, we've noted that it's associated with meaning, and this meaning has to do with the significance of life itself. Force is concrete, literal, and arguable. It requires proof and support. The sources of power, however, are inarguable and aren't subject to proof. The self-evident isn't arguable. That health is more important than disease, that life is more important than death, that honor is preferable to dishonor, that faith and trust are preferable to doubt and cynicism, that the constructive is preferable to the destructive—all are self-evident statements not subject to proof. Ultimately, the only thing we can say about a source of power is that it just "is."

Every civilization is characterized by native principles. If the principles of a civilization are noble, it succeeds; if they're selfish, it falls. As a term, *principles* may sound abstract, but the consequences of principle are quite concrete. If we examine principles, we'll see that they reside in an invisible realm within consciousness itself. Although we can point out examples of honesty in the world, honesty itself as an organizing principle central to civilization does not independently exist anywhere in the external world. True power, then, emanates from consciousness itself; what we see is a visible manifestation of the invisible.

✢ ✢ ✢

Pride, nobility of purpose, sacrifice for quality of life—all such things are considered inspirational, giving life significance. But what actually inspires us in the physical world are things that symbolize concepts with powerful meanings for us. Such symbols realign our motives with abstract principle. A symbol can marshal great power because of the principle that already resides within our consciousness.

Meaning is so important that when life loses meaning, suicide commonly ensues. When life loses meaning, we first go into depression; when life becomes sufficiently meaningless, we leave it altogether. Force has transient goals; when those goals are reached, the emptiness of meaninglessness remains. Power, on the other hand, motivates us endlessly. If our lives are dedicated, for instance, to enhancing the welfare of everyone we contact, our lives can never lose meaning. If the purpose of our life, on the other hand, is financial success, what happens after it's been attained? This is one of the primary causes of depression in middle-aged men and women.

The disillusionment of emptiness comes from failing to align one's life with the principles from which power originates. A useful illustration of this phenomenon can be seen in the lives of great musicians, composers, and conductors of our own times. How frequently they continue productive careers into their 80s and 90s, often having children and living vigorously until a ripe old age![1] Their lives have been dedicated to the creation and embodiment of beauty, which incorporates and expresses enormous power. We know clinically that alignment with beauty is associated with longevity and vigor—because beauty is a function of creativity, such longevity is common in all creative occupations.

New Paradigms

The philosophic position of positivism, based on the premise that nothing is real except as it is quantifiable, is native to the sciences. The sources of power, however, are invisible and intangible. The fallacy of logical empiricism is clear from its essential premise. To say that nothing is real unless it's measurable is already an abstract position, is it not? This proposition itself isn't tangible, visible, or measurable; the argument of tangibility is itself created from the intangible.

Even if such a position were valid, who would want to live without pride, honor, love, compassion, or valor? Despite the pathetic implications of this argument, let's address it nevertheless.

Does power have any tangible basis? Does it proceed exclusively from the undefinable, the mystical, philosophic, spiritual, or abstract? Is there anything more we can know about power that would make sense to those who are oriented only to that left-brain world, which, regardless of its computerized sophistication, remains only a system of mechanical measurements?

Before we proceed, let's remind ourselves that the most advanced artificial intelligence machines in the world are unable to feel joy or happiness. Force can bring satisfaction, but only power brings joy. Victory over others brings us satisfaction, but victory over *ourselves* brings us joy. But as previous chapters have shown, not only can these qualities now be measured, they can be accurately calibrated. To make this fact more comprehensible to reason, let's continue our tour through some easily understood concepts from advanced theoretical physics.

We needn't be intimidated by these concepts; to the contrary, their implications for daily life, though profound, are quite simple. We don't have to understand the molecular structure of rubber in order to benefit from having tires on our cars. Even though their proofs may be complex, Einstein's Theory of Relativity, Bell's Theorem, and so on, can all be stated in a few easily understandable sentences.

Several recently defined concepts have relevance in understanding the nature of power. One is physicist David Bohm's theory, which states that there is both a visible and an invisible universe.[2] This idea shouldn't be daunting; many things that we have a daily familiarity with, such as x-rays, radio and TV waves, aren't visible either. An "enfolded" universe runs parallel to the visible, "unfolded" universe, which is itself merely a manifestation of that enfolded, invisible universe.

Thus, for instance, did the idea of building the world's tallest building rally support—eventually the result was that an invisible concept became the Empire State Building in the visible world. The enfolded universe is connected with human consciousness, as inspiration arises in the mind of a creator. Bohm says meaning links mind and matter like opposite sides of a coin.[3] Another useful concept is Rupert Sheldrake's notion of morphogenetic fields, or M-fields.[4] These invisible organizing patterns act like energy templates to establish forms on various levels of life. It's because of the distinctiveness of M-fields that identical representations of a species are produced. Something similar to M-fields also exists in energy fields of consciousness, underlying thought patterns and images—a phenomenon termed "formative causation." The idea that M-fields assist learning has been verified by wide-scale experimentation.[5]

When Sir Roger Bannister broke the four-minute mile, he created a new M-field. The belief system prevailing in human consciousness had been that the four-minute mile was a limit of human possibility. Once the new M-field was created, many runners suddenly began to run sub-four-minute miles. This occurs every time mankind breaks into a new paradigm, whether it's the capacity to fly (an M-field created by the Wright Brothers), or the capacity to recover from alcoholism (an M-field created by Bill W., the founder of Alcoholics Anonymous). Once an M-field is created, everyone who repeats the accomplishment reinforces the power of that M-field.

We're all familiar with the fact that new ideas often seem to arise in the minds of several far-removed people at the same time. Somehow, the M-field acts as an organizing principle, like a sort of general magnetic attraction. An M-field doesn't have to move anywhere—it's a standing energy field that's present everywhere. Once it's created, it exists as a universally available pattern throughout the invisible universe.

Chaos Theory

The next concept we need to consider in more detail is the *chaos theory* (nonlinear dynamics). Its first application was in the examination of weather. Over the centuries, the study of it had established the consensus that there was no definable, predictable mathematical pattern to weather (just as it had also been determined that there was no mathematical way to prove when a dripping faucet will drip, or even to explain how a droplet is formed). Chaos merely means a mass of apparently meaningless data—for instance, dots—in which one can't see any inherent organizing pattern. With the advent of advanced computer technology, it was discovered that inner organizing patterns could be found by computer analysis in what looked disorganized—that which appears to be incoherent actually has an inner coherence.

Such analysis revealed patterns that often look like the figure eight folded back upon itself, frequently with a funnel effect, so that the graphic itself has a repeatable geometric configuration. What science has realized is what mystics have claimed throughout the centuries: That the universe is indeed coherent, unified, and organized around unifying patterns.[6]

Nonlinear dynamics has verified that there really is no chaos in the universe; the appearance of disorder is merely a function of the limits of perception. This came as a disturbing revelation to left-brain people, but seemed self-evident to right-brain types. Creative people merely write, paint, sculpt, or design what they already see within their own minds—after all, we don't dance from logic, we dance from feeling patterns. We make our choices from values, and values are associated with intrinsic patterns.

The accepted chain of causality as commonly understood in the basic sciences occurs as the sequence A→B→C. In this scheme of material determinism, nothing is inherently free, but only the result of something else. It's thereby limited; what this system really defines is the world of force. Force A results in Force B and is transmitted to Force C with consequence D. D, in turn, becomes the beginning of another series of chain reactions, *ad infinitum*. This is the left-brain world, mundane and predictable. It's the limited paradigm that the conventional sciences operate from: familiar, controllable, able to be charted, but uncreative—determined, and therefore limited, by the past. It isn't the world of genius, but to many it feels safe. It's the world of productivity and practicality—but to creative people, it seems pedestrian, prosaic, and uninspiring.

It's one thing to conceive of the Empire State Building; it's something else to make it happen. To make a thing happen requires motivation. Motivation is derived from meaning. Therefore, the visible and invisible worlds are linked together, as we've already diagramed it:

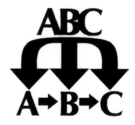

Here we see the concept ABC, which within the invisible, enfolded universe will activate emergence into the visible world to result in A→B→C. Thus, the visible world is created from the invisible world, and is therefore influenced by the future.[7] The capacity of the invisible concept to materialize is based on the power of the original concept itself. We might say that the right brain "gets the pattern" and the left brain "makes it visible." An ABC may be either a high-energy attractor or a low-energy attractor. Certain concepts and values apparently have greater power than others. (Thus far, science has only defined that attractors may have either high energy or low energy.)

Simply stated, powerful attractor patterns make us go strong, and weak patterns make us go weak. Some ideas are so weakening that merely holding them in mind hinders a test subject from being able to keep his arm up at all. Other concepts are so powerful that when they're held in mind, it's impossible to force down the subject's arm with any amount of exertion. This was a universal clinical observation. Powerful patterns are associated with health; weak patterns are associated with sickness, disease, and death. If you hold forgiveness in mind, your arm will be very strong—but if you hold revenge, your arm will go weak.

For our purposes, it's really only necessary to recognize that power is what makes you go strong, while force makes you go weak. Love, compassion, and forgiveness, which may be mistakenly thought of as submissive by some, are, in fact, profoundly empowering. Revenge, judgmentalism, and condemnation, on the other hand, inevitably make you go weak. Therefore, regardless of moral righteousness, it's a simple clinical fact that in the long run, the weak cannot prevail against the strong. That which is weak falls of its own accord.

Individuals of great power throughout human history have been those who have totally aligned themselves with powerful attractors. Again and again, they have stated that the power they manifested was not of themselves. Each has attributed the source of the power to something greater than himself.

All of the Great Teachers throughout the history of our species have merely taught one thing, over and over, in whatever language, at whatever time. All have said, simply: Give up weak attractors for strong attractors.

In examining these attractors, we'll notice that some weak patterns tend to imitate (in form only) more powerful patterns. These we'll call *imitators*. Thus, the German people under the Third Reich were deceived by *p*atriotism because they thought it was *P*atriotism. The demagogue or the zealot tries to sell us imitators as the real thing. Demagogues, to this end, always put forth a great deal of rhetoric . . . those who move from power need say very little.

PART II

WORK

CHAPTER NINE

Power Patterns in Human Attitudes

The ability to differentiate between high- and low-energy patterns is a matter of perception and discrimination that most of us learn by painful trial and error. Failure, suffering, and eventual sickness result from the influence of weak patterns; success, happiness, and health proceed from powerful attractor patterns. Therefore, it's well worth taking a few minutes to scan the list of contrasting patterns below, which have been researched and calibrated to determine their respective criteria. This exhaustive list is an educational tool operating from the principle of closure. Reflection on the many contrasting pairs of qualities can initiate a consciousness-raising process, so that one gradually becomes aware of patterns operating in relationships, business affairs, and all the various interactions that make up the fabric of life. On the left are adjectives describing powerful (positive) patterns, which calibrate above 200; on the right, weak (negative) patterns, which calibrate below 200.

Abundant	Excessive	Detached	Removed
Accepting	Rejecting	Determined	Stubborn
Admitting	Denying	Devoted	Possessive
Aesthetic	Artsy	Diplomatic	Deceptive
Agreeable	Condescending	Doing	Getting
Allowing	Controlling	Educating	Persuading
Appreciative	Envious	Egalitarian........	Elitist
Approving	Critical	Empathetic	Pitying
Attractive	Seductive	Encouraging	Promoting
Authoritative ..	Dogmatic	Energetic	Agitated
Aware..............	Preoccupied	Enlivening........	Exhausting
Balanced	Extreme	Envisioning	Picturing
Beautiful	Glamourous	Equal	Superior
Being	Having	Erotic	Lustful
Believing	Insisting	Essential	Apparent
Brilliant...........	Clever	Eternal	Temporal
Candid	Calculating	Ethical	Equivocal
Carefree	Frivolous	Excellent..........	Adequate
Challenged......	Impeded	Experienced	Cynical
Charitable	Prodigal	Fair	Scrupulous
Cheerful	Manic	Fertile	Luxuriant
Cherishing	Prizing	Flexible...........	Rigid
Choosing-to	Having-to	Forgiving	Resenting
Civil	Formal	Free	Regulated
Concerned	Judgmental	Generous	Petty
Conciliatory	Inflexible	Gentle	Rough
Confident........	Arrogant	Gifted	Lucky
Confronting	Harassing	Giving	Taking
Conscious........	Unaware	Global	Local
Considerate	Indulgent	Gracious	Decorous
Constructive....	Destructive	Grateful	Indebted
Contending	Competing	Harmonious	Disruptive
Courageous	Reckless	Healing...........	Irritating
Defending	Attacking	Helpful	Meddling
Democratic	Dictatorial	Holistic	Analytic

Honest	Legal	Principled	Expedient
Honoring	Enshrining	Privileged	Entitled
Humble	Diffident	Prolific	Barren
Humorous	Somber	Purposeful	Desirous
Impartial	Righteous	Receiving	Grasping
Ingenious	Scheming	Releasing	Tenacious
Inspired	Mundane	Reliant	Dependent
Intentional	Calculating	Requesting	Demanding
Intuitive	Literal	Respectful	Demeaning
Inventive	Prosaic	Responsible	Guilty
Inviting	Urging	Satisfied	Sated
Involved	Obsessed	Selective	Exclusive
Joyful	Pleasurable	Serene	Dull
Just	Punitive	Serving	Ambitious
Kind	Cruel	Sharing	Hoarding
Leading	Coercing	Significant	Important
Liberating	Restricting	Sober	Intoxicated
Long-term	Immediate	Spontaneous ..	Impulsive
Loyal	Chauvinistic	Spiritual	Materialistic
Merciful	Permissive	Steadfast	Faltering
Modest	Haughty	Striving	Struggling
Natural	Artificial	Surrendering ..	Worrying
Noble.............	Pompous	Tender	Hard
Nurturing........	Draining	Thoughtful......	Pedantic
Observant	Suspicious	Thrifty	Cheap
Open	Secretive	Timeless	Faddish
Optimistic	Pessimistic	Tolerant	Prejudiced
Orderly	Confused	Tractable	Contrary
Outgoing........	Reserved	Trusting	Gullible
Patient	Avid	Truthful	False
Patriotic	Nationalistic	Unifying..........	Dividing
Peaceful	Belligerent	Unselfish	Selfish
Polite	Obsequious	Valuing............	Exploitive
Powerful	Forceful	Virtuous	Celebrated
Praising	Flattering	Warm.............	Feverish

Just reading over this list makes you a different person—merely to become acquainted with the differences between these poles begins to increase one's inner power. With these distinctions in mind, we'll start to notice things we never observed before. Such revelations occur because, as the reader will discover, the universe favors power.

Moreover, the universe doesn't forget. There are many sides to the question of karma, but every choice of who and how to be is a choice of great consequence, as all of our choices reverberate through the ages. Thousands of reports of near-death experiences, as reflected in such bestselling books as Dannion Brinkley's *Saved by the Light* or B. J. Eadie's *Embraced by the Light* (which calibrates at 595), confirm that we shall eventually have to accept responsibility for every thought, word, and deed we generate, and will reexperience exactly the same suffering we've caused. It's in this sense that we each create our own heaven or hell.

The universe holds its breath as we choose, instant by instant, which pathway to follow; for the universe, the very essence of life itself, is highly conscious. Every act, thought, and choice adds to a permanent mosaic; our decisions ripple through the universe of consciousness to affect the lives of all. Lest this idea be considered either merely mystical or fanciful, let's remember that fundamental tenet of the new theoretical physics: Everything in the universe is connected with everything else.[1]

Our choices reinforce the formation of powerful M-Fields, which are the attractor patterns that influence others whether we wish them to or not.[2] Every act or decision we make that supports life supports *all* life, including our own. The ripples we create return to us—this, which may once have seemed a metaphysical statement, is now established as scientific fact.[3]

Everything in the universe constantly gives off an energy pattern of a specific frequency that remains for all time and can be read by those who know how. Every word, deed, and intention creates a permanent record. Every thought is known and recorded forever. There are no secrets; nothing is hidden, nor can it be. Our spirits stand naked in time for all to see—everyone's life, finally, is accountable to the universe.

CHAPTER TEN

Power in Politics

To better understand the critical difference between force and power and the implications of this distinction for our own lives, it's helpful to examine human endeavor on a larger scale. The interactions of men and governments provide many clear illustrations.

Looking at history from our unique perspective, we'll naturally be reminded of the powerful example set by the American Revolution, which first formally established freedom as an inalienable right, setting a precedent for centuries to come. Principles that calibrate as high as 700 affect mankind over great courses of time. The pen is indeed mightier than the sword—for power originates from the mind, whereas force is rooted in the material world.

A related pivotal event in global history, which we've already referred to and will again, came about in this century through the power of a solitary man: Mahatma Gandhi, a 90-pound "colored" who single-handedly overcame the British Empire, which was then the greatest force in the world, ruling two-thirds of the face of the globe.[1]

Not only did Gandhi bring the British Empire to its knees, he effectively brought the curtain down on the centuries-old drama of colonialism, and he did it by simply standing for a principle: the intrinsic dignity of man and his right to freedom, sovereignty, and self-determination.[2] Fundamental to this principle, in Gandhi's view, was the fact that such rights come to man by virtue of the divinity of his creation. Gandhi believed that human rights aren't granted by any earthly power, but are ingrained in the nature of man himself because they're inherent in his creation.[3]

Violence is force, but since Gandhi was aligned with power instead of force, he forbade all use of violence in his cause.[4] And because he expressed universal principles (which calibrate at 700), he was able to unite the will of the people. When the will of the people is so united by and aligned with universal principle, it's virtually unconquerable. Colonialism (calibrated at 175) is founded in the self-interest of the ruling country. Gandhi demonstrated, for the world to witness, the power of selflessness versus the force of self-interest.[5] (The same principle has also been demonstrated quite dramatically in South Africa by Nelson Mandela.)[6]

Power accomplishes with ease what force, even with extreme effort, cannot. Thus, in our own time, we've seen the almost effortless toppling of communism in Russia as a governmental form, after half a century of the most ominous—and ultimately ineffectual—military confrontation of history. The political naïveté of the Russian people, long used to the tyrannical rule of czars, didn't allow them the civic wisdom to understand that a totalitarian dictatorship was being established in the name of "communism." Similarly, the German people were deceived by Hitler, who rose to power in the name of national socialism, only to establish a virtual tyranny. A distinctive characteristic of force in politics is that it cannot tolerate dissent. Both rules depended on the pervasive use of force through secret police; Joseph Stalin, who also put millions to death, relied on his KGB, as Hitler did his SS.

Adolf Hitler assembled the greatest military machine the world had ever seen. On the simple level of force, his military was unbeatable; yet he could not defeat a tiny island across the English Channel because of the power expressed by Winston Churchill, who unified the will of his people through principles of freedom and selfless sacrifice. Churchill stood for power, Hitler for force.[7] When the two meet, power always eventually succeeds; in the long run, if it's deeply founded in the will of the people, power is immune to force.

Force is seductive because it emanates a certain glamour, whether that glamour is manifested in the guise of false patriotism, prestige, or dominance; conversely, true power is often quite unglamourous. What could be more glamourous than the Luftwaffe or the Gestapo of Nazi Germany during World War II? These elite branches embodied romance, privilege, and style, and certainly had enormous force at their disposal—including the most advanced weapons of the day and an *esprit de corps* that cemented their might. Such is the glamour of the formidable.

The weak are attracted to, and will even die for, the

glamour of force. How else could something so outrageous as war even occur? Force often seizes the upper hand temporarily, and the weak are attracted by those who seem to have overcome weakness. How else could dictatorship be possible?

One characteristic of force is arrogance; power is characterized by humility. Force is pompous; it has all the answers. Power is unassuming. Stalin, who strutted military autocracy, has gone down in history as an arch-criminal.[8] The humble Mikhail Gorbachev, who wore a plain suit and easily admitted to faults, has been awarded the Nobel Peace Prize.

Many political systems and social movements begin with true power, but as time goes on, they become co-opted by self-seekers and end up relying increasingly on force until they finally fall in disgrace. The history of civilization demonstrates this repeatedly. It's easy to forget that the initial appeal of communism was idealistic humanitarianism, as was that of the union movement in the United States, until it became a refuge of petty politicians.[9]

To fully comprehend the dichotomy we're discussing, it's necessary to consider the difference between politicians and statesmen. Politicians, operating out of expediency, rule by force after gaining their position through the force of persuasion—often calibrating at a level less than 200. Statesmen represent true power, ruling by inspiration, teaching by example, and standing for self-evident principle. Statesmen invoke the nobility that resides within all men and unifies them through what can best be termed "the heart." Although the intellect is easily fooled, the heart recognizes the truth. Where the intellect is limited, the heart is unlimited; where the intellect is intrigued by the temporary, the heart is only concerned with the permanent. Force often relies upon rhetoric, propaganda, and specious argument to garner support and disguise underlying motivations. One characteristic of truth, though, is that it needs no defense; it's self-evident. That "all men are created equal" requires no justification or rhetorical persuasion. That it's wrong to gas people to death in concentration camps is self-evident; it requires no argument. The principles that true power is based upon never require vindication, as force inevitably does—there are always endless arguments about whether force is "justified" or not.

It's clear that power is associated with that which supports life, and force is associated with that which exploits life for the gain of an individual or an organization. Force is divisive and, through that divisiveness, weakens, whereas power unifies. Force polarizes. The jingoism that has such obvious appeal to a militaristic nation just as obviously alienates the rest of the world.

Power attracts, whereas force repels. Because power unifies, it has no true enemies, although its manifestations may be opposed by opportunists whose ends it doesn't serve. Power serves others, whereas force is self-serving. True statesmen serve the people;[10] politicians exploit people to serve their own ambitions. Statesmen sacrifice themselves to serve others; politicians sacrifice others to serve themselves. Power appeals to our higher nature, force to our lower nature. Force is limited, whereas power is unlimited.

Through its insistence that the ends justify the means, force sells out freedom for expediency. Force offers quick, easy solutions. In power, the means and the end are the same, but ends require greater maturity, discipline, and patience to be brought to fruition. Great leaders inspire us to have faith and confidence because of the power of their absolute integrity and alignment with inviolate principles. Such figures understand that you can't compromise principle and still retain your power. Winston Churchill never needed to use force with the British people; Gorbachev brought about total revolution in the largest political monolith in the world without firing a shot; Gandhi defeated the British Empire without raising a hand in anger.

Democracy and the United States of America

Democracy is eventually being acknowledged universally as the superior form of government. Around the globe, there's a rising call for freedom; many nations with a heritage of repression are learning the lessons necessary for the establishment of liberty. Following conventional science, historians usually try to explain such sequences of political events through an A➤B➤C causality; this, however, is merely the apparent sequential unfolding of something with a much greater power, the ABC attractor pattern that a society evolves from.

The power of the United States, or any other democracy, arises from the principles upon which it is founded. Thus we can find the basis of power by examining such documents as the Constitution of the United States, the Bill of Rights, and the Declaration of Independence; and acknowledged expressions of the spirit of democracy, such as the Gettysburg Address.

If we calibrate the relative power of each line of these documents, we find the highest attractor pattern of all. In the Declaration of Independence, which the power of the entire United States government emanates from, it says: "We hold these truths to be self-evident, that all men are created equal, that they are endowed by their Creator with certain unalienable Rights, that among these are Life, Liberty, and the pursuit of Happiness" (calibrated at 700).

These sentiments are echoed in the Gettysburg Address, where Abraham Lincoln reminds us that this nation was conceived in Liberty and " . . . dedicated to the proposition that all men are created equal" and that "this nation, under God, shall have a new birth of freedom—and that government of the people, by the people, for the people, shall not perish from the earth" (also calibrated at 700).

If we examine the actions and statements of Lincoln himself during the trying years of the Civil War, we'll find, with absolute certainty, that he was devoid of all hatred. He had compassion, rather than malice, for the South—for he understood better than anyone else that the battle was really between man's higher and lower natures. He therefore represented the "self-evident truths" he referred to, and personally mourned the price that he knew had to be paid.[11]

The Declaration of Independence states, "We hold these truths to be self-evident"—that human rights are endowed by nature of man's creation and are *inalienable;* that is, they don't derive as a decree from force, nor are they granted by any transitory ruler. Democracy recognizes the divine right of the ruled, rather than the ruler. It isn't a right by virtue of title, wealth, or military superiority, but instead is a profound statement of the essence of man's nature, defining principles intrinsic to human life itself: liberty and the pursuit of happiness. (Mahatma Gandhi's power base calibrates identically with the power base of the Declaration of Independence and the Constitution; all are essentially concerned with freedom, liberty, and the equality of all men by virtue of endowment by a divine higher power.)[12]

Interestingly, if we calibrate the power of the attractor field of theocracy, we find it consistently lower than that of any democracy that also recognizes the Creator as the ultimate authority. The makers of the Declaration of Independence were astute in drawing a very clear distinction between that which is *spiritual* and that which is *religious*. And they must have intuitively, if not rationally, known the marked difference between the power of the two. Religion is often associated with force, sometimes disastrously so, historically and today; whereas spiritual concepts such as loyalty, freedom, and peace don't create strife or conflict, much less war. Spirituality is always associated with nonviolence.

If we examine the application of the Bill of Rights today, however, we find that its power in several areas has dwindled. The right to freedom from unreasonable search and seizure, as well as freedom from cruel and unusual punishment, have both been eroded over the years by expediency. The spirit of the United States Constitution has become sufficiently dimmed so that laws that are blatantly unconstitutional are frequently proposed and often passed without a murmur of protest. Pockets of totalitarianism exist within government itself; our society routinely tolerates totalitarian tactics by both federal and local agencies, manifested in the conspicuous use of intimidation. Unfortunately, we've gotten so used to an atmosphere of fear and violence that it comes as a surprise to Americans abroad that the threat of government intrusion or police force doesn't even exist in many foreign countries.

It's most important to remember that to violate principle for practical expediency is to relinquish enormous power. The rationalization that the execution of criminals deters crime, for instance, doesn't hold up under study; and the end does *not* justify the means. The consequence of this violation of principle is reflected in the crime statistics of the United States, where murder is so common it doesn't even make the newspapers' front pages.

Because we fail to differentiate principle from expediency, the average person lacks the discernment to understand the difference between *p*atriotism and Patriotism, between *a*mericanism and Americanism, between *g*od and God, between *f*reedom and Freedom, between *l*iberty and Liberty. Thus, "Americanism" is used as a justification by white supremacy groups (calibrated at 150) and lynch mobs, just as warmongering throughout history has been conducted in the name of "God." The misinterpretation of liberty as license tells us that many people don't know the difference between *f*reedom and Freedom.

Learning the difference between principles and their imitators requires experience and educated judgment. The exercise of such discretion is necessary for moral survival in the modern world in general, but is imperative in those grayest of areas, where ethical ambiguity has been elevated from convention to art form: the political arena and the marketplace of daily commerce.

CHAPTER ELEVEN

Power in the Marketplace

Man has freedom of choice, without which there would be no accountability or responsibility. The ultimate choice, really, is whether to align with a high-energy attractor field or a low-energy field. The same weak attractor patterns that have brought down governments, social movements, and entire civilizations routinely destroy organizations and careers as well. One makes one's choice and then takes the consequences.

Nowhere are these consequences more dramatically visible than in the realm of business—yet this is also the area where failure could most easily be avoided, if a few basic concepts were clearly understood. Attractor fields can be quickly calibrated, whether in a product, company, or employee. In our research, the differences between businesses that have failed and businesses that have succeeded have proved so marked that excellent predictive accuracy can be expected. All too often, the "buyer"—who can be a voter, investor, or truth-seeker, as well as a purchaser—is captured by the glamour of an imitator pattern that on the surface appears to be a high-energy attractor pattern. People are dazzled by superficial style and slick presentation, like those naïve investors who recently bought silver only to find that the entire commodity market had been manipulated. Our notorious savings-and-loan fiascoes and their perpetrators could easily have been identified long before the scandals surfaced. Similar disasters can be avoided by simply examining whether a business endeavor is associated with a high or a low attractor pattern. This identification can become almost instinctive once one understands the difference between the operation of force and power in commerce.

Efficiency Can Be Expensive

Sam Walton, the founder of Wal-Mart, provided a model of how power comes from aligning with high-energy attractor patterns. The ABC he conceived has resulted in the A→B→C that is the rapidly growing Wal-Mart colossus. (The basic principles involved are spelled out in the book *Sam Walton* by Vance Trimble.)[1]

In the aisles of many of today's giant stores, there seem to be no available employees whatsoever; the gross indifference to customer goodwill is shocking. Wal-Mart's employees, in contrast, are trained to be accommodating, warm, and energetic—to reflect a humane energy field in their workplace. Their jobs have meaning and value because they're aligned with Service, a commitment to the support of life and human value. All Wal-Marts feature an area where you can rest your feet and decide about purchases—such allocation of space to meet simple human needs would never pass the scrutiny of scientific management calculations in terms of gross sales per square footage. But such "efficiency" expertise has discarded, along with human compassion, the market allegiance of millions of customers. Computers don't feel; more attention would be paid to feelings if it was realized that *feelings determine purchases.*

A commercial factor of great, but often unrecognized, importance is the "family" feeling of employees—their loyalty to their organization. This is a very prominent quality in successful companies. Employees who feel nurtured and supported are those who smile genuinely at customers. Another characteristic of such an environment is low employee turnover, whereas cold and impersonal companies have very rapid employee turnover. Employee shortage is always an expression of a low-energy attractor pattern. Critical factor analysis of a large cut-rate drug chain that had just filed for Chapter 11 revealed that the few dollars saved by not having extra employees at the checkout counter regularly cost countless thousands of dollars in sales; such shortsightedness is common in businesses dominated by low-energy fields.

To be a success, it's necessary to embrace and operate from the principles that produce success, not just imitate the actions of successful people—for to really do what they do, it's necessary to *be like they are*. Companies that have imitated some of Wal-Mart's features, hoping to regain their market share, haven't been successful because they merely imitated the A→B→C instead of aligning with the ABC from which those features emanated.

Our research on attractor patterns correlates closely with the conclusions arrived at by Thomas Peters and Robert Waterman in their book *In Search of Excellence*, which is a detailed analysis of several great businesses.[2] They concluded that successful companies were those that had "heart," as opposed to strictly left-brain, scientifically managed companies. In reading this study, one can't help but be struck by the inadequacy of many marketing survey procedures: The statisticians simply don't know what questions to ask.

In addition to counting the millions that companies make, analysts might well assess the multimillions that they *don't* make. A suitable example is the decline of the U.S. auto industry. One would think that from the success of Rolls-Royce or the Volkswagen Beetle, it would be apparent that espousing a philosophy of planned obsolescence rather than enduring quality demonstrates a gross miscalculation. Our research indicated years ago that by following the high-energy attractor patterns we've already identified, Detroit could reclaim the auto market. Truly creative innovation is required in order to recapture the imagination of the public, and enduring quality must supplant efficiency, as the price of a new car rises ever higher.

Sensibly enough, not many Americans are happy to shell out such sums in full knowledge that the investment will shortly be lost. Obviously, what the depreciating car loses isn't any real, innate value: The inflated price of glamour and novelty doesn't reflect any actual worth. After all, people will gladly pay $50,000 or more for a used Rolls-Royce, knowing that 20 years from now it will still be classic in style and mechanically sound, with a high resale value.

Our research indicates that Americans would willingly pay such high prices for cars if their intrinsic worth were equivalent to their purchase price, so as to protect the investment; also, if the cars would run well and maintain value for a long time, ideally a lifetime. (For instance, a modular car in which such items as the motor and drive train were easily removable and replaceable—with a lifetime guarantee—would be a sure winner.) Attractor research tells us that customers are willing to pay for quality, and that good products would sell themselves without slick advertising gimmicks. Since integrity and excellence are aligned with power, they speak for themselves.

One of the most profitable and simple applications of critical factor analysis is in the field of advertising. The use of the simple kinesiologic technique we've described can instantly reveal whether an advertising campaign or given commercial is weak or strong.

Companies pay enormous sums to reach the greatest possible audiences, but this strategy can backfire when a widely viewed commercial that makes viewers go weak damages the company's image. An ad that makes people go strong will always produce a positive feeling about the product. Similarly, advertisers who buy time during TV programs that make people go weak will find their product unconsciously associated with these negative feelings. By analyzing a commercial in detail, one can ascertain the elements that have a weakening, negative effect—the voice of the announcer; the mannerisms of an actor; or the use of certain words, concepts, or symbols. That some companies repeatedly produce tasteless and even embarrassing commercials reflects low attractor fields prevalent in their advertising and marketing departments.

Beyond the surface world of commerce, society provides numerous other marketplaces where fulfillment of human needs is sought, bartered, stolen, coerced, and denied. It's a simple fact of life that satisfaction of needs leads to contentment; frustration breeds violence, crime, and emotional turmoil. If the missions of government-regulatory institutions were realigned to support the fulfillment of human needs, rather than mounting moralistic, black-and-white campaigns to stamp out "social problems," these institutions could become powerful forces for human betterment.

Perceptual fields are limited by the attractor patterns that they're associated with. This means that the capacity to recognize significant factors in a given situation is limited by the context that arises from the level of consciousness of the observer. The motive of the viewer automatically determines what is seen; causality is, therefore, ascribed to factors that are, in fact, a function of the biases of the observer and aren't at all instrumental in the situation itself. The concept of "situational ethics" tells us that the right or wrong of behavior can't be determined without reference to context. As each conditioning factor colors the picture, shades of gray are introduced that alter the significance of the whole scenario.

One indication of a low-energy attractor field is a struggle of opposites. Whereas power always results in a win-win solution, force produces win-lose situations; the consequent struggle indicates that the correct solution hasn't been found, as when the assertion of one group's interests violates those of another, or the rights of the accused conflict with those of the victim. The way to finesse a high-energy attractor field solution is to seek the answer that will make all sides happy and still be practical. Such solutions involve utilization of both the tolerant right brain as well as the judgmental left brain.

One basic principle has the power to resolve the problems of the social marketplace: *Support the solution instead of attacking the supposed causes.* Attack is in itself inherently a very weak attractor pattern (150), leading through fear to intimidation, coercion and, eventually, moral corruption. The "vice squad" becomes just that, turning city streets into jungles of crime.

Objective examination reveals that most intractable "social problems" appear unsolvable due to the persistence of either sentimentality or juvenile moralizing. Neither of these positions is based in truth, and, therefore, all approaches proceeding from them are weak. Falsehood makes us go weak; acting from false positions typically results in the use of force. Force is the universal substitute for truth. The gun and the nightstick are evidence of weakness; the need to control others stems from lack of power, just as vanity stems from lack of self-esteem. Punishment is a form of violence, an ineffectual substitute for power. When, as in our society, the punishment rarely fits the crime, it can hardly be effectual; punishment is based on revenge at the weak energy level of 150.

Supporting the solution of human needs, on the other hand, creates a no-cost resolution that brings serenity; attacking the artificially created "problem" is always expensive, in addition to criminalizing society. Only the childish proceed from the assumption that human behavior can be explained in black-and-white terms. Denying basic biologic needs and instinctual drives is futile. Blocking normal sexual outlets merely results in the creation of abnormal sexual outlets. The solutions that have power are the ones realistically based at the level of Acceptance (350) rather than condemnation (150, the level of Anger). In Amsterdam, one section of the city is traditionally designated as a red-light district, quiet and serene with a pastoral atmosphere; its streets are safe. In Buenos Aires, parts of parks are set aside for lovers. The police patrol these areas to protect rather than harass, and all is peaceful.

Another example is the previously cited inability of our government to solve the problem of drug use. Again, the mistake is in looking at the problem moralistically and acting out of force in a punishing role. The original critical error was the failure to differentiate between hard drugs and soft drugs. Hard drugs (narcotics) are addicting, with severe withdrawal effects, and have been traditionally associated with crime. Soft drugs (recreational) are nonaddicting, don't induce withdrawal, and are usually initially handled by amateurs. By criminalizing soft drugs, the government created a new criminal syndicate, wealthy and international in scope. Shortages of cheap, relatively harmless recreational material on the streets were quickly filled by hard-drug merchants, and the peaceful, largely innocuous drug culture became criminalized and vicious.

Successful solutions are based on the powerful principle that resolution occurs by fostering the positive, not by attacking the negative. Recovery from alcoholism can't be accomplished by fighting intoxication, but, rather, only by choosing sobriety. The "war to end all wars" did no such thing, nor could it possibly have done so. Wars—including wars on "vice," "drugs," or any of the human needs regularly traded for in the great hidden social marketplace that underlies conventional commerce—can only be won by choosing peace.

CHAPTER TWELVE

Power and Sports

The theoretical understanding that we've come to in our study of consciousness provides a context that may be applied to any field of human activity. Examining sports is a good illustration because sport is so widely observed and extensively documented. Great sports heroes have been celebrated throughout history at least as much as notable figures in science, the arts, or any other area of cultural achievement. Sports figures symbolize the possibilities of excellence for all of us—and at the level of the champion, they represent mastery.

What is it in athletics that brings a crowd to its feet and commands such intense, enthusiastic loyalty? At first, we might think that it's pride, a fascination with competition and triumph. But while these motives may produce pleasure and excitement, they don't account for the far greater emotions of respect and awe elicited by a display of athletic excellence. What animates the crowd is an intuitive recognition of the heroic striving required to overcome human limitation and achieve new levels of prowess. High states of consciousness are also frequently experienced by athletes. It's widely documented that long-distance runners frequently attain sublime states of peace and joy. This very elevation of consciousness, in fact, often inspires the prolonged transcendence of pain and exhaustion necessary to achieve higher levels of performance. This phenomenon is commonly described in terms of pushing oneself to the point where one suddenly breaks through a performance barrier and the activity becomes effortless; the body then seems to move with grace and ease of its own accord, as though animated by some invisible force. The accompanying state of joy is quite distinct from the thrill of success; it's a joy of peace and oneness with all that lives.

It's notable that this transcendence of the personal self and surrender to the very essence or spirit of life often occurs at a point just beyond the apparent limit of the athlete's ability. The seeming barrier is predicated by the paradigm of one's own past accomplishments or of what has been recognized as theoretically possible. Take, for instance, the historic "four-minute mile": Until Roger Bannister tore down that barrier, it was universally accepted that it wasn't humanly possible to run any faster; Bannister's greatness wasn't just in breaking the record, but in breaking through that paradigm to a new model of human possibility. This breakthrough to new levels of potential has correspondences in every field of human endeavor; in many diverse enterprises, those who have achieved greatness have given parallel accounts of the circumstances surrounding their accomplishments.

We've made calibrations of various kinds of records of athletic achievement, including movies. Of all the movies about sport studied, the French film *The Big Blue* produced the highest calibration.[1] This is the story of Jacques Mayol, the Frenchman who held the world record for deep-sea diving for many years (until very recently). The movie calibrates at the extraordinary energy level of 700 (universal truth), and has the capacity to put viewers into a high state of consciousness—the manager of one movie theater that showed it described audiences wandering out lost in silence or crying with a joy they couldn't describe.

Through the use of slow-motion photography, the movie achieves an accurate depiction of the world's greatest deep-sea diver in elevated states of consciousness. A subjective sensation of slow-motion, beauty, and grace is frequently noted in higher states; time seems to stop, and there's an inner silence, despite the noise of the world.

We see throughout the film that Jacques Mayol maintains this state by the intensity of his concentration, which keeps him in an almost constant meditative condition. In this mode, he transcends ordinary human limitations, for he becomes enabled to achieve great feats through altered physiology. The deeper he dives, the slower his heartbeat becomes, and his blood distribution concentrates almost entirely in his brain. (This also happens in porpoises.) His best friend, himself a highly evolved athlete, dies in an attempt to match Mayol's feat because he hadn't reached the level of consciousness required to transcend the normal limits of the body.

The subjective experience of effortless bliss also occurs in other types of exceptional physical performance, such as that of the world-famous Sufi dancers known as *whirling dervishes,* who, through discipline and exhausting practice, become able to move effortlessly through space over long periods of time with dazzling precision.

The most highly developed martial arts clearly demonstrate how motive and principle are of ultimate importance in extraordinary athletic achievement.[2] The most frequently heard admonition to trainees is: "Stop trying to use force."[3] Schools devoted to these arts produce masters whose overriding concern is victory of the higher self over the lower through control, training, and commitment to goals aligned with true power.[4] Alignment with these high-power attractor patterns isn't limited to the exercise of the discipline itself but becomes an entire lifestyle. Thus, when the power of the principle is transferred to the practitioner, the results begin to be manifested everywhere in his life.

The hallmark of true greatness in athletic achievement is always humility (such as that exhibited by Pablo Morales after winning his gold medals in the 1992 Summer Olympics). Such athletes express gratitude, inner awe, and an awareness that their performance wasn't merely the result of an individual effort—that maximum personal effort brought them to the breakthrough point from which they were then transported by a power greater than that of the individual self. This typically is expressed as the discovery of some aspect of the self hitherto unknown, or unexperienced in its pure form.

Pride and Sports

Through kinesiology, we can demonstrate that if one is motivated by any of the energy fields below Courage, one goes weak. The notorious Achilles' heel that brings down not just athletes but the potentially great in all areas of human achievement is *pride*. Pride, calibrated at 175, not only makes the performer go weak, but it can't provide the motivational power of love, honor, or dedication to a higher principle (or even to excellence itself). If we ask a powerful athlete to hold in mind the hope of defeating his opponent, or becoming a star, or making a lot of money, we'll see that he goes weak and we can put down his trained, muscular arm with minimal effort. The same athlete holding in mind the honor of his country or his sport, the dedication of his performance to someone he loves, or even the sheer joy of maximum effort for the sake of excellence, goes powerfully strong, and we cannot push down his arm with even the greatest effort.

Thus, the competitor who is motivated by pride or greed, or interested primarily in defeating an opponent, will go weak at the moment of the starting gun and be unable to achieve the maximum continued effort necessary for great achievement. At times, we see an athlete start poorly for such reasons—but, as the contest progresses and selfish goals are forgotten, he improves his performance. We also see the opposite happen when an athlete starts well because he's competing for the honor of his country, his team, or of the sport itself, but then, as he nears the goal, the anticipation of personal glory or triumph over a rival makes him lose strength and form, and he fumbles.

One unfortunate sequence of consciousness occurs

when an athlete sets a new record during qualifying trials, arousing new personal ambitions, but during the final competition, goes to pieces to the puzzlement of the audience. If top performers are imbued with the belief that their excellence isn't a personal accomplishment, but a gift belonging to all of mankind as a demonstration of man's potential, they'll go strong and remain so through any event.

The scale of consciousness may be seen in one aspect as a scale of ego, with the level of 200 being the point where selfishness begins to turn to selflessness. At the rarefied plane of Olympic competition, the disastrous consequences, both in private and in public life, of motivations emanating from levels below 200 are all too clearly illustrated by the recent scandal involving a well-known figure skater. This athlete's excessive zeal to capture an Olympic medal and defeat her rival—by any means available—led her to abandon the power of ethical principle and descend to the grossest level of force. There could hardly be a more telling example of how submission to a negative attractor field can produce the rapid collapse of an otherwise promising athletic career.

Where higher motivations toward excellence give access to the realm of grace and power, self-centered motivations of personal gain draw one almost magnetically into the realm of force. The reaping of recognition—even in the symbolic form of a medal, not to mention the financial reward that may accompany it—has little to do with true athletic greatness, which proceeds from an attainment of stature of the spirit; this is what we laud in the champion. Even if the competitor does not surrender to the lust for wealth and fame, the drive to attain dominance in one's sport, rather than to simply manifest all the excellence that one is capable of, has its own corrupting, egocentric effect—the negative forces associated with the level of Pride. There's nothing intrinsically wrong with some manifestations of pride. We all may well be proud when we take the America's Cup or our Olympians win medals, but that's a different kind of pride. It's an honoring of human achievement that transcends personal pride. We honor the endeavor, not the personal accomplishment, which is only the occasion and expression of something greater, universal and innate in the human heart. The Olympics, one of the greatest dramas of human striving, and one that captures everyone's imagination, provides a context that should counteract personal pride. The entire setting inspires the competitor to move from personal pride to an esteem that is an expression of unconditional love—one that also honors one's opponents for their dedication to the same lofty principles.

The media tends to evoke the downside of sports and undermines the athlete, because celebrity status either consciously or unconsciously elicits this egotism. Great athletes need to gird themselves against this source of contamination. Humility and gratitude seem to be the only effective shields against the onslaughts of media exploitation. Athletes in the traditional martial arts employ specific exercises to overcome any tendency toward egotism. The dedication of one's skill, performance, or career to a higher principle provides the only absolute protection.

True athletic power is characterized by grace, sensitivity, inner quiet, and paradoxically, gentleness in the noncompetitive lives of even fierce competitors. We celebrate the champion because we recognize that he has overcome personal ambition through sacrifice and dedication to higher principles. The great become legendary when they teach by example. It isn't what they have, nor what they do, but what they have become that inspires all of mankind, and that's what we honor in them. We should seek to protect their humility from the forces of exploitation that accompany acclaim in the everyday world. We need to educate the public that the abilities of these athletes and their great performances are gifts to mankind to be respected and defended from the abuse of the media and corporate commerce.

The Olympic spirit resides within the heart of every man and woman. Great athletes can, by example, awaken awareness of that principle in all people. These heroes and their spokesmen have a potentially powerful influence on all of mankind, literally the power to lift the world on their shoulders. The nurturing of excellence and recognition of its value is the responsibility of all men, because the quest for excellence in any area of human endeavor inspires us all toward the actualization of every form of man's yet unrealized greatness.

CHAPTER THIRTEEN

Social Power and the Human Spirit

When we cheer the spirit of the true athlete, what we applaud is a demonstration of all of the significances the word *spirit* entails for us: courage, tenacity, commitment, alignment with principle, demonstration of excellence, honor, respect, and humility.[1] To *inspire* implies filling with spirit; *dispirited* means dejected, hopeless, defeated. But what exactly does the term *spirit* signify? The collective totality of human experience can be comprehended in phrases such as "team spirit" or when we exhort people to "get in the spirit." That spirit is a highly pragmatic factor, which can determine the difference between victory and defeat, is well known by military commanders, coaches, and CEOs. An employee or other group member who doesn't enter into the spirit of the group enterprise soon finds himself without a job or group.

So it's clear that *spirit* refers to an unseen essence, which never changes, even though its expression varies from one situation to another.[2] This essence is vital; when we lose our spirit, we die—we *ex*pire from lack of that which *in*spires.

Clinically speaking, then, we can say that spirit equates with life; the energy of life itself can be termed *spirit*. Spirit is the alive-ness that accompanies, and is an expression of, alignment with life energy. The power of high-energy attractor patterns is anabolic, sustaining life; their opposites are catabolic, eventually leading to death. True power = life = spirit, whereas force = weakness = death. When an individual has lost or lacks those qualities we term *spiritual,* he becomes devoid of humanity, love, and self-respect; he may even become selfish and violent. When a nation veers from its alignment with the spirit of man, it can become an international criminal.

It's a common error to identify spirituality with religion. We noted previously that the United States Constitution, the Bill of Rights, and the Declaration of Independence clearly differentiate between the spiritual and the religious. The United States government is forbidden to establish any religion, lest it impair the freedom of the people; yet these same documents presume that government's authority derives from spiritual principles.[3]

In fact, the founders of the world's great religions would be shocked at the profoundly unspiritual deeds wrought in their names through history—many of which would make a heathen shudder. Force always distorts truth for its own self-serving purposes. Over time, the spiritual principles upon which religions are based become distorted for expedient ends, such as power, money, and other worldliness. The spiritual is tolerant, yet religiosity is commonly intolerant; the former leads to peace, the latter to strife, bloodshed, and pious criminality. There remains, however, buried within every religion, the spiritual foundation that it originated from.[4] Like religions, entire cultures are weakened when the principles that they're based upon are obscured or contaminated by false interpretation.

To more fully understand the nature of spirit in power and how it originates and operates as a social movement, we'll do well to study a contemporary spiritual organization of enormous power and influence—about which everything is of public record—one that's avowedly aligned with the spirit of man, yet flatly states that it is *not* religious. That is the 55-year-old organization known as *Alcoholics Anonymous (AA)*.

The Power of 12-Step Programs

We all know something about Alcoholics Anonymous, because its adherents number in the millions, but also because it has become woven into the very fabric of modern society. AA and its offshoot organizations have been estimated to affect, in one way or another, the lives of about 50 percent of Americans at this time. Even where the 12-step-based self-help groups don't enter lives directly, they affect everyone indirectly because they reinforce certain values by example. Let's study the power principles that AA is based upon and how this foundation came about historically, and examine the impact that these principles have within the general population, as well as among members. We can look at what AA is and also what it is not, and learn from both.

According to its preamble, AA is "not allied with any sect, denomination, politics, or organization." In addition, it has "no opinion on outside matters." It's neither for nor against any other approach to the problem of alcoholism. It has no dues or fees, no ceremonies, trappings, officers, or laws. It owns no property; it has no edifices. Not only are all members equal, but all AA groups are autonomous and self-supporting.[5] Even the 12 basic steps by which members recover are specified as only "suggestions." The use of coercion of any kind is avoided and is emphasized by slogans such as "One day at a time," "Easy does it," "First things first," and, most important, "Live and let live."[6]

Alcoholics Anonymous respects freedom, in that it leaves choice up to the individual. Its identifiable power patterns are those of honesty, responsibility, humility, service, and the practice of tolerance, goodwill, and brotherhood. AA doesn't subscribe to any particular ethic, has no code of right and wrong or good and bad, and avoids moral judgments. AA doesn't try to control anyone, including its own members. What it does instead is chart a path. It merely says to its members, "If you practice these principles in all of your affairs, you'll recover from this grave and progressive fatal illness, and regain your health and self-respect, and the capacity to live a fruitful and fulfilling life for yourself and others."[7]

AA is the original example of the power of these principles to cure hopeless disease and change the destructive personality patterns of members. From this paradigm came all subsequent forms of group therapy, through the discovery that groups of people coming together on a formal basis to address their mutual problems have enormous power: Al-Anon for the spouses of AA members; then Alateen for their children; then Gamblers Anonymous, Narcotics Anonymous, Parents Anonymous, Overeaters Anonymous, and so on. There are now close to 300 anonymous 12-step self-help organizations dealing with every form of human suffering. Americans, as a result of all of this, have now largely turned from condemning self-destructive behaviors to recognizing that these conditions are indeed curable diseases.

From a practical viewpoint, the sizable impact of self-help organizations on society can be counted on, not only in the relief of human suffering and the reconstitution of families, but in savings of billions of dollars. Absenteeism, automobile insurance rates, welfare, health care, and penal system costs are all greatly moderated by the widespread behavioral change produced by this movement. The cost of state-provided counseling and group therapy alone for the millions of troubled individuals served would be staggering.

By the millions, the members of these organizations unanimously agree that admitting the limitations of their individual egos allowed them to experience a true power, and that it's that power that brought about their recovery—which hitherto nothing on Earth, including medicine, psychiatry, or any branch of modern science, had been able to do.

The History of Alcoholics Anonymous

We can make some important observations from the story of how the prototype 12-step organization, Alcoholics

Anonymous, came into existence. Back in the 1930s, alcoholism was accepted, as it had been over the centuries, as a hopeless, progressive disease that had baffled medical science and religion as well. (In fact, the prevalence of alcoholism among the clergy itself was alarmingly high.) All forms of drug addiction were thought to be incurable, and when they reached a certain stage, victims were simply "put away."

In the early 1930s, a prominent American businessman (known to us as Rowland H.), had sought every cure for his alcoholism, without avail. He then went to see the famous Swiss psychoanalyst Carl Jung for treatment. Jung treated Rowland H. for approximately a year, by which time he'd achieved some degree of sobriety. Rowland returned to the United States full of hope . . . only to fall ill again with active alcoholism.

Rowland went back to Switzerland to see Jung again and ask for further treatment. Jung humbly told him that neither his science nor art could help him further, but that throughout man's history—rarely, but from time to time—some who had abandoned themselves completely to some spiritual organization and surrendered to God for help had recovered.[8]

Rowland returned to the United States dejected, but he followed Jung's advice and sought out an organization of that time called the Oxford Groups. These were groups of individuals who met regularly to discuss living life according to spiritual principles, very much like those adopted later by AA. Through these means, Rowland in fact recovered, and his recovery was a source of astonishment to another concerned party named Edwin T., or "Ebby," who was also a desperate alcoholic beyond all help. When Rowland told Ebby of how he had recovered, Ebby followed suit and also got sober. The pattern of one person helping another with the same problem then extended from Ebby to his friend Bill W., who had been hospitalized frequently for hopeless, incurable alcoholism and whose condition was medically grave. Ebby told Bill that his recovery was based on service to others, moral housecleaning, anonymity, humility, and surrendering to a power greater than himself.[9]

Bill W. was an atheist, and found the idea of surrendering to a higher power unappealing, to say the least. The whole idea of surrender was abhorrent to Bill's pride; consequently, he sank into an absolute, black despair. He had a mental obsession with, and a physical allergy to, alcohol—which condemned him to sickness, insanity, and death, a prognosis that had been clearly spelled out to him and his wife, Lois. Ultimately, Bill gave up completely; at this point he had the profound experience of an infinite Presence and Light and felt a great sense of peace. That night, he was finally able to sleep, and when he awoke the next day, he felt as though he'd been transformed in some indescribable way.[10]

The efficacy of Bill's experience was confirmed by Dr. William D. Silkworth, his physician at what was then Town's Hospital, on the west side of New York City. Silkworth had treated more than 10,000 alcoholics and, in the process, had acquired enough wisdom to recognize the profound importance of Bill's experience. It was he who later introduced Bill to the great psychologist William James's classic book, *The Varieties of Religious Experience.*

Bill wanted to pass his gift on to others, and as he himself said, "I spent the next few months trying to sober up

drunks, but without success." Eventually, he discovered
that it was necessary to convince the subject of the hopelessness of his condition—in modern psychological terms,
to overcome his *denial.* Bill's first success was Dr. Bob, a
surgeon from Akron, Ohio, who turned out to have a
great aptitude for the spiritual—he later became a co-
founder of AA. Until his death in 1956, Dr. Bob never took
another drink (neither did Bill W., who died in 1971.)[11]
The enormous power that was realized through Bill W.'s
experience has manifested itself externally in the millions
of lives that have been transformed because of it. In *Life's*
listing of the 100 greatest Americans who ever lived, Bill
W. is credited with being the originator of the entire self-
help movement.[12]

+ + +

The story of Bill W. is typical of individuals who have
been channels of great power—the principles they convey
in a brief career reorder the lives of millions over long periods of time. Jesus Christ, for instance, taught for only
three short years, and yet his teachings transformed all of
Western society for the generations since; man's encounter
with these teachings lies at the center of Western history
for the last 2,000 years. The highest calibrations of attractor power fields that we've discovered have invariably
been associated with the teachings of the great spiritual
masters of history.

There's always a diminishment from the calibrated
power of the energy field of the great masters' original
teachings to their current practice in the form of organized
religion (see Chapter 23). Yet the original principles

themselves retain their innate power pattern; it's merely their expression that's become weaker. The teachings themselves have the same profound power they always did. The power of a principle remains unchanged throughout time. Whether we fully understand them or not, these principles are the ideals for which mankind strives. From our own struggles to better ourselves, we learn compassion for those still in the grip of inner conflict; out of this grows a wisdom, including compassion, for the entire human condition.

If we refer to the principles of advanced theoretical physics, and the results of our own attractor research, it will be obvious that in a universe in which everything is connected with everything else, unseen power accomplishes things for us that we never do by ourselves. As we've said before, we can't see electricity, x-rays, or radio waves, but we know of their intrinsic power by virtue of their effects. Similarly, we constantly observe the effects of power in the world of thoughts and feelings, although until now, it hadn't been considered possible to measure a thought.

When we discuss high-power attractor fields, we frequently can allude to them only by means of symbols. National flags are just dyed patterns on pieces of material, from a physical viewpoint, but men are willing to die for what they symbolize. Empowerment, as we've said, comes from meaning. Those things that have the greatest meaning to us arise from the spiritual, not the material, world.

Thus far, we've seen that alignment with the principles associated with high-power attractor energy fields can result in Olympic achievement; success in commerce; political victory on an international level; and recovery from hopeless, progressive diseases. But these same attractor patterns are also responsible for the finest music ever written. They're the basis of the eminent religious teachings, the world's grand art and architecture, and the wellspring of all creativity and genius.

CHAPTER FOURTEEN

Power in the Arts

The great works of art, music, and architecture that have come down to us through the centuries are enduring representations of the effect of high attractor patterns. In them, we see a reflection of the commitment of our civilization's master artists to perfection and grace, and thereby to the ennoblement of humanity.

The fine arts have always provided the venue for man's highest spiritual strivings in the secular realm. From as far back as the time of the ancient Greek sculptor Phidias, it has been the role of the arts to realize, in physical media, the ideals of what man could and should be. Art sets down a distilled expression of the human spirit, one that's tangible in form and accessible to all.

Great art not only brings forth the ordered essence of human experience, but of the world we live in, too—this is what we call *beauty*. Like the theoretical physicist, the artist finds order in apparent chaos. For example, where there were only blocks of meaningless marble, Michelangelo saw *David* and the *Pieta*, and with his chisel, removed the surrounding stone to liberate those perfected images. And while contemplating the random patterns of a meaningless plaster wall in the Sistine Chapel, he conceived a wondrous ABC through the *inspiration* of art—and through the *technique* of art, he actualized the A→B→C known today as *The Last Judgment.*

The bequest of the arts to mankind is internal, too: In beholding realized beauty, a sensitivity to the beautiful is implanted in us, enabling us to discover, and create, our own aesthetic rewards in the apparently disordered jumble of existence.

Art and love are man's greatest gifts to himself; and there can be no art without love. Art is always the making of the soul, the craft of a human being's touch—which can be corporeal or of the mind and spirit—so it has been since Neanderthal times, and so it will always be. Thus, we find that computer-generated art and even great photographs never calibrate as highly as original paintings. A most interesting kinesiological experiment, which anyone can try, is to test the strength of a person who's looking at an original painting. Compare that result to what happens when you test them while they're looking at a mechanical reproduction of that painting. When a person looks at something that has been handcrafted, he goes strong; when he looks at a reproduction, he goes weak. This is true regardless of pictorial content—an original of a disturbing subject will make the subject go stronger than a copy of a pleasant subject. Dedicated artists put love into their work, and there's great power in both the human touch and human originality. Therefore, kinesiology provides a fail-safe detector of art forgery.

Carl Jung emphasized over and over again the relation of art to the dignity of man and the importance of the human spirit in art. Jung himself (and his work) calibrates highest out of all of the famous psychoanalysts in history. (Many of the others, aligned with such attractor patterns as material determinism, produced significantly lower scores.)

Music is in some ways the most subtle of the arts, for it's the least concrete. However, in bypassing left-brain rationality to appeal directly to our subconscious right-brain sense of pattern, it's at the same time the most visceral and emotional. It also provides the easiest example of how attractor patterns order reality: If you wish to comprehend the difference between chaos and meaning, thereby attaining an effective definition of *art,* simply contemplate the difference between noise and music.

In this description of the creative process, contemporary Estonian composer Arvo Pärt, whose work is often described as "transcendental" or "mystical," condenses much of what we've observed regarding the crucial role of artistic genius in the unfolding of attractor patterns:

> To write, I must prepare myself for a long time. Sometimes it takes five years. . . . In my life, my music, my work, in my dark hours, I have the certain feeling that everything outside this one thing has no meaning. The complex and many-faceted only confuses me, and I must search for unity. What is it, this one thing, and how do I find my way to it? Traces of this thing appear

in many guises and everything that is unimportant falls
away. . . . Here I am alone with silence. I have discovered that it is enough when a single note is played. . . .
That is my goal. Time and timelessness are connected.
This instant and eternity are struggling within us.[1]

Among the arts, it's music that most readily brings
tears to our eyes, springs us to our feet, or inspires us to
pinnacles of love and creativity. We've already noted that
longevity seems to be a corollary of an association with the
attractor fields of classical music, whether one is a performer, conductor, or composer. Classical music often
demonstrates extremely high inherent power patterns.

But of all of the arts, architecture is the most tangible
and influential in the lives of men everywhere. We live,
shop, go to work, and seek our entertainment in buildings;
thus, the form of the structure itself deserves the utmost
attention, because its influence is a background to so
much human activity.

Of all of the world's architecture, the great cathedrals
elicit a special awe. Their energy patterns have calibrated
the highest among architectural forms. This appears to be
the result of several factors. Our experience of cathedrals
can combine a number of art forms simultaneously—such
as music, sculpture, or painting—as well as spatial design.
Moreover, these edifices are dedicated to the divine; that
which is begotten in the name of the Creator is aligned with
the highest attractor patterns of all. The cathedral not
only inspires, but unifies, teaches, symbolizes, and serves
all that's noblest in man.

Beauty in architecture, however, need not be expan-
sive or grand in scale. There are few architectural settings

more charming than the little thatched cottages that dot the Irish countryside, where each one is more quaint and picturesque than the last. Innate appreciation for the aesthetic allows as much for traditional, simple domestic architecture as it does for elegant statements of majesty and grandeur. Well-conceived public architecture speaks with historical authenticity of the beauty of form combined with utility. Function and beauty are impressively joined in the great subway stations of Russia and in the design and layout of many new high-rise apartment buildings in Canada. Older cultures seem to have always understood the practicality of beauty—that that which is designed without beauty quickly deteriorates. An architecturally ugly neighborhood becomes part of a feedback loop of blight and violence; the sleazy, dehumanized housing projects of urban ghettos manifest their weak power patterns in squalor and crime. But it should be remembered that depending on which attractor pattern one aligns with, the destitution of the ghetto can be an excuse for depravity *or* the inspiration to rise above it. (After all, it isn't the facts of one's environment, but one's attitude toward them, that determines whether one will be defeated or victorious.)

Grace is the expression of the power of aesthetic sensitivity, and power is always manifested with grace, whether in beauty of line, style, or expression. We associate grace with elegance, refinement, and economy of effort. We marvel at the grace of the Olympic athlete, just as we're uplifted by the grace of the Gothic vault. Gracious power patterns acknowledge and support life, and respect and uphold the dignity of others. In addition, grace is an aspect of unconditional love. Graciousness also implies generosity—not merely material generosity, but generosity of spirit, such as the willingness to express thanks or acknowledge the importance of others in our lives. Grace is associated with modesty and humility, for power doesn't need to flaunt itself; force always must show off, because it originates in self-doubt. Great artists are thankful for their power, whatever its expression, because they know it's a gift that benefits all of mankind.

Beauty has expressed itself in so many various ways, in disparate cultures, throughout different periods of time, that we have good reason to say it's in the eye of the beholder. However, we should note that it's only the *vehicle* of beauty that changes—the *essence* of beauty does not change, only the form that it's perceived in. It's interesting that people of advanced consciousness are able to see beauty in all forms. To them, not only is all of life sacred, but all form is beauty.

CHAPTER FIFTEEN

Genius and the Power of Creativity

Creativity and genius are at the center of high-energy attractors. No human talents are more relevant to the creation of new M-fields or for the expansion of the enfolded universe; in fact, these are the explicit domains of creativity and genius. Yet there's a scarcity of information about the essential nature of either quality—these closely allied processes remain shrouded in mystery.

Human history is the record of man's struggle to comprehend truths that have appeared obvious to those of genius. *Genius* is by definition a style of consciousness characterized by the ability to access high-energy attractor patterns. It isn't a personality characteristic, nor is it something that a person "has" or "is." A universal characteristic of genius is humility; after all, those in whom we recognize genius commonly disclaim it, as they've always attributed their insights to some higher influence.

The process of animating genius most commonly involves first formulating a question, then waiting an indefinite interval for consciousness to work with the problem—until suddenly, the answer appears in a flash, in a form that's characteristically nonverbal. For example, great musicians throughout history have stated that they didn't plan their music, but simply wrote down what they heard within their own minds.[1] The father of organic chemistry, F. A. Kekulé, saw the molecular structure that he based the ring theory on in a dream. And, in an illuminated moment, Albert Einstein had the revolutionary insight that then took him years to translate into provable mathematics.[2] Indeed, one of the main problems of genius is how to transform what's perceived in one's private understanding into a visible expression that's comprehensible to others. The revelation itself is usually complete and self-explanatory to the person who receives it, but to make it so to others may take a lifetime.[3]

Genius thus seems to proceed from sudden revelation rather than conceptualization, but there *is* an unseen process involved: Although the genius's mind may appear stalled and frustrated with the problem, what it's really doing is preparing the field. There's a struggle with reason that eventually leads, like a Zen koan, to a rational impasse from which the only way forward is to leap from a lower attractor energy pattern to a higher one.

Attractor energy patterns have harmonics, as do musical tones. The higher the harmonic's frequency, the higher the power. What the genius arrives at is a new harmonic. Every advance in human consciousness has come through a leap from a lower attractor pattern to its higher harmonic. Posing the original question activates an attractor; the answer lies within its harmonic. This is why it's said that the question and the answer are merely two sides of one coin, and that one can't pose a question unless the answer already exists—otherwise there would be no pattern that the question could be formulated from.[4]

Recognized geniuses may be rare, but genius resides within all of us. There's no such thing as "luck" or "accident" in this cosmos; and not only is everything connected to everything else, no one is excluded from the universe—we're *all* members. Consciousness, like physicality, is a universal quality; because genius is a characteristic of consciousness, genius is also universal. It follows that that which is universal is available to each and every person.

The process of creativity and genius are inherent in human consciousness. Just as every human has within himself the same essence of consciousness, so is genius a potential that resides within everyone—it simply waits for the right circumstance to express itself. Each of us has had moments of genius in our lifetimes, perhaps only known to ourselves or to those close to us. We suddenly make a brilliant move or decision, or say exactly the right thing at the right moment, without quite knowing why. Sometimes we might even like to congratulate ourselves for these fortuitous events, but in truth we really don't know where they came from.

Genius is often expressed through a change of perception—a modifying of context or paradigm. The mind struggles with an unsolvable problem, poses a question, and is open to receive an answer. The source that this answer comes from has been given many names, varying from culture to culture and time to time; in the arts of Western civilization, it's traditionally been identified with the Greek goddesses of inspiration called the *Muses*. Those who are humble and grateful for illumination received tend to continue to have the capacity to access genius; those who credit the inspiration to their own ego soon lose this capacity, or are destroyed by their success. High power, like high voltage, must be handled with respect.

Genius and creativity, then, are subjectively experienced as a *witnessing;* it's a phenomenon that bypasses the individual self or ego. The capacity to finesse genius can be learned—though often only through painful surrender—when the phoenix of genius arises out of the ashes of despair after a fruitless struggle with the unsolvable. Out of defeat comes victory; out of failure, success; and out of humbling, true self-esteem.

One of the problems in attempting to understand genius is that it takes near-genius to recognize it. The world frequently fails to identify genius altogether; society often gives acclaim to its work without noting the intrinsic genius of its creation itself. Until one acknowledges the intrinsic genius within oneself, one will have great difficulty recognizing it in others—we can only acknowledge without what we realize within. For example, Mikhail Gorbachev was the subject of enormous worldwide attention, but at the same time, the world never really did acknowledge his *genius:* Single-handedly, and in only a few short years, he completely revolutionized one of the greatest empires on Earth, and his only sources of power were his inspiration and vision. (Had the communist regime been based on power, nothing could have overturned it; because it was based on force, it was destined to come to an end under the hand of a charismatic leader who was aligned with power.)[5]

✛ ✛ ✛

Genius is one of the greatest untapped resources of our society. It's no more specific than it is personal—people of genius frequently have multiple talents in different realms, and they might have answers to a diversity of problems. Yet society suffers a great loss because it doesn't know how to nurture its geniuses, and in fact is often either indifferent or hostile to them. This is unfortunate, for they characteristically don't cost much to maintain. The lifestyle of those we term *genius* is typically simple, and they're seldom interested in money or fame. Genius is characterized by an appreciation for resources and the economy of integrity, because the genius values life and sees the intrinsic worth of all of its expressions. Since time and resources are considered precious, doing more than is necessary is viewed as a waste; therefore, people of genius often lead very quiet lives and usually only come forth, very reluctantly, when there's a cause that must be supported.

Because they are in touch with an endless source of supply, geniuses experience only a minimum of want (such simplicity seems a common characteristic of true success in general)—for there's no need to "get" when you already "have." The basis of this nonmateriality, this seeming naïveté, is a radical understanding of the nature of the universe itself: That which supports life is supported by life;

survival is thus effortless, and giving and receiving are one and the same.

Genius is notoriously interpreted as unconventionality or eccentricity. It's true that such people, due to their alignment with high-energy attractors, have a different perspective on life; therefore, things have a different significance for them than they do for the average person. The genius is frequently inspired to intense activity by insights beyond our understanding.

Genius isn't stardom—those who attain prominence are a very small minority. There remains a legion of geniuses who achieve no such status; many appear in no way noteworthy and may, in fact, have never had formal higher education. What characterizes this type is the capacity to exhaustively utilize what experience they have, and to capitalize on it by the dedication necessary to reach a high degree of mastery. Many productive geniuses aren't recognized until years after they've died. In fact, the gift—or curse—of genius often brings about unfortunate consequences during such an individual's lifetime.

One characteristic of genius is the capacity for great intensity, which is often expressed in a cyclic fashion. That is, the personality of the genius sometimes seems to incorporate polar extremes: When inspired, he may work 20 hours a day to realize a solution while it's still fresh in his mind; these periods of intense activity tend to be interspersed with intervals of apparent stasis that are actually times of fermentation, which is a necessary part of the creative process. Geniuses understand the need to make space for ideas to crystallize, for creativity occurs under appropriate inner, not outer, circumstances. The stage is often set by complete distraction—we all know stories of people who have gotten the answers to complex problems while sitting in traffic on the freeway.

A primary reason that so many people fail to recognize, and therefore empower, their own genius is because in the popular mind, genius is confused with a high IQ. This is a gross misunderstanding, which has arisen from the fact that many celebrated geniuses in the fields of mathematics and physics indeed have high IQs; however, in those fields, the IQ necessary to comprehend the work is a prerequisite. It would be more helpful to see genius as simply an extraordinarily high degree of insight in a given area of human activity. After all, there are droves of noncerebral geniuses in many fields—such as art, music, design, and invention—whose innovative, creative talents fall within certain limited parameters.

Keep in mind that IQ is merely a measure of academic capacity for logically comprehending symbols and words. From our studies, it appears that the alignment of one's goals and values with high-energy attractors is more closely associated with genius than anything else. Genius can be more accurately identified by perseverance, courage, concentration, enormous drive, and absolute integrity—talent alone is certainly not enough. Dedication of an unusual degree is required to achieve mastery, and in the simplest definition, one could say that genius is the capacity for an extraordinary degree of mastery in one's calling. A formula followed by all geniuses, prominent or not, is: *Do what you like to do best, and do it to the very best of your ability.*

◉ ◉ ◉

CHAPTER SIXTEEN

Surviving Success

The tragic downfall of many geniuses, after they've been discovered and celebrated by the public, illustrates that there is success, and then there is *Success*. The former frequently jeopardizes life, while the latter enhances it. True success enlivens and supports the spirit; it has nothing to do with isolated achievements, but instead relates to being accomplished as a total person, and attaining a lifestyle that benefits not only the individual but everyone around them. Truly successful people's lives are empowered by the context of their accomplishments.

Contrast that with what the tabloid world calls success, which often erodes the "successful" person's health and relationships—spiritual collapse is commonplace in the lives of the rich and famous. This kind of success is merely celebrity, and the capacity of celebrity to destroy is documented daily: Famous people constantly succumb to failed marriages, addiction, alcoholism, suicide, or other untimely demises. If we listed the names of all of the celebrities whose careers were blighted by such tragedies, it would fill a score of pages—the movie stars, the pop stars, the writers . . . the list goes on and on. In addition to such notorious examples of the price of celebrity, there are countless other "successful" lives ruined by drug problems or the twisting of personality—whereby formerly decent people become vain, cruel, self-centered, and inordinately self-indulgent.

It isn't just that such people have acquired too much wealth, fame, or attention; it's that these influences distorted their egos and reinforced what might be called the small self instead of the big Self. The small self is the part of us that's vulnerable to flattery; the big Self is an aspect of our more evolved nature, which is humble and grateful for success. The self aligns with weak attractor patterns; the Self is aligned with high-energy attractor fields.

Whether it uplifts or destroys us depends not upon success itself, but on how it's integrated into our personalities. Whether we're proud or humble; whether we're egotistic or grateful; whether we deem ourselves better than others because of our talents or consider them a gift for which we're thankful—these are the determining factors. We all know people for whom just a bit of success is corrupting—who become arrogant, officious, and controlling when given even a small taste of authority. By the same token, we also know people of much greater authority who are cordial, sensitive, and caring.

When we come to know the powerful figures of the world—captains of industry, presidents of banks, Nobel

Prize winners, and members of legendary families—it's striking to see how many are open, warm, sincere, and view success as a responsibility, or "noblesse oblige." These are truly successful people—whether visiting potentates or servants, they're notable, courteous, and considerate to all, *treating everyone as an equal.* The truly successful have no inclination to act arrogantly, for they consider themselves not better that others, just more fortunate. They see their position as a *stewardship,* a responsibility to exercise their influence for the greatest benefit of all.

What allows the truly successful to be so gracious, open, and giving can be explained through our formula of causality:

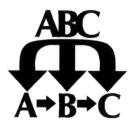

The truly successful identify with the ABC. They realize that they're a channel acted through to create success in the outer world. As much as they identify with success, they have no anxiety about losing it, for solid confidence comes from the knowledge that the source of success is "in here." But a person who views his success in the realm of A→B→C will always be insecure, since the source of his success is "out there." By believing that the source of power lies outside oneself, one becomes powerless and vulnerable and, therefore, defensive and possessive. True success originates within, independent of external circumstances.

The ladder of success seems to have three main steps: (1) Initially, it's what one "has" that counts—that is, status depends upon visible signs of material wealth; (2) as one progresses, status is afforded by what one "does," rather than what one has—at this level on the ladder, one's position and activities bring significant social status, but the attraction of social roles loses glamour as one achieves mastery and matures, for it's what one has accomplished that is important; (3) and finally, one is concerned only with what one has become as a result of life's experiences—such people have a charismatic "presence" that is the outer manifestation of the grace of their inner power. In their company, we feel the effect of the powerful attractor energy patterns that they're aligned with and that they reflect. Success comes as the automatic consequence of aligning one's life with high-power energy patterns.

Why is true success so relatively effortless? It might be likened to the magnetic field created by an electric current running through a wire: The higher the power of the current, the greater the magnetic field that it generates—and the magnetic field itself then influences everything in its presence. There are very few at the top; the world of the mediocre, however, is one of intense competition, and the bottom of the pyramid is crowded. Charismatic winners are sought out; losers have to strive to be accepted. People who are loving, kind, and considerate of others have more friends than they can count; accomplishment in every area of life is reflected back to those who are aligned with successful patterns. And the capacity to be able to discern the difference between the strong patterns of success and the weak patterns leading to failure is now available to each of us.

CHAPTER SEVENTEEN

Physical Health and Power

We become healthy, as well as wealthy, by being wise. But what is wisdom? According to our research, it's the result of aligning with high-power attractor patterns—although we tend to find a mixture of energy fields in the average life, the pattern with the highest power dominates. We've now explored sufficient material to be able to introduce a basic dictum of nonlinear dynamics and attractor research: *Attractors create context*. In essence, this means that one's motive, which arises from the principles that one is committed to, determines one's capacity to understand and, therefore, gives significance to one's actions.

The effect of alignment with principle is never more striking than in its physiological consequences. Vibrant health follows alignment with high-energy attractor patterns; alignment with weak patterns results in disease.

That this syndrome is specific and predictable, and can be proven through a demonstration meeting the scientific criterion of 100 percent replicability, is a fact that by now is familiar. The human central nervous system clearly has an exquisitely sensitive capacity to differentiate between life-*supportive* and life-*destructive* patterns. High-power attractor energy patterns, which make the body go strong, release brain endorphins and have a tonic effect on all of the organs; adverse stimuli release adrenaline, which suppresses immune response and instantaneously causes both weakness and even breakdown of specific organs, depending on the nature of the stimulus.

This clinical phenomenon forms the basis for such treatments as chiropractic, acupuncture, reflexology, and many others. These therapies, however, are usually designed to correct the *results* of an energy imbalance, but unless the basic attitude that's *causing* the energy imbalance is corrected, the illness tends to return. People by the millions in self-help groups have demonstrated that health and recovery from the entire gamut of human behavioral problems and illnesses comes as a result of adopting attitudes correlated with high-energy attractor patterns (that is, spiritual).

Generally speaking, physical and mental soundness are attendant upon positive attitudes, whereas poor physical and mental health are associated with such negative attitudes as resentment, jealousy, hostility, self-pity, fear, anxiety, and the like. In the field of psychoanalysis, positive attitudes are called *welfare emotions,* and the negative ones are called *emergency emotions.* Chronic immersion in emergency emotions results in ill health and a gross weakening of one's personal power.

How does one overcome negative attitudes so as to avoid this deterioration of power and health? Clinical observation indicates that the patient must reach a decision: A sincere desire for change allows one to seek higher attractor energy patterns in their various expressions. For instance, one doesn't get over pessimism by associating with cynics; the popular idea that you're defined by the company you keep does have some clinical basis. Attractor patterns tend to dominate any field; thus, all that's really necessary is to *expose* oneself to a high-energy field and one's inner attitudes will spontaneously begin to change. This is a well-known phenomenon among self-help groups—it's reflected in the saying, "Just bring the body to the meeting." If you merely expose yourself to the influence of higher patterns, they begin to "rub off," or, as it's been said, "You get it by osmosis."

Traditional medicine generally holds that stress is the cause of many human disorders and illnesses. The problem with this diagnosis is that it doesn't accurately address the *source* of the stress. It looks to blame external circumstances, without realizing that *all stress is internally generated by one's attitudes*. I must emphasize again that it isn't life's events, but one's reaction to them, that activates the symptoms of stress. As we've already discovered, a divorce can bring about agony or relief; and challenges on the job can result in stimulation or anxiety, depending on whether one's supervisor is perceived to be a teacher or an ogre.

Our attitudes stem from our positions, and our positionality has to do with motive and context. According to the overall way that we interpret the meaning of events, the same situation may be tragic or comic. Physiologically speaking, in the choice of attitude, one chooses between anabolic endorphins or catabolic adrenaline.

The Power of Nutrition

It would be foolish to claim that the only impacts on our health are those originating internally, for impersonal elements of the physical world can also increase or decrease our strength. Here, too, kinesiological testing is valuable: It will clearly show that synthetics, plastics, artificial coloring, preservatives, insecticides, and artificial sweetener (just to mention a few) make the body go weak; whereas substances that are pure, organic, or made by human hands tend to make us go strong. If we experiment with vitamin C, for example, we find that organic is far superior to chemically produced—one makes you go strong and the other does not. Likewise, eggs from organically fed free-range chickens have much more intrinsic power than eggs from caged and chemically fed chickens. The health-food movement seems to have been right all along.

Unfortunately, neither the American Medical Association nor the National Council on Food and Nutrition have a history of being enlightened in the field of nutrition. The scientific community now finally recognizes that nutrition is related to behavior and health, but this simple observation caused quite a controversy 20 years ago when the book *Orthomolecular Psychiatry* stated that nutrition affects the chemical environment of the brain and bloodstream, influencing various behaviors, emotions, and mental disorders.[1]

More recently, a series of papers on a 20-year study showed that a regimen of certain vitamins prevented the development of a neurological disorder called *tardive dyskinesia,* a frequently irreversible disorder that occurs in a high percentage of patients on long-term treatment with major tranquilizers.[2] In a study of 61,000 patients, treated by 100 different doctors over a 20-year period, the introduction of vitamins B_3, C, E, and B_6 decreased the expected rate of this terrible neurologic disorder from 25 percent to .04 percent.[3] (Among 61,000 patients protected by high-dosage vitamin therapy, only 37, rather than the predicted nearly 20,000, developed the disorder.)[4]

The paper was largely ignored in the United States because there was still no context to give it credibility. The medical profession has simply been uninterested in nutrition, and organized medicine has traditionally been less-than-kind to innovators. It's helpful to remember that it's a foible of human nature to stoutly defend an established position despite overwhelming evidence against it; the only healthy way to deal with such lack of recognition is *acceptance.* Once we really understand the human condition, we'll feel compassion where we once might have felt condemnation. Compassion is one of the highest of all of the energy attractor power patterns. As we shall see, our capacity to understand, forgive, and accept is directly linked to our personal health.

CHAPTER EIGHTEEN

Wellness and the Disease Process

Throughout the ages, it's been a common observation that certain diseases are associated with particular emotions and attitudes. The medieval concept of "melancholy," for instance, connected depression with impairment of the liver; in contemporary times, many physical disorders have been clearly linked with the emotion of stress.

That emotions do have physiologic consequences is well documented. In the early days of psychoanalysis, research to identify particular diseases with specific psychological conflicts gave rise to the whole field of psychosomatic inquiry. We've all heard about the connection between heart disease and "type A" personalities, and how suppressed anger results in hypertension and strokes. The presumption has been that, through neurotransmitter variations in different areas of the brain that are associated with controlling different organs, emotions affect hormonal change.

In more recent years, concern over the spread of AIDS has been a great incentive for researchers to study the body's immune system. Generally, it appears that what's experienced as stress results in suppression of the thymus gland, and the body's defenses are consequently impaired. But the various research approaches to this topic fail to examine the relationship between belief systems and attitudes, and the resulting context of perception that determines the nature of individual experience. The origin of stress is always related to the organism's tendency to respond to stimuli in specific and characteristic patterns. Drawing on what we already know from the mathematics of nonlinear dynamics and attractor research—which has been clinically confirmed by kinesiology and acupuncture—we can derive a formulation of the basic nature of the disease process itself.

An idea or constellation of thoughts presents itself in consciousness as an attitude that tends to persist over time; this attitude is subsequently associated with an attractor energy field of corresponding power or weakness. The result is a particular perception of the world, and appropriate events are created to trigger the specific emotion. All attitudes, thoughts, and beliefs are also connected with various pathways—called *meridians* of energy—to all of the body's organs. Through kinesiologic testing, it can be demonstrated that specific acupuncture points are linked with specific attitudes, and the meridian, in turn, serves as the energy channel to specific muscles and body organs.[1] These specific meridians have traditionally been named according to the organs that they energize—for instance, the heart meridian, gallbladder meridian, and so on.[2] There's nothing mysterious about these vital internal communications, and they can be demonstrated in seconds to anyone's satisfaction—for as we know, if one holds a particular negative thought in mind, a very specific muscle will go weak; if one then replaces the thought with a positive idea, the same muscle will instantly go strong.[3] The connection between mind and body is immediate, so the body's responses shift and change from instant to instant in response to one's train of thought and the associated emotions.

We've referred to the law of sensitive dependence on initial conditions, drawing from the science of nonlinear dynamics and its mathematics.[4] Remember that this describes the manner in which a minuscule variation in a pattern of inputs can result in a very significant change in the eventual output. This is because the repetition of a slight variation over time results in a progressive change of pattern, or, when the increment increases logarithmically, in a leap to a new harmonic. The effect of the minute variation becomes amplified until it eventually affects the entire system and a new energy pattern evolves—which, by the same process, may then result in a further variation, and so on.

In the world of physics, this process is called *turbulence,* and is the subject of an enormous amount of research, especially in the field of aerodynamics, which combines both physics and mathematics. When such turbulence occurs in the attractor fields of consciousness, it creates an emotional upset that continues until a new level of equilibrium is established.

When the mind is dominated by a negative worldview,

the direct result is a repetition of minute changes in energy flow to the various body organs. The subtle field of over-all physiology is affected in all of its complex functions— mediated by electron transfer, neural hormonal balance, nutritional status, and the like. Eventually, an accumulation of infinitesimal changes becomes discernible through measurement techniques, such as electron microscopy, magnetic imaging, x-ray, or biochemical analysis—but by the time these changes are detectable, the disease process is already quite advanced.

We could say that the invisible universe of thought and attitude becomes visible as a consequence of the body's habitual response. If we consider the millions of thoughts that go through the mind continually, it isn't surprising that the body's condition could radically change to reflect prevailing thought patterns, as modified by genetic and environmental factors.[5] It's the *persistence* and repetition of the stimulus that, through the law of sensitive dependence on initial conditions, results in the observable disease process. The stimulus that sets off the process may be so minute that it escapes detection itself.

If this scheme of disease formation is correct, then all illness should be reversible by changing thought patterns and habitual responses. In fact, spontaneous recoveries from every disease known to man have been recorded throughout history. (This phenomenon was the subject of the TV news show *20/20* on April 8, 1994.) Traditional medicine has documented spontaneous "cures," but has never had the conceptual tools with which to investigate them. (As an aside, it's interesting to note that even thoroughly modern surgeons are rather reluctant to operate on anyone who's convinced that he's going to die during the surgery—because such patients frequently do just that.)

In AA, it's said that there can be no recovery until the subject experiences an essential change of personality.[6] This is the basic change first manifested by AA founder Bill W.—a profound transformation in his total belief system, followed by a sudden leap in consciousness.[7] Such a major metamorphosis in attitude was first formally studied by the American psychiatrist Harry Tiebout, who treated a hopeless alcoholic who was the first woman in AA. She underwent a profound change of personality to a degree unaccountable through any known therapeutic method. In the first of a series of papers on this observation, Tiebout documented that she was transformed from an angry, self-pitying, intolerant, and egocentric creature to a kind, gentle, forgiving, and loving person.[8] This example is important because it clearly demonstrates how key this element of transformation is in the recovery from any progressive or hopeless disease.

In every studied case of recovery from hopeless and untreatable disease, there has been this major shift in consciousness so that the attractor patterns that resulted in the pathologic process no longer dominated. The steps necessary for recovery from such grave illness were formalized by the first 100 alcoholics who recovered from their disease; these became the well-known 12 steps suggested by AA and all of the 12-step recovery groups that have followed.[9] The fact that pursuing these steps has resulted in the recovery of millions of people suggests that this experience may have a universal applicability to *all* disease processes. The advice Carl Jung gave Rowland H.— "Throw yourself wholeheartedly into any spiritual group that appeals to you, whether you believe in it or not, and hope that in your case a miracle may occur"[10]—may hold true for anyone who wishes to recover from a progressive disease.

In spontaneous recovery, there's frequently a marked increase in the capacity to love and the awareness of the importance of love as a healing factor. Numerous best-selling books have told us that to love is to live healthily— but love of our fellow man can ensue only when we stop condemning, fearing, and hating each other. Such radical change, however, can be disorienting; the courage to endure the temporary discomfort of growth is required, and the mind tends to resist change as a matter of pride. Recovery from any disease process is dependent on willingness to explore new ways of looking at one's self and life, which includes the capacity to endure inner fears when belief systems are shaken. People cherish and cling to their hates and grievances, so to heal humanity, it may be necessary to pry entire populations away from lifestyles of spite, attack, and revenge.

A prime difficulty with thoughts and behaviors associated with the energy fields below 200 is that they cause counterreactions. A familiar law of the observable universe is that force results in equal and opposite counterforce; all attacks, therefore, whether mental or physical, result in counterattack. Malice literally makes us sick; we're always the victims of our own vindictiveness. Even secret hostile thoughts result in a physiological attack on one's own body.

On the other hand, like love, laughter heals because it arises through viewing a small context from a larger and more inclusive one, which removes the observer from the victim posture. Every joke reminds us that our reality is transcendent, beyond the specifics of events. Gallows humor, for instance, is based upon the juxtaposition of the opposites of a paradox; the relief of basic anxiety then results in a laugh. One of the frequent accompaniments of sudden enlightening realizations is laughter: The cosmic joke is the side-by-side comparison of illusion with reality.

Humorlessness, in contrast, is hostile to health and happiness. Totalitarian systems are notably devoid of humor at any level—laughter, which brings acceptance and freedom, is a threat to their rule. After all, it's difficult to oppress people who have a good sense of humor. Beware the humorless—whether in the form of a person, institution, or belief system—for it's always accompanied by an impulse to control and dominate, even if its proclaimed objective is to create prosperity or peace.

Peace can't be created this way; peace is the natural state of affairs when what's preventing it is removed. Relatively few people are genuinely committed to peace as a realistic goal, for in their private lives, most people prefer being "right" at whatever cost to their relationships or themselves. A self-justified positionality is the real enemy of peace. When solutions are sought on the level of coercion, no peaceful resolutions are possible.

Because of their inherent dishonesty, systems associated with very weak attractor fields are ineffective and become wasteful and cumbersome. Take, for example, the health-care industry: It's so overburdened with fear and regulation that it can barely function. The industry itself demonstrates how controlling attempts only become compounded into a burgeoning bureaucratic morass—complexity is costly, and systems are as weak and inefficient as the attitudes that underlie their construct. Healing from individual illness (or the healing of the health-care industry itself) can only occur by the progressive steps of elevation of motive and abandonment of self-deception, so a new clarity of vision is attained. There aren't any villains here; the fault is in the misalignment of the system itself.

If we say that health, effectuality, and prosperity are the natural states of being in harmony with reality, then anything less calls for internal scrutiny rather than the projection of blame on things outside of the system involved. Attractor patterns obey the laws of their own physics, even if they're not Newtonian; to forgive is to be forgiven. As is repeatedly observed, in a universe where everything is connected with everything else, there's no such thing as an "accident," and nothing is outside of the universe. Since the power of causes is unseen and only the manifestation of effects is observable, there's an illusion of "accidental" events. An abrupt and unexpected incident may appear to be random, unrelated to observable causes, but its actual origin can be traced through research. For instance, a sudden illness always has discernible antecedents; even accident-prone-ness involves numerous small preparatory steps before "accidents" occur.

A disease process is evidence that something is amiss in the workings of the mind, and that's where the power to effect a change resides. Treating an illness as a physical process only, within the A→B→C world of effects, doesn't correct the origin of the dysfunction, and covers it up instead of curing it. It's possible for a lifelong affliction to heal rapidly with a mere shift of attitude; but even though this shift may seem to occur in a split second, it may in actuality take years of inner preparation.

Keep in mind that the critical point in any complex system is that which the least power is required to alter the whole system—for instance, a move of even one pawn on the chessboard completely changes the possibilities of the game. Every detail of the belief system that we hold has consequences for better or for worse. It's for this reason that there's no such thing as an incurable or hopeless condition—somewhere, at some time, somebody has recovered from it through the process described.

To have compassion for oneself and all of mankind is instrumental—not only in recovery, but for any major advancement of consciousness—as we go through the painful struggles of evolution. Only then do we become healers as well as healed, and only then may we hope to be cured of any malaise, physical or spiritual.

Does all of this mean that if we learn to operate on the level of unconditional love, we'll become immortal? Unfortunately, the protoplasm of the physical body is vulnerable to its own genetic programming, as well as to its external environment. But from the viewpoint of levels of consciousness at 500 and above, it appears that death itself is only an illusion; life goes on unimpeded by the limitation of perception that results from being localized in a physical body: Consciousness is the vital energy that both gives life to the body and survives beyond it in a different realm of existence.

◉ ◉ ◉

PART III
MEANING

CHAPTER NINETEEN

The Database of Consciousness

Noting the ubiquity of archetypal patterns and symbols, Carl Jung coined the phrase "collective unconscious"—which refers to the bottomless, subconscious pool of all of the shared experiences of the human race.[1] We may think of it as a vast, hidden database of human awareness, which is characterized by powerful, universal organizing patterns. Such a database, comprised of all of the information ever available to human consciousness, implies stunning inherent capabilities; it's far more than just a giant storehouse of information awaiting a retrieval process. The great promise of the database is its capacity to "know" virtually anything the moment it's "asked," for it's able to tap in to all that has ever been experienced anywhere in time.

This database is the origin of all information obtained sub- or suprarationally—by intuition or premonition; by divination or dream; or simply by "lucky" guess. It's the foundation of genius, the well of inspiration, and the source of "uncanny" psychic knowledge, including "foreknowledge." It is, of course, the inventory drawn upon by kinesiological testing. Thinkers who are troubled by the notion of "paranormal" or nonrational knowledge usually balk at logical—or illogical—inconsistencies with Newtonian concepts of simultaneity, causality, or time and space. But it's a bigger universe than that.

These same thinkers will scan the evening sky and find pleasure in identifying favorite constellations . . . but there aren't any constellations. That familiar pattern of "stars" is made up of points of light originating from totally unrelated sources—some millions of light-years away; some in different galaxies; some actually separate galaxies themselves; many have, millennia since, burnt out and ceased to "exist." Those lights have no spatial or temporal relationship; it isn't only the shape of a dipper, bear, or man, but the very pattern—the "constellation" itself— that's projected on the sky by the eye of the beholder. Yet the zodiac is still "real" because we *conceive* it; astrology still "exists," and for many people, it's quite a useful tool in explaining themselves and their relationships. And why shouldn't it be? The database of consciousness is, after all, an infinite resource.

✝ ✝ ✝

The database behaves like an electrostatic condenser with a field of potentiality, rather than a battery with a stored charge. A question can't be asked unless there's already the potentiality of the answer. The reason for this is that the question and answer are both created out of the same paradigm and, therefore, are exactly symmetrical—there can be no "up" without an already existent "down." Causality occurs as simultaneity rather than as sequence; *synchronicity* is the term used by Jung to explain this phenomenon in human experience.[2] As we understand from our examination of advanced physics, an event "here" in the universe doesn't "cause" an event to occur "there"—instead, both appear at the same time. What's the connection between these events, then, if it isn't a Newtonian linear sequence of cause and effect? Obviously, the two are related or connected to each other in some invisible manner, but not by gravity or magnetism, or even by a cosmic field of such magnitude that it includes both events. The "connection" between any two events occurs only in the observer's consciousness—he "sees" a connection and describes a "pair" of events, hypothesizing a relationship. This relationship is a concept in the mind of the observer; it isn't necessary that any corollary external event exist in the universe. Unless there's an underlying attractor pattern, nothing can be experienced. Thus, the entire manifest universe is its own simultaneous expression and experience of itself.

Omniscience is omnipotent and omnipresent. There's no distance between the unknown and the known—the known is manifest from the unknown merely by the asking. For example, the Empire State Building was born in the mind of its architects—human consciousness is the agent that can transform an unseen concept into its

manifested experience, which is therefore frozen in time.
What "happened" on Fifth Avenue in New York City in
1931 is there for all to see, and what "happened" in the
consciousness of its creators also stands recorded in the
database for all to see to this day—both exist complete, but
in different sensory domains. By transferring concept into
concrete and steel, the architects simply enabled the rest
of us to experience their vision.

We "normal" humans are completely preoccupied
with our function as transformers of concepts from the invisible level, ABC, to the sensorially perceptible A→B→C.
Extraordinary individuals live primarily in the world of
ABC (those who live beyond that, in the completely formless domain of pure consciousness itself, we call *mystics*).
To such individuals, the origin of everything is obvious;
they're uninterested in the process of making things visible and manifest. In everyday life, these are the creative
people who spawn new enterprises and then turn over their
execution and management to others. Mystics, who are
even more advanced, conclude that only *their* ABC level
of awareness is "real" and the observable world is a dream
or illusion. It should be pointed out, however, that this is
only another limited point of view. There is neither real nor
nonreal, only that which *is*. That which is, is so, from all
viewpoints or none.

Existence without form isn't imaginable, yet at the
same time it's the ultimate reality—this includes both yin
and yang; the unmanifest and the manifest; the formed and
the formless; the seen and the unseen; the temporal and the
timeless. Thus, the real world is simultaneously the *R*eal
world, for that which is All Possibility must include within
it all that is. Creation is, therefore, continuous, or there

could be no creation at all. To look for the "beginning" of creation is to proceed from an artificial notion of time—the "start" of something that's outside of time cannot, therefore, be located in time. The "big bang" can only occur in the mind of an observer.

The universe is very cooperative—as much as it isn't different from consciousness itself, the universe is happy to create whatever we wish to find "out there." The problem is with the concept of *cause* itself, which presumes that a time warp, a sequence, or a string of events will make sense. If we step outside of time, there are no causes at all. We could say that the manifest world originates out of the unmanifest, but that again would be inferring a sequential causal series in time, that is, unmanifest→manifest. Once beyond the warp of time, with its implicit restriction of comprehension to terms of mere sequence, there is no backwards or forwards. It's then just as valid to say, reciprocally, that the manifest universe causes the unmanifest; at a certain level of understanding, this is demonstrably true. If, for example, we look at electrons lined up on one side of a space and protons lined up on the other in an equal balance, how can we say which side causes the other to line up? Similarly, though healing is a consequence of compassion, compassion isn't its "cause." In an energy field of 600 or higher, almost anything will heal.

The source of all life and all form is, of necessity, greater than its manifestations; yet, it's neither different nor separate from the manifestations to any degree. There's no conceptual artifact of separation between creator and created. As scripture states, that which is, was, and always shall be.

Time, then, is much like a hologram that already stands complete; it's a subjective, sensory effect of a progressively moving point of view. There's no beginning or end to a hologram, it's already everywhere, complete—in fact, the appearance of being "unfinished" is part of its completeness. Even the phenomenon of "unfoldment" itself reflects a limited point of view: There is no enfolded and unfolded universe, only a becoming awareness. Our perception of events happening in time is analogous to a traveler watching the landscape unfold before him. But to say that the landscape unfolds before the traveler is merely a figure of speech—nothing is actually unfolding; nothing is actually becoming manifest. There's only the progression of awareness.

These paradoxes dissolve in the greater paradigm that includes both opposites, wherein oppositions as such are only related to the locations of the observer. This transcendence of opposition occurs spontaneously at consciousness levels of 600 and above. The notion that there's a "knower" and a "known" is in itself dualistic, in that it implies a separation between subject and object (which, again, can only be inferred by the artificial adoption of a point of observation). The Maker of all things in heaven and on Earth, of all things visible and invisible, stands beyond both, includes both, and is one with both. Existence, is, therefore, merely a statement that awareness is aware of its awareness and of its expression as consciousness.

Ontology need not be speculative—it is, after all, only the theology of existence; anyone who's aware that he exists already has access to its highest formulations and beyond. *There is only one absolute truth;* all the rest are semi-facts spawned from the artifacts of limited perception and positionality. "To be or not to be" isn't a choice; one may decide to be this or that, but to *be* is, simply, the only fact there is.

All of the foregoing has been expressed at various times in man's intellectual history by sages who have moved beyond duality in their awareness. But even then, to claim that the comprehension of the nonduality of existence is superior to its realization as dual is again to fall into an illusion. There is, ultimately, neither duality nor nonduality; there's only *awareness*. Only awareness itself can state that it's beyond all concepts such as "is" or "is not." That must be so, because "is" can be conceived only by consciousness itself.

Awareness itself is beyond even consciousness. Therefore, it may be said that the Absolute is unknowable exactly because it's beyond knowing, or beyond the reach of consciousness itself. Those who have attained such a state of awareness report that it can't be described and can have no meaning for anyone without the experience of that context. Nonetheless, this is the true state of Reality, universally and eternally—we merely fail to recognize it. Such a recognition is the essence of enlightenment and the final resolution of the evolution of consciousness, to the point of self-transcendence.[3]

◎ ◎ ◎

CHAPTER TWENTY

The Evolution of Consciousness

Thousands of calculations—and innumerable calibrations drawn from kinesiologic testing of individuals and from historical analysis—indicate that the average advance in the level of consciousness throughout the global population is little more than five points during a lifetime. Apparently, even though one undergoes untold millions of individual experiences in one's life, only a few lessons are usually ever learned. The attainment of wisdom is slow and painful, and few are willing to relinquish familiar views (even if they're inaccurate); resistance to change or growth is considerable. It would seem that most people would rather die than alter those belief systems that confine them to lower levels of consciousness— if this is true, then what's the prognosis for the human condition? Is a five-point advance per generation all that can be expected? This troubling question deserves our attention.

In the first place, as we can observe from the distribution of levels of consciousness throughout the world population, great masses of our species are at the low end of the evolutionary scale, still relying on force to compensate for their actual powerlessness. More advanced, individual cultures exhibit more variation. For example, the Japanese capitalized on the lessons of World War II and collectively made a major jump in their evolution; on the other hand, America's level of consciousness sank as a result of the Vietnam War—what was actually learned as yet remains to be seen.

Unfortunately, our entertainment tends to trade on emotional sensationalism, and therefore gravitates toward violence. Murder is nightly family fare on television; our children grow up on a steady mental diet of it. Americans have learned to enjoy the gruesome—and the more bizarre, the better. Cruelty and havoc are becoming the status quo. In 1993, an initiative requiring children to have parental permission to carry guns failed in the city of Phoenix, Arizona; soon after, the news reported the handgun killing of a two-and-a-half-year-old toddler by another child, who was just three years old himself. It seems that society institutionalizes certain self-propagating levels of consciousness that consequently become an ingrained characteristic of various social strata.

Nonetheless, there remains free choice and therefore a considerable potential for individual mobility and variety of experience, which makes alternate options available. From our study of advanced theoretical physics, nonlinear dynamics, and the nature of nonlinear equations, it's clear that, at least in theory, choice is not only possible, but inevitable. It's out of regularity that irregularity appears; all attractor patterns are connected to each other, if only by a single "strand," so to speak. But how exactly do transformational choices occur? What leads to them? Who makes them and why? This is a subject where few principles have been defined.

Growth and development are irregular and nonlinear; practically nothing is known about the essential nature of growth, or any "process" in nature for that matter. No one has ever studied the nature of *life itself,* only its images and consequences. There simply hasn't been adequate mathematics to comprehend it; linear differential equations brought us to approximations, but not to essence. When we bear witness to the simple sprouting of a bud or leaf, incredible wonders are performed through an intrinsic wizardry that we really have no understanding of whatsoever.

As is commonly observed, growth—both individual and collective—can take place either slowly or suddenly. It isn't limited by restraints, but by tendencies. Innumerable options are open to everyone all the time, but they're relatively infrequently chosen, because people want the context that would make such options attractive. One's range of choice is ordinarily limited only by one's vision.

Context, value, and *meaning* are merely different terms for a subtle web of energy patterns within an overall organizing attractor energy field—which is itself only part of a still larger one, and so on, in an infinite continuum throughout the universe, until it eventually includes the total field of consciousness itself. While the sheer magnitude of such a complex of energy patterns seems beyond human cognizance, its totality is nonetheless comprehended by individuals whose consciousness reaches the 600 to 700 range, which gives us some idea of the enormous capacity for understanding possessed by those with advanced consciousness.

The most important element in facilitating an upward movement in consciousness is an attitude of willingness, which opens up the mind through new means of appraisal to the possible validity of new hypotheses. Although motives for change are as multitudinous as the innumerable facets of the human condition, they're most often found to arise spontaneously when the mind is challenged in the face of a puzzle or a paradox. In fact, certain disciplines (such as Zen) deliberately create such an impasse in order to finesse a leap of awareness.

On our scale of consciousness, there are two critical points that allow for major advancement. The first is at 200, the initial level of empowerment: Here, the willingness to stop blaming and accept responsibility for one's own actions, feelings, and beliefs arises—as long as cause and responsibility are projected outside of oneself, one will remain in the powerless mode of victimhood. The second is at the 500 level, which is reached by accepting love and nonjudgmental forgiveness as a lifestyle, exercising unconditional kindness to all persons, things, and events *without exception*. (In 12-step recovery groups, it's said that there are no justified resentments—even if somebody "did you wrong," you're still free to choose your response and let resentment go.) Once one makes this commitment, he begins to experience a different, more benign world as his perceptions evolve.

Holograms and Perceptions

It's initially very challenging to understand that attitudes can alter the world one experiences—and that there are numerous valid ways of experiencing it. But, as in viewing a hologram, what you see depends completely on the position that you view it from. So what position, then, is "reality"?

In fact, *this is a holographic universe.* Each point of view reflects a position that's defined by the viewer's unique level of consciousness. If you're on this side of the hologram, your perception will hardly agree with that of the observer on the other side. "He must be crazy!" is a common reaction to such wide discrepancy. And even though it's been said many times that the world is made of mirrors, this just isn't true. The world is a set of holograms in limitless dimensions that seem to be fixed in time and place and offer only a single reflection. Auditory experience, for example, is part of a holographic series of attractor fields of all of the sounds that ever were. The physical world is tactile, too. It has texture, color, dimension, and spatial relationships such as position and shape. Again, each of these is part of an underlying sequence that, with all of the other qualities, goes "back in time" to the original source of its existence, which is *now.*

A hologram, we might say, is in and of itself a process. There's nothing fixed in a three-dimensional hologram. And what then of a *four*-dimensional hologram? It would include all possible instances of itself simultaneously. To change seems to be to move through time, but if time itself is transcended, then there's no such thing as sequence. If all is now, there's nothing to follow from here to there.

Each hologram is in itself an evolutionary projection from an endless nonlinear matrix of events that aren't causally related, but instead synchronous. Then, at the perceptual level of 600 to 700, what was, what is, and what will be are comprehended wordlessly within the complete, simultaneous holographic possibility.[1] The term *indescribable* here begins to take meaning.

Let's attempt to better understand all of this through a concrete example. Imagine a "bum" on a street corner: In an upscale neighborhood stands an old man in tattered clothes, alone and leaning against the corner of an elegant brownstone. Look at him from the perspective of various levels of consciousness, and note the inconsistency in how he appears to different people and viewpoints.

- From the bottom of the scale, at a level of **20 (Shame)**, the bum is seen to be dirty, disgusting, and disgraceful. From level **30 (Guilt)**, he'd be blamed for his condition: He deserves what he gets; he's probably a lazy welfare cheat. At **50 (Hopelessness)**, his plight would appear desperate, a damning piece of evidence to prove that society can't do anything about homelessness. At **75 (Grief)**, the old man looks tragic, friendless, and forlorn.

- At a consciousness level of **100 (Fear)**, we might see the bum as threatening, a social menace: Perhaps we should call the police before he commits some crime. At **125** (**Desire**), he might represent a frustrating problem—why doesn't somebody do something? At **150** (**Anger**), the old man might look like he could be violent; or, on the other hand, one could be furious that such horrible conditions exist in our country today. At **175** (**Pride**), he could be seen as an embarrassment or as lacking the self-respect to better himself. At **200** (**Courage**), we might be motivated to wonder if there is a local homeless shelter—all he needs is a job and a place to live.

- At **250** (**Neutrality**), the bum looks okay, maybe even interesting. "Live and let live," we might say—after all, he's not hurting anyone. At **310** (**Willingness**), we might decide to go down and see what we can do to cheer up that fellow on the corner; maybe we'd be motivated to volunteer some time at the local shelter. At **350** (**Acceptance**), the man on the corner appears intriguing: He probably has an interesting story to tell; he's where he is for reasons we may never understand. At **400** (**Reason**), he's a symptom of the current economic and social malaise, or perhaps a good subject for in-depth psychological study.

- At the **higher levels,** the old man begins to look not only interesting, but friendly—and then lovable. Perhaps we'd then be able to see that he was, in fact, one who had transcended social limits and gone free, a joyful old guy with the wisdom of age in his face and the serenity that comes from indifference to material things. At **600 (Peace),** he's revealed as our own self in a temporary expression.

When approached, the bum's response to these different levels of consciousness would vary with them. With some, he'd feel secure—with others, frightened or dejected. Some would make him angry, others would delight him; some he'd avoid, others he'd greet with pleasure. (And so it's said that we meet what we mirror.)[2]

So much for the manner in which our level of consciousness—that is, the world we encounter as passive observers—decides what we see. It's true that we'll react to things in a fashion predicated by the level that we perceive them from, that is to say, external events may define conditions, but they don't determine the consciousness level of human response. To illustrate this point, let's take a look at our current penal system.

Placed in an identical and extremely stressful environment, different inmates react in ways that vary extraordinarily according to "where they're coming from." Prisoners whose consciousness is at the lowest end of the scale sometimes attempt suicide in jail; others become psychotic and delusional with guilt. Some fall into despondency, go mute, and stop eating; still others sit with head in hands, trying to hide incipient tears of grief. A common expression is fear, which is manifested either through paranoid defensiveness or blatant sycophancy. Other prisoners react with a great degree of violent and assaultive rage. Pride is everywhere, in the form of macho bragging and dominance.

In contrast, some inmates find the courage to face the truth of why they're incarcerated, and begin to look at their lives honestly . . . and there are always those who just "roll with the punches" and try to get some reading done. At the level of Acceptance, we see prisoners who seek out help and join support groups. It isn't unusual for an inmate to take a new interest in learning, perhaps by studying in the prison library, or even becoming a jailhouse lawyer (some of history's most influential books were written behind bars). A few prisoners go through a transformation of consciousness and become loving and generous caregivers to their fellow inmates. And it's not unheard of for a prisoner aligned with higher energy fields to grow deeply spiritual, or even to actively pursue enlightenment. Some even become saintly.

How we react depends upon the world we're reacting to. Who we become, as well as what we see, is determined by *perception*—which can be said, simply, to create the world.

It's interesting to note that the further down the scale of consciousness a person is, the harder it is for him to maintain eye contact; at the low end, visual contact is avoided altogether. In contrast, as we go up the scale, the ability to hold prolonged, and finally almost endless, gazes at great depth becomes characteristic. We're all familiar with the guarded glance of guilt, the glare of hostility, and the unblinking open-eyed-ness of innocence. *Remember that power and perception go hand in hand.*

The Mechanics of Perception

How, then, does perception work? What are its mechanics? That perception is subjectively unique is evidenced by common observation: We're all familiar with the example of a mock trial in law school, wherein different witnesses relate wildly divergent accounts of the same event. The mechanism of perception is like a movie theater where the projector is consciousness itself. The forms on the film are the attractor energy patterns, and the moving pictures on the screen are the world that we perceive and call "reality." We could say that the configurations on the film are the ABC attractor fields in mind and the moving picture on the screen is the A→B→C observed as the phenomenal world.

This schema provides a model for a better understanding of the nature of causality, which occurs on the level of the film, not the level of the screen. Because the world routinely applies its efforts to the screen of life at the level of A→B→C, these endeavors are ineffectual and costly. Causality stems from the attractor patterns of levels of energy, the ABCs of the configurations imprinted on the film of mind, illuminated by consciousness.

The nature of the stream of consciousness—its pattern of thought, perception, feeling, and memory—is the consequence of entrainment of the attractor energy fields that dominate. Keep in mind that *this domination is voluntary*—it isn't imposed, but is the outcome of one's own choices, beliefs, and goals.

By consensus, we synchronize with a field pattern that implies specific styles of processing and influences all of our decisions according to its accompanying set of values and meanings. What appears as an important and exciting piece of information from the perspective of one level might be boring or even repulsive at another level. Truth is subjective, and that can be frightening. The current elevation of science to the status of infallible oracle is an expression of our insecure compulsion to feel that there's some kind of a measurable, universally predictable, objective world "out there" that we can rely upon.

But in transcending the emotional distortions of perception, science itself creates yet another conceptual distortion due to the limitation of its parameters. Out of necessity, science must remove data from its context in order to study it—but in the end, it's only the context that gives the data its whole significance or value. The eventual discovery arrived at by advanced theoretical physics can be reached from any organized field of human knowledge: The more detailed one's analysis of the structure of "out there" is, the more one discovers that what one is examining is, in fact, the nature of the intricate processes of consciousness in here. There's nothing "out there," other than consciousness itself. The habitual tendency to believe otherwise is our fundamental illusion, a vanity of the human mind, which tends always to view its transitory subject as "mine."

Objectively, it can be seen that thoughts really belong

to the consciousness of the world; the individual mind merely processes them in new combinations and permutations. What are seen to be truly original thoughts appear only through the medium of genius and are invariably felt by their authors to be a gift, found or given, not self-created. It may be the case that we're each unique, as no two snowflakes are alike . . . however, *we're still just snowflakes.*

We all inherit the human condition of mind in our unasked-for birth. To transcend the limitations of the mind, it's necessary to dethrone it from its tyranny as sole arbiter of reality. The vain mind confers its imprint of authenticity on the movie of life it happens to be viewing; the mind's very nature is to convince us that its unique view of experience is the genuine article. Each individual secretly feels that *his* particular experience of the world is accurate.

In our discussion of the levels of consciousness, we noted that one of the downsides of Pride is denial. Every mind engages in denial in order to protect its "correctness"—this begets the fixity and resistance to change that prevents the average consciousness from advancing much more than five points in a lifetime. Great leaps in levels of consciousness are always preceded by surrender of the illusion that "I know." Frequently, the only way one can reach this willingness to change is when one "hits bottom," that is, by running out a course of action to its end in the defeat of a futile belief system. Light can't enter a closed box; the upside of catastrophe can be an opening to a higher level of awareness. If life is viewed as a teacher, then it becomes just that. But unless we become humble and transform them into gateways to growth and development, the painful life lessons that we deal ourselves are wasted.

We witness, observe, and record apparent processions of experience. But even in awareness itself, nothing actually happens. Awareness merely registers what's being experienced; it has no effect on it. Awareness is the all-encompassing attractor field of unlimited power identical with life itself. *And there's nothing the mind believes that isn't erroneous at a higher level of awareness.*

The mind identifies with its content. It takes credit and blame for what it receives, for it would be humbling to the mind's vanity to admit that the only thing it's doing is experiencing, and, in fact, only *experiencing experiencing.* The mind doesn't even experience the world, just sensory reports of it. Even brilliant thoughts and deepest feelings are only experience; ultimately, we have but one function—to experience experience.

The major limitation of consciousness is its innocence. Consciousness is gullible; it believes everything it hears. Consciousness is like hardware that will play back any software that's put into it. We never lose the innocence of our own consciousness; it persists, naïve and trusting, like an impressionable child. Its only guardian is a discerning awareness that scrutinizes the incoming program.

Over the ages, it's been noted that merely observing the mind tends to increase one's level of consciousness.[3] A mind that's being watched becomes more humble and begins to relinquish its claims to omniscience—a growth in awareness can then take place. With humility comes the capacity to laugh at oneself and increasingly be less the *victim* of the mind and more its *master.*

From thinking that we "are" our minds, we begin to

see that we have minds, and that it's the *mind* that has thoughts, beliefs, feelings, and opinions—eventually, we may arrive at the insight that all of our thoughts are merely borrowed from the great database of consciousness and were never really our own. Prevailing thought systems are received, absorbed, identified with, and, in due time, replaced by new ideas that have become fashionable to us. As we place less value on such passing notions, they lose their capacity to dominate us, and we experience progressive freedom of—as well as from—the mind. This, in turn, ripens into a new source of pleasure; fittingly, the pleasure of existence itself matures as one ascends the scale of consciousness.

CHAPTER TWENTY-ONE

The Study of Pure Consciousness

Traditional philosophy has studied various aspects of consciousness, and the expressions of consciousness as mind or emotion have been the subjects of the clinical sciences, but the nature of *consciousness itself* has never been clinically examined in any comprehensive sense.

In medicine, the presumption that consciousness is nothing more than a function of the brain is reflected in such statements as, "The patient regained consciousness"—this routine, narrow depiction has assumed that consciousness is a mundane physical phenomenon, a self-evident priority for experience about which nothing more needs to be said.

The one recurrent focus of interest on the subject has been speculation regarding what happens to man's consciousness at death. Does the power of life and awareness arise from a physical basis? Does the body sustain conscious life, or is it the other way around—the power of life sustains the body? Since the way the question is asked will be defined by the questioner's preconception of causality, his level will predetermine the nature of his answer. Each questioner, therefore, will derive an answer representative of his level of consciousness.

To the materialistic scientist, the question would appear nonsensical, a fruitless exercise in redundancy. To those at the other pole (or the "enlightened"), the question would seem comical, and the limited perception it reveals would elicit compassion. The common man might take the authority of either position on faith, or might look to conventional religious teachings to answer the question.

All discussions of life, death, and the final fate of consciousness must necessarily reflect differences of context. The reciprocal of René Descartes's famous phrase, "I think, therefore I am," is "I am, therefore I think." Because thinking takes place as form, Descartes is correct—that which has form must already have existence in order to have form. "I am" is a statement of awareness, witnessing that the capacity for experience is independent of form.[1] Descartes implies that consciousness is only aware of itself when it assumes form. But the enlightened throughout history have disagreed, customarily stating that consciousness is beyond form and is, indeed, the very omnipotent matrix out of which form arises. Modern physicists concur—an example is David Bohm's concept of an "enfolded" and "unfolded" universe.

Without consciousness, there would be nothing to experience form. It could also be said that form itself, as a product of perception with no independent existence, is thus transitory and limited, whereas consciousness is all-encompassing and unlimited. How could that which is transitory (with a clear beginning and ending), create that which is formless (all encompassing and omnipotent)? However, if we see that the notion of limitation itself is merely a product of perception with no intrinsic reality, then the riddle solves itself: Form becomes an expression of the formless. Metaphysically, consciousness is an aspect of "Is-ness" and "Being-ness" and is implicit to man's definition of himself as *human*. *Human*-ness is only one expression of *being*-ness.

The operation of consciousness in human beings is the greater subject of our study. Although consciousness itself may be intangible, it's intrinsic to all human behavior. For purposes of this work, the problem is how to clinically explain the connection between consciousness and behavior in an accurate, meaningful way that can be scientifically studied. Fortunately, kinesiology categorically demonstrates the physical expression of awareness through the instantaneous reaction of the body to events experienced within consciousness. The technique affords us an elegant methodology, with an unmistakable established end point that can be calibrated, documented, and reproduced experimentally.

Characteristics of Pure Consciousness

Our vision of consciousness is aligned with our concept of self: The more limited the sense of self, the smaller the parameter of experiencing is. Restricted paradigms of reality are global in their effects—for example, our studies of the "poor" have made it evident that "poorness" isn't just a financial condition, but that the "poor" are also poor in friendships, verbal skills, education, social amenities, resources, health, and their overall level of happiness. Poorness, then, can be seen as a quality characteristic of a limited self-image, which then results in a scarcity of resources.[2] It isn't a financial condition, but a level of consciousness. The energy of that level of awareness calibrates at about 60.

The identification and experience of *self* could be limited to a description of one's physical body. Then, of course, we might well ask, how does one know that one has a physical body? Through observation, we note that the presence of the physical body is registered by the senses. The question then follows, what is it that's aware of the senses? How do we experience what the senses are reporting? Something greater, something more encompassing than the physical body, has to exist in order to experience that which is lesser—and that something is the *mind*. A person identifies with his body because his mind is experiencing his body. Patients who have lost sizable portions of their bodies report that their sense of self remains undiminished; such a person will say, "I'm still just as much *me* as I ever was."

The question then arises: How does one know what's being experienced by the mind? By observation and introspection, one can witness that thoughts have no capacity to experience themselves, but that something both beyond and more basic than thought experiences the sequence of thoughts, and that that something's sense of identity is unaltered by the content of thoughts.

What is it that observes and is aware of all of the

subjective and objective phenomena of life? It's *consciousness itself* that resonates as both awareness and experiencing, and both are purely subjective. Consciousness itself isn't determined by content; thoughts flowing through consciousness are like fish swimming in the ocean. The ocean's existence is independent of the fish; the content of the sea doesn't define the nature of the water itself. Like a colorless ray, consciousness illuminates the object witnessed—which explains its traditional association throughout world literature with "light."[3]

Identification solely with the content of consciousness accounts for the experience of self as limited. In contrast, to identify with consciousness itself is to know that one's actual self is unlimited. When such circumscribed self-identifications have been surmounted so that the sense of self is identified as consciousness itself, we become "enlightened."[4]

One characteristic of the experience of pure consciousness is a perception of timelessness (or timelessness of perception). Consciousness is experienced as beyond all form and time and seen as equally present everywhere. It's described as "Is-ness" or "Being-ness" and, in the spiritual literature, "I-am-ness."[5] Consciousness doesn't recognize separation, which is a limitation of perception. The enlightened state is a "Oneness" where there is no division into parts. Such division is only apparent from a localized perception; it's only an accident of a point of view.

Similar descriptions throughout the history of thought are in accord with the studies of William James. In the famous Gifford lectures, James described the experience of consciousness itself as rare, unique, indescribable, and "beyond mind"—a thought-free state of Knowingness that's complete, all-inclusive, with neither need nor want, and beyond the limitation of experiencing the merely individualized, personal self.[6]

Another attribute of pure consciousness is the cessation of the ordinary flow of thoughts or feelings—a condition of infinite power, compassion, gentleness, and love. In this state, self becomes Self. There's an accompanying recognition of the very origin of the capacity to experience self as Self, which is the culmination of the process of eliminating limited identifications of self.[7]

The steps necessary to be taken to facilitate awareness of Self as consciousness have been well detailed historically. Numerous techniques and behaviors have been prescribed to facilitate the removal of obstacles to expanded awareness; these can be found in the practice of various spiritual disciplines. The one process common to all such teachings is the progressive elimination of the identification of self as finite.[8]

Enlightenment is said to be relatively rare, not so much because of the difficulty of following the necessary steps to get there, but because it's a condition of interest to very few, particularly in modern society. If we were to stop 1,000 people in the street and ask them, "What is your greatest ambition in life?" how many would say, "To be enlightened"?

Contemporary Recognition of Higher Consciousness

The growing level of interest in consciousness as a scientific subject was evidenced by the first international conference regarding it. Entitled *Toward a Scientific Basis of Consciousness,* the conference was held at the University of Arizona Health Sciences Center in Tucson, Arizona, on April 12–17, 1994. This was an international, interdisciplinary convocation of impressively credentialed scholars—however, among the numerous eminent presenters and the wide range of highly specialized subjects dealt with, there was little inquiry beyond rational/materialistic explanations of consciousness as a purely physical phenomenon.

In fact, approaches to the subject of consciousness are as varied as human experience itself. This book has cited many of the cutting-edge insights of modern inquiry into this issue in passing. In order to more clearly proceed to our own conclusions, it may be helpful to review the evolution of contemporary thought on this matter.

The presence of some variety of consciousness is ordinarily considered to be the distinguishing characteristic of what's living as opposed to what's not. Life is the expression of consciousness in the observable or experiential world of form. But the totality of human experience attests that consciousness is both manifest and unmanifest. The awareness of consciousness within form is common; the awareness of pure consciousness, beyond form, is exceptional.

The "experience" of pure consciousness itself, devoid of all content, has been consistently reported throughout human history—and the reports have always been the same.[9] Many who attain that state go on to become the Great Teachers of history, and have profoundly influenced human behavior. Such beings, in the course of their few short years, have been capable of creating a realization by millions of people, over millennial periods, of the contextual significance of existence. Because these teachings haven't concerned the material world as experienced through the senses, they've been labeled *spiritual*.[10]

Before the recent interest of scientists in the subject, the study of consciousness was exclusively the concern of spiritual teachers and their students. But in the last 20 years, the considerable interest of numerous theoretical physicists has turned, as we've seen, to the correlation between advanced theoretical physics and the nonmaterial universe. The deepening of popular cultural focus since the 1960s created a receptive audience for spinoffs of this exploration, in such books as Fritjof Capra's *The Tao of Physics*, and Robert Ornstein's *The Psychology of Consciousness*, which are now considered to be classics. The occurrence of higher states of consciousness, traditionally thought to be extremely rare, grows more common as the M-field of the new paradigm spreads: Recent surveys indicate 65 percent of respondents report having had experiences previously categorized as *spiritual*.

Because science is by its very nature concerned only with observable phenomena, it has never been attracted to spiritual concepts as a subject for consideration, despite the fact that many great scientists throughout history have personally testified to subjective experiences of pure consciousness occurring in the course of, and frequently crucial to, their work.[11] But the exploding field of nonlinear dynamics has provoked curiosity and commentary regarding the nature of existence and consciousness itself, expressed in such books as Ian Stewart's *Does God Play Dice?: The Mathematics of Chaos*. The new concept of a "science of wholeness" became the subject of popular works such as *Looking Glass Universe,* by John Briggs; and

Turbulent Mirror, by Briggs and F. David Peat. Recently, astronomers, mathematicians, brain surgeons, and neurologists (as well as physicists) have been caught up in a tide of enthusiasm about the significance of the new discoveries. It's frequently been pointed out that man is unable to observe or recognize an event until there's a prior context and language for naming the event. This inability, called *paradigm blindness,* is the direct consequence of a limitation of context.[12] So it was that the extension of the new intellectual substructure that's pervading the physical sciences only slowly created the potential for new views and approaches in the "human" sciences, such as psychology.

Although Abraham Maslow long ago discussed "peak experiences," the mainstream literature of psychology never addressed the subject of consciousness itself—with the exception of such classics as *The Varieties of Religious Experience* by William James, which has long been considered the standard scientific work on the psychology of consciousness as spiritual experience. Eventually, transpersonal psychology went beyond the bounds of experience and clinical psychology to investigate those aspects of human experience that were purely subjective. Unusual experiences, or abilities once discounted as hoax or hallucination, finally became the subject of parapsychology, legitimizing experimental attempts to verify experiences such as extrasensory perception (ESP).

The field of psychiatry originally arose from the attempt to address the tangible origin of the intangibles in human behavior and disease. Psychiatry, as a branch of medicine, concerned itself with pathology; therefore, it dealt almost exclusively with the lower levels of consciousness and their neurophysiologic correlates; consciousness as such remained outside the paradigms of psychiatry.

In medicine, physicians who worked from a larger paradigm of the healing process and included nontraditional modalities in their therapeutic approaches became known as *holistic* practitioners, a designation that at first carried distinct overtones of unprofessionalism among the ranks of the medical establishment. But the contributions of pioneering individuals in this field—especially in such areas as recovery from heart attacks, or the use of prayer to speed up recuperation in surgical patients—demanded serious recognition.

Elizabeth Kübler-Ross brought the attention of the professions, as well as the public, to the phenomena of dying and near-death experiences as reported by patients. Out-of-body experience also eventually became a relatively common subject, as more and more surgical patients reported that they witnessed their entire operations and heard everything that was said in the operating room.[13] Thelma Moss became well known for her work with Kirlian photography—which records the radiation emitted by, or the aura surrounding, an object in a high-frequency electric field, such as around fingertips. Her photographs of the energy body of a full leaf remaining after it had been cut in two are quite renowned.[14] Finally, even acupuncture has gained a place of some respect in the American health field, with many physicians learning the technique—despite the fact that traditional medicine hasn't recognized any energies other than mechanical, electrical, or chemical.

Holistic approaches operate from a different context of the nature of human consciousness than traditional medicine does, and the emphasis is on *healing* rather than on *treating*. Though their connection with the theoretical breakthroughs of recent decades may not appear explicit, the alternate therapies employed by holistic-health caregivers—whether they're physicians, alternative practitioners, or lay healers, and however widely they differ in their approach and method—all have one common element. All holistic approaches are based on techniques to influence not protoplasm as such, but an *energy field* that surrounds, courses through, and conditions the human body.[15]

Outside of the medical domain, the phenomenal success of the 12-step self-help movement, to which I've frequently alluded, has impressively established that healing can be brought about through the practice of *principles of consciousness*. The capacity to heal desperate conditions, which was recognized by Jung in his work with Rowland H.—the first link, as we've seen, in the long chain of healings that eventually became the worldwide AA movement—lay distinctly within the realm of higher consciousness. The profound spiritual experience held out as hope by Jung to Rowland, very much akin to the transformations of enlightenment, was the essence of the message passed on to Bill W., the founder of AA.[16] It is notable that Bill W. characterized AA as "the language of the heart."[17]

All these trails blazed in the pioneering of theoretical and applied human wisdom have a common point of convergence—or perhaps it might be better said that they share a common point of origin. Bill W.'s revelation from the depths of despair didn't proceed from conceptual rationality or any other introspective focus of self, but from a leap to higher consciousness, a transport of Self to a Presence of Infinite Light and Power.[18] That this transformational experience has led to the recovery of millions is merely testimony to the power of energy fields that calibrates at 600 or more—that's the level where there's a crossover of the experience of consciousness from form to formless.

This formless power, the "higher power" of the worldwide 12-step self-help movement and the basis for its millions of recoveries,[19] is the same wellspring of power that all of these far-flung branches of intellectual exploration have been not so much thrusting forward toward as working their way back to. It's the power of pure consciousness itself.

CHAPTER TWENTY-TWO

Spiritual Struggle

We can reinterpret the struggle of man's spiritual enterprise from the understanding of consciousness at which we've arrived. Pure consciousness itself—which is described as "Is-ness," "Being-ness," or "I-amness"—represents the infinite potential, power, and energy source of *all* of existence, identified as "Deity," "God," or "Divinity." Within this potential, the Unmanifest becomes Manifest, like the avatar (such as Christ or Buddha) whose energy field calibrates at 1,000 (maximum). These individuals set up attractor patterns of such enormous force that the mind, with its holographic capacity to react globally to attractor fields, is subject to them.

Of lesser significance, but still enormously powerful, are the "ordinary" enlightened teachers who have taught the path to the realization of the "Self." The Self has been described by the

enlightened throughout time as infinite, formless, change-
less, all-present, unmanifest-and-manifest.[1] Here is the
Oneness, the All-ness, and God-ness of all that exists, indistinguishable from the Creator, whose power in the
human realm is a giant attractor field that allows and encompasses variation (free will) so that "all paths lead to
Me." In our studies, teachings and other works that deal
with this subject typically calibrated at 700.

At the energy field of 600, ordinary thought ceases. Beyond temporal linear process, existence is witnessed as
Knowing-ness, omnipresence, and nonduality. Because
existence has no locality, the "me/you" duality and consequent illusion of separation disappears.[2] This state is
peace beyond all understanding—or infinite, unconditional love. It's all-encompassing, all-knowing, all-present,
omnipowerful, and coincident with the Self, which is the
awareness that the Manifest is one with the Unmanifest.

Truly spiritual states can be said to appear at a calibrated level of about 500 (Love) and continue on to infinity. Teachers who calibrate in the high 500s and the
600s are frequently recognized as saints; their state of
consciousness is often described as "sublime."[3]

It is a common experience for as-yet-unenlightened
devotees to enter such a sublime state when in the presence
of teachers whose energy fields calibrate at 550 and over—
this happens through the process of "entrainment," which
is the dominance of a powerful attractor field. Until the
devotee arrives at the higher state of awareness, this state
won't persist outside of the higher energy field of the
teacher.[4] Advanced spiritual seekers often fluctuate in and
out of this "presence of the Beloved" as they approach enlightenment; this loss of the higher state and descent to a

lower one is identified in both Eastern and Western literature as an "anguish of the soul."[5]

Spiritual work, like other intensive pursuits—such as sports—can be arduous and frequently requires the development of specific tools for the task, including an extremely focused intent and unfailing concentration. The difficulty of inner work results from the great effort required to escape from the familiar gravity of lower attractor fields and move to the influence of a higher field. In order to relieve this struggle, all religions issue restrictions against exposing oneself to the lower energy fields; it's only from an authoritarian viewpoint that such error is depicted as "sin." A more liberal viewpoint accepts man's dalliance in lower energy fields as a pardonable "failing."

But attitudes, emotions, and behaviors characteristic of the energy fields below 200 do, in fact, generally preclude spiritual experience. The classical *chakra* system recognized by many spiritual disciplines correlates almost exactly with the Map of Consciousness that has emerged from our studies. The level of 600 corresponds to the crown chakra, 500 to the heart, 200 and up to the solar plexus—while the lower attitudes and emotions of spite, envy, resentment, and jealousy are associated with the spleen. The base chakra has to do with animal survival and the absorption with what prohibits spiritual progress; thus, all spiritual teachings advise against "worldliness," suggesting avoidance of attachment to sex or money.[6]

The lower regions are also the center of addictions; one can be fixated at any of the lower levels. Almost all of these energy fields, and the behaviors associated with them, now have given rise to specific self-help groups, all of which concur that without a spiritual context, recovery is quite unlikely. In consciousness-raising programs in general, a universal dictum is that one is powerless *until one tells the truth*. All spiritually oriented self-help groups require this first step: They're unanimous in believing that an open mind and willingness to improve are necessary prerequisites to progress; in other words, one must have reached an energy field of 200 in one's development to be healable. Lingering within the influence of fields below this entails a real danger of becoming so deeply entrained that one can't escape. This isn't always so, however—history has noted many occasions of individuals in the very depths of entrainment suddenly breaking through to a high level of consciousness.

Such sudden breakthroughs are still seen on occasion in modern society; this, as we've seen, was the precise experience of Bill W., which resulted in the founding of AA. This experience seems typically to be characterized by a total transformation of consciousness and liberation from the entrainment of lower attractor fields and a sudden emergence into higher awareness. (This type of experience—common in the early days of AA, when its members were frequently "last-gaspers"—isn't reported by "high bottom" members, who constitute the majority of newcomers to AA today.)

Just as the entrainment or influence of the higher energy fields has an anabolic, or growth-enhancing, effect on a subject, entrainment by lower attractor fields has a catabolic, or destructive, effect; the most widespread example in today's culture is the influence of some forms of violent pop music. Among our test subjects, punk rock, death rock, and gangster rap music made every subject go weak, confirming earlier observations made by Dr. John Diamond.[7]

In a more recent study of students (reported in *The Arizona Republic,* July 4, 1994), Dr. James Johnson of the University of North Carolina found rap music to increase tolerance for and predisposition to violence while promoting materialism and reducing immediate interest in academics and long-term success.

A common experience observed in therapy groups and clinics is that drug abusers don't recover if they continue to listen to heavy metal rock music—in fact, a one-year follow-up of inpatient and outpatient cocaine addicts from Sedona Villa, a branch of Camelback Hospital of Phoenix, Arizona, indicated that not a single cocaine abuser who continued to listen to this violent and negative music recovered.[8] Self-help groups for the addicted invariably recommend avoiding the influence (that is, the energy fields) of former lifestyle associations. These addicts found that leaving the drug wasn't enough; to do so was merely to attack the A➤B➤C of addiction. As long as they couldn't make the commitment of will to entirely leave the influence of the field—of which the music, like the drug, was simply a manifestation—they couldn't escape entrainment to the low-energy attractor, the ABC of addiction.

Recovered addicts who leave the energy field of their self-help programs rather predictably relapse.[9] Besides having relinquished the infusion of the combined power of their fellow members, their assertion that one can "go it alone" is a notorious symptom of an oncoming relapse, because it indicates an infiltration of arrogance and pride, calibrating at 175, which is well below the power of the energy field required for healing.

The same principle, of course, operates in the other direction. To seek enlightenment is to seek entrainment to the most powerful attractor patterns. The key, again, is *will,* a constantly repeated act of choice. Here, the chaos-theory principle of sensitive dependence on initial way of spiritual progress. In all spiritual disciplines, the opening wedge predicated for advancing one's awareness is described as "willingness." History shows what has been clinically shown as well: A persistent willingness is the trigger that activates a new attractor field and allows one to begin to leave the old. We may visualize a lesser attractor field approaching a greater one, at which point the introduction of a third element (free will, the decisive consequence of choice and evolution) suddenly creates a crossover (a "saddle-pattern"), and change takes place.

In Eastern spiritual disciplines, it's accepted that the devotee alone, unaided by a guru, is unlikely to make much progress.[10] The AA experience is that a true alcoholic is unable to recover without the help of a sponsor. In sports, great coaches are sought after because their influence inspires maximum effort. A devotee can abet his own progress by merely focusing on an advanced teacher and thereby aligning with that teacher's energy field; in our testing, it was repeatedly shown that holding the image of an advanced spiritual teacher in mind made every subject go strong, regardless of his personal beliefs.

✟ ✟ ✟

The agency of change in spiritual struggles of personal metamorphosis is always beyond the power of the seeker. Great saints, such as Francis of Assisi, have typically asserted that they were mere channels of a higher power—they've taken no credit for personal initiative in achieving their state, which they attributed to Grace.[11] This is illustrative of the instrumentation where the newcomer from a lesser level of awareness, who places himself in the influence of a higher awareness, is transformed "by osmosis" (entrainment). Even casual observers frequently note this conspicuous absence of agency on the part of the person so clearly transmuted by an invisible force.

Therefore, when someone suddenly goes from the influence of a lower attractor field to that of a higher one, it's often acclaimed as a miracle. The unfortunate verdict of human experience is that few escape the energy fields that gradually come to dominate their behaviors. A currently popular spiritual program designed to facilitate such escape is *A Course in Miracles*.[12] The purpose of this course of spiritual psychology is to prepare the necessary groundwork to precipitate a sudden jump in consciousness through encouraging a total change of perception. In a more traditional fashion, prayer and meditation also provide points of departure to rise from the influence of a lower energy field into a higher one.

Physicians who have risen to energy fields at 500 and above have become powerful healers, accomplishing striking successes with treatments that others are unable to achieve similar results from (and thereby producing paradoxical data in many double-blind studies). Such inexplicable variances show the intervention of power unaccountable by the routine, causal explanation that predominates in medicine. In a holographic world, any "single" event is the result of all events in the universe;

"events" as such have no self-existent reality. The universe *is* man's consciousness—it requires a comprehension beyond intellect. The achievements of pure reason are the great landmarks of cultural history. They've made man the master of his external environment; and to some degree, on the physical plane, of his internal environment. But reason has its limits, in more ways than one: The intellectual brilliance of the 400 level, so dazzling and enviable to those in the 300s, quickly pales for those who have transcended it. From a higher perspective, it's all too clear how tedious and trivial reason's infatuation with itself can become. Reason is the mirror of the mind's vanity; ultimately, there are few things more boring to observe than self-admiration.

Rationality, the great liberator that's freed us from the demands of our lower natures, is also a stern warden, denying our escape to the planes above and beyond intellect. For those entrained at the level of the 400s, reason itself becomes a cap, a ceiling in spiritual evolution. It's striking how many of history's great names calibrate at 499—Descartes, Newton, Einstein, and dozens more—it's a sticking point, an enormous barrier; the fight to overcome it is the most common, and frequently the lengthiest, of spiritual struggles.

It isn't unheard of for very advanced scientists, who are thoroughly entrained by the influences of the level of Reason, to have sudden breakthroughs and emerge into a realm of global wholeness.[13] The world of spirituality is coincident with the world of nondeterministic science and nonlinear systems, as we've attempted to show. Our research and this presentation, in fact, are designed to facilitate rational recognition of spiritual phenomena by

· those who are predominantly linear and accustomed to the "left-brain" mode. Perhaps the construct of our map of the anatomy of consciousness can illuminate somewhat the nature of ultimate causality by illustrating that *the power of creation proceeds from the top down, rather than from the bottom up.*

It's our hope, though, not to dogmatize, but to assist the reader in a process of self-revelation, as our desire is to address not merely that figment designated as the reader's rational self, but his entire consciousness. In our study, it's the total person that reacts to the test stimuli. Although the subject's mind may not be aware of what's going on, his total being certainly is, or there would be no consistency to our findings. This reminds us of the observation of advanced spiritual teachers—that the devotee has only to discover . . . that which he already knows.

CHAPTER TWENTY-THREE

The Search for Truth

Although it may sound cynical at first, we must admit that for everyday operational purposes, truth is whatever is subjectively convincing at one's current level of perception. At the lower levels of consciousness, propositions are accepted as true even when they're illogical, unfounded, and express tenets neither intellectually provable nor practically demonstrable. This isn't a phenomenon restricted to the lunatic fringe: Locally, far more often than we'd like to admit, innocent people are convicted and jailed on the testimony of clearly irrational and biased witnesses; and globally, the basis for perennial wars (such as those in Slavic Europe or the Middle East) is an insane belief in the justice of revenge, which virtually guarantees endless conflict.

With few exceptions, even religions that ostensibly represent the teachings of Jesus Christ—

the "Prince of Peace"—have never forbidden war or the killing of other human beings under "justifiable" circumstances—justifiable, of course, to those doing the killing; their victims probably wouldn't appreciate the justification. Such self-contradictory behavior, which is diametrically opposed to the underlying principles of a faith, will appear less surprising if we apply critical factor analysis to calibrate the evolution, or devolution, of spiritual teachings over time.

Let's take a look at the worlds' foremost religious teachings in this new light.

Christianity

The level of truth originally expounded by Jesus Christ calibrates at 1,000—the highest level attainable on this plane. By the second century, the level of truth of the practice of his teachings had dropped to 930, and by the sixth century, to 540. By the time of the Crusades, at the beginning of the 11th century, it had fallen to its current 498. A major decline in the year A.D. 325 was apparently due to the spread of misinterpretations of the teachings originating from the Council of Nicaea. Students of religious history will find it interesting to calibrate Christianity's level of truth before and after Paul, Constantine, Augustine, and so on.[1]

It should be noted that the Lamsa translation (from the Aramaic) of the New Testament calibrates at 750, and the King James Version (which was translated from the Greek) at 640. Just as there is a wide range in the level of truth of various translations, so there is a wide variation between different Christian practices. Most major persuasions—

Roman Catholicism, Anglicanism, Christian Science (and many small denominations, such as the Quakers)—calibrate in the high 500s. Specialized interpretations, such as that of the contemporary *Course in Miracles,* or the 14th-century mysticism of Meister Eckhart, calibrate at 600. As in the case of Islam (see next page) however, extreme fundamentalist groups with explicit reactionary political agendas can calibrate as low as 125.

Buddhism

The level of truth of the teaching of the Buddha was also originally at 1,000; by the sixth century A.D., the level of truth in practice had dropped to an average of 900. These teachings have deteriorated less than any other religion: Hinyana Buddhism (the lesser vehicle) still calibrates at 890; Mahayana Buddhism (the greater vehicle) calibrates at 960; Zen Buddhism is 890.

Hinduism

The teachings of Lord Krishna calibrated at 1,000 and have weakened over time, but the truth of the current practice still calibrates at 850.

Judaism

The teachings of Abraham calibrated at 985; the practice that was current at the time of Moses calibrated at

770—the level of truth of the Torah. Modern Judaism calibrates at 499. The Kabbalah is 720; the Zohar is 730.

Islam

The level of consciousness of Mohammed was 740, and the Koran calibrates at 720. The kernel of Islamic faith is an expression of loving acceptance and inner peace, but the evolution of practical dogma was intertwined from the start with the politics of territorial expansion in the form of *jihad*, or religious warfare. The truth of Islamic teachings had dropped severely by the end of the Crusades. In modern times, the ascendence of fanatic nationalistic religious movements, characterized by paranoia and xenophobia, has rapidly eroded the spiritual essence of this faith. At the present time, the level of truth of the teachings of militant Islamic fundamentalism is 130.

✛ ✛ ✛

When we look at the decline of the level of truth of the world's great religions, we notice that those that are the most "yin" have remained relatively pure throughout the ages, whereas those that are more "yang" (involved in worldly affairs) have degraded markedly, until the militant extremist faction of the most aggressive religion has actually sunk below the critical level of integrity at 200. The more dualistic the creed, the greater its vulnerability to misinterpretation seems to be. Dualism promotes a split between belief and action and the disorientation of levels of truth. When this occurs, the spiritual essence can be confused in translation into physical expression. Thus, the conceptual Christian Soldier (of the spirit) becomes, through a distorted "literal" translation, a self-justified battlefield killer.

The Hindus did not fall into the error of confusing levels of interpretation; the battle described in the opening of the Bhagavad Gita was never misinterpreted to suggest that Lord Krishna taught that believers are to engage in actual warfare. The Buddha's view—that the cause of all pain and suffering is ignorance, which is the only "sin" possible, and that one's duty is to be compassionate toward others and pray for them—is also hardly susceptible to such distortion.

The downfall of all lofty spiritual teachings has been their misinterpretation by the less enlightened; each level of consciousness predefines its own limited capacity for perception and comprehension. Until one has become enlightened oneself, or at least experienced the higher states of consciousness, all spiritual teachings remain hearsay and are thus prone to distortion and misunderstanding—scripture can be quoted to justify any position. The "righteous" are always dangerous because of their imbalanced perception and their consequent indifference to moral violence. Within any religion, fundamentalist sects always calibrate lowest, often operating at the same level of consciousness as criminality; their hallmark is egocentric extremism and irrationality. But with 85 percent of the human population calibrating below the critical level of 200, error is easily disseminated and readily accepted around the world.

Cults proliferate because the general public has no objective criterion with which to distinguish truth from falsehood. Using the tools of this study, we may identify any purportedly spiritual movement that calibrates below the level of 200 a "cult." As we've seen above, cults aren't just isolated, renegade phenomena—they also thrive as tolerated subgroups within the world's great religions, distorting teachings and subverting their intent.

Cults needn't be formally religious at all. The ultimate cult, of course, is the antireligion, based on antidivinity known as "Satanism." It has no explicit religious agenda of its own, as it defines itself through the antithesis and reversal of benign principles—and in one form or another, it's always been with us. As up implies down—and light, darkness—man's socially organized search for truth, and his commitment to attaining higher spiritual levels, has always implied the socially organized spread of falsehood and submission to the lowest energy fields. Examination of the nature of antireligion demonstrates, in fact, the enormously destructive power of negative energy fields. Examples are unfortunately ready at hand.

The trappings of Satanism grew as fashions of a popular youth subculture, its primary vehicle being an overt musical genre. But principles are implicit in trappings, and principles generate attractor fields. The effects are all too familiar to any clinical psychiatrist who practices near an urban area—the destruction of energy fields spreads like disease. Victims become desensitized to distinctions between good and evil, a value inversion that can be clinically examined. Habitués are found to directly display "blown-out" acupuncture systems and desynchronization of the cerebral hemispheres in response to repetitive negative patterns of the associated music—the net result is, in effect, a hypnotic trance during which the listener is highly susceptible to the violent and profane suggestions of the lyrics. In this sense, these children become literally enslaved and prone to later bouts of irrational destruction where they truthfully "don't know why" they act out these posthypnotic suggestions. And the influence persists.

Continued weakening of the body and its immune system—long after the music stops—is accompanied by an inversion of kinesiological response. Negative stimuli that would make a normal person go weak cause a strong response, while those that would make a normal person strong now produce a weak one. Unaware that they're the victims of a potent negative energy field, the members of this culture sink into sometimes inescapable subservience to forces beyond their comprehension. Youth subjected to such physical, emotional, and sexual abuse can suffer permanent damage to the brain's neurotransmitter balance, becoming adult depressives who habitually seek out abusive partners and must endlessly struggle against an inclination to suicide that is, in fact, a lingering form of posthypnotic suggestion.[2]

We may wish to deny that such a spiritual plague, reminiscent of the Dark Ages, could remain so injurious in our enlightened society; but such perverse influences don't operate in a moral vacuum or arise from a social matrix that doesn't already incorporate preconditions for their growth. The paradox of our puritanical society is that it encourages constant seduction but denies satisfaction, so a perpetual frustration of normal outlets eventually finds release in perverse ones. If we look more closely, we may find that other elements of what we call "civilization" in fact foster the persistence of such "perversions."

✝ ✝ ✝

While the young are being programmed by specialized TV and computer games that glorify violence, their parents are being brainwashed by adult media. Kinesiological testing showed that a fairly typical TV show caused test subjects to go weak *113 times* during a single episode. Each of these weakening events suppressed the observer's immune system and reflected an insult to the viewer's central as well as autonomic nervous system. Invariably accompanying each of these 113 disruptions of the acupuncture system were suppressions of the thymus gland; each insult also resulted in damage to the brain's delicate neurohormonal and neurotransmitter systems. Each negative input brought the watcher closer to eventual sickness and to imminent depression—which is now the world's most prevalent illness.

Subtle grades of depression kill more people than all the other diseases of mankind combined. There is no antidepressant that will cure a depression that's spiritually based, for the malaise doesn't originate from brain dysfunction, but from an accurate response to the desecration of life. The body is the reflection of the spirit in its physical expression, and its problems are the dramatization of the struggles of the spirit that gives it life. A belief that we ascribe to "out there" has its effect "in here." Everyone dies by his own hand—that's a hard clinical fact, not a moral view.

✝ ✝ ✝

The attempt to impose standards of would-be absolute Good and Evil is, in fact, one of the greatest moral pitfalls. But without moralizing, we can plainly state that whatever calibrates above 200 supports life and may therefore be functionally defined as "good"; whereas whatever calibrates below 200 is destructive, nonsupportive of life and can thus be declared functionally "evil." Through testing, we can prove that a false premise such as "the end justifies the means" is operationally evil, yet this is a routinely accepted justification for much of human behavior, from the peccadilloes of commerce to the enormities of war. Such spiritual ambiguity, leading ultimately to irretrievable confusion between functional good and evil, has always been the Achilles' heel of human society.

The process of perverting truth through a failure of discernment is responsible for providing the vehicle for the decline in the world's great religions (noted previously in this chapter). Religions that fall below the level of 500 may preach love, but they won't be able to practice it. And no religious system that encourages war can claim spiritual authority without the blatant hypocrisy that's made atheists of many honest men.

Society is collectively most vulnerable when the capacity to distinguish between attractors and imitators, or to perceive nuances of differing levels on consciousness, is dulled. This is how civil abuses become law and political extremists persuade with righteous slogans. The children of violence become its perpetrators because a confused society that's lost the capacity for discernment necessary to protect its own consciousness can hardly hope to protect its young.

An individual's level of consciousness is determined by the principles to which one is committed. To maintain progress in consciousness, there can be no wavering from principle, or the individual will fall back to a lower level. Expediency is never an adequate justification. If it's wrong to kill another human being, that principle can allow *no* exceptions, regardless of how emotionally appealing a construct may be used to justify the exception. Thus, a society that condones capital punishment will always have a problem with murder—*both are products of the same level of perception.* After all, to the murderer, the killing of the victim is a justifiable exception.

Once a principle is breached, its mutated form propagates like cancer. A society that supports killing—whether in war, by the police, or by the penal system—can't at the same time effectively stop "criminal" killing. To kill is to kill is to kill; there's no escaping that fact. The decision to kill or not is a basic issue on the path to real power; but this rudimentary step hasn't even been addressed by 85 percent of the world's population or by virtually any of its governments. Koko—the famous simian resident of the Primate Research Institute, who has worked for some years with a psychologist and developed a sophisticated sign language vocabulary—is truthful, affectionate, intelligent, and trustworthy; her integrity calibrates at 250. Thus, one is safer with Koko, a gorilla, than with 85 percent of the humans on the planet.

Injury to man's "spiritual eye" has resulted in dimness of moral vision and blindness to truth—which afflict 85 percent of the earth's population who linger below the level of integrity. The great issue that confronts mankind as a whole is the healing of this spiritual blindness. The more immediate "problem" of Right and Wrong that always diverts our societal focus only exists as a function of perception based at the lower levels of consciousness. Little children must be taught that dangerous behaviors are "wrong," but as they grow older, discernment should replace moralism. Whether or not it's wrong to kill other human beings may be a moral dilemma at lower levels of consciousness; at higher levels the very question is ridiculous. Conventional morality is, therefore, only a provisional substitute for a faculty of higher consciousness. Moralism, a by-product of duality, becomes insignificant as the consciousness level rises through the 500s, and is irrelevant at the level of 600.

Merely to reach a stage where one functions primarily from reason requires a major evolution in consciousness to the 400s, which is a very powerful level in world society—Freud, Einstein, and Descartes calibrate at 499, the level of humanism.[3] But reason, so vulnerable to loss of perspective through self-absorption, has in the long run never provided man with any solid moral, or even intellectual, certainty. Again and again it has, to the contrary, led from the chaos of ignorance to an equally baffling cerebral maze. In a world of mass confusion, we desperately need a reliable, accurate, objectively verifiable yardstick to measure truth with. Hopefully, this book has presented such a tool. Any increased infusion of the influence of truth into the collective human consciousness gives us cause for greater hope than what tends inevitably to be a rather gloomy overview.

We've established that consciousness is capable of discerning any change of energy to a degree of $\log 10^\infty$. This means that there is no possible event in the entire universe that isn't detectable by the exquisite sensitivity of consciousness itself. The energy of human thought, though minute, is nonetheless absolutely measurable. A thought that emanates from the 100 level of consciousness will typically measure between log $10^{-800 \text{ million}}$ to $10^{-700 \text{ million}}$ microwatts. On the other hand, a loving thought at the consciousness level of 500 measures approximately log $10^{-35 \text{ million}}$ microwatts.

Although only 15 percent of the world's population is above the critical consciousness level of 200, the collective power of that 15 percent has the weight to counterbalance the negativity of the remaining 85 percent of the world's people. Because the scale of power advances logarithmically, a single avatar at a consciousness level of 1,000 can, in fact, totally counterbalance the collective negativity of all of mankind. Kinesiological testing has shown that:

One individual at level 700	*counterbalances*	70 million individuals below level 200
One individual at level 600	*counterbalances*	10 million individuals below level 200
One individual at level 500	*counterbalances*	750,000 individuals below level 200
One individual at level 400	*counterbalances*	400,000 individuals below level 200
One individual at level 300	*counterbalances*	90,000 individuals below level 200
Twelve individuals at level 700	*equal*	one avatar at 1,000

(There are currently 12 persons on the planet who calibrate at 700.)

Were it not for these counterbalances, mankind would self-destruct out of the sheer mass of its unopposed negativity. The difference in power between a loving thought ($10^{-35 \text{ million}}$ megawatts) and a fearful thought ($10^{-750 \text{ million}}$ microwatts) is so enormous as to be beyond the capacity of the human imagination to easily comprehend. We can see from the analysis above, however, that even a few loving thoughts during the course of the day more than counterbalance all of our negative thoughts.

As we've said, from a social-behavioral viewpoint, truth is the set of principles that people live by, regardless of what they might say they believe. We've seen that there are different truths—subjective, operational, hypothetical, and intellectual—and then there is factual data. The legitimacy of any of these is dependent upon the context of a given perceptual level. Truth isn't functional unless it's meaningful, and meaning, like value, relies on a unique perceptual field. Facts and data may be convincing at one level and irrelevant at another. Functional validity of information received also varies with the intellectual level and capacity for abstraction of the recipient. To be operational, truth must not simply be "true" but knowable; yet each level of truth is unknowable to the levels below it and has no validity beyond its own territory. Thus, we can conclude that all levels of truth as we know it—within the dimension of ordinary human function—are examples of *dependent truth*, whose veracity is totally contingent on a given set of parameters. Even our revered "scientific truth" is also defined by conditions, and therefore subject to dispute and error. Statistical inference has become a propaganda tool, and the statistical distortions by which anything can be proven about anything have alienated our credence.

Is there any impersonal truth, independent of individual condition or context?

Truth, as detected by the research methods illustrated through this book, derives its validity from ultimate sources far beyond the influence of any localized perceptual field. It respects neither personality nor opinion and doesn't vary with any condition of test subject or environment.

Ignorance does not yield to attack, but it dissipates in the light, and nothing dissolves dishonesty faster than the simple act of revealing the truth. The only way to enhance one's power in the world is by increasing one's integrity, understanding, and capacity for compassion. If the diverse populations of mankind can be brought to this realization, the survival of human society and the happiness of its members is secure.

The initial effect of taking responsibility for the truth of one's life is to raise lower energy levels to 200, which is the critical level that power first appears and the stepping-stone to all of the higher levels. The Courage to face truth leads eventually to Acceptance, where greater power arises at the level of 350. Here, there's sufficient energy to solve the majority of man's social problems. This, in turn, leads to the yet greater power available at 500, the level of Love. Knowing our own—and everyone else's— human foibles gives rise to forgiveness, and then to compassion. Compassion is the doorway to grace, to the final realization of who we are and why we're here, and to the ultimate source of all existence.

◎ ◎ ◎

CHAPTER TWENTY-FOUR

Resolution

A thorough absorption of the material presented in this book has been shown to be able to raise one's level of consciousness by an average of 35 points. Since the progression of consciousness during the average human lifetime on this earth is only five points, such an increase in individual awareness is an enormous benefit in and of itself. And, as advanced theoretical physics and nonlinear dynamics have shown, any individual increase also raises the consciousness of *everyone* on the planet to some degree.

To become more conscious is the greatest gift anyone can give to the world; moreover, in a ripple effect, the gift comes back to its source. While the level of consciousness of mankind as a whole stood at a perilous 190 for many centuries, in the mid-1980s, it suddenly jumped to the hopeful level of 207. For the first time in its history, man is now on safe ground from which to continue his upward march . . . and this promise of new hope comes none too soon.

Today, many of the topics we've discussed are exploding in the news media: (1) the perversion of religion to the ends of political savagery; (2) the deepening depravity of crimes; (3) the involvement of children in violence; (4) moral confusion in politics; and (5) the bizarre violence of cults. All of these subjects appear against a backdrop colored by the prevalence of lies as social tender and a lack of consensus as to individual and collective responsibility toward one's fellow man.

This social confusion and paralysis stems from the dearth of guidelines to base decisions upon. Hopefully, this book has taken a step toward filling that void with what is, in fact, an essay on the science of Morality. By "Morality," we don't refer to petty moralistic judgments of right and wrong, but to an at once objective *and* personal basis from which to make decisions and evaluations regarding the highest conduct of our lives.

In a social framework, we can certainly choose to refuse passive submission to any political system that falls below the level of 200; we should instead apply our newly developed faculties of examination and correction to it. It's now possible, for instance, to establish clear criteria for selecting holders of public office. Each office requires a specific minimum level of awareness in order to be effective; in general, any government official who falls below 200 won't solve problems but will create them.

The larger social issue is how, in view of the dark side of mankind's behavior, one can maintain compassion. It's a relative world; everyone acts from his own level of truth and therefore believes that his actions and decisions are "right"—it's this very "rightness" that makes fanatics so dangerous. But the real danger to society doesn't come from overt bigotry—such as white supremacism (which calibrates at 150)—as such damage can at least be monitored. The really grave danger to society lies in the silent and invisible entrainment that stealthily conquers the psyche. In this process, negative attractor fields are covered up by rhetoric and the manipulation of symbols. Moreover, it isn't the obvious message of the negative input that destroys consciousness, but the energy field that accompanies it.

The extreme negativity of many popular works of pseudophilosophy, for example, is obvious if one tests these books. But even being forewarned can't defend us against unwitting entrainment by invisible energy fields that activate when these works are read. One may think that he can maintain his psychic independence by refuting the work intellectually, but mere exposure to the material has a profound negative effect that continues even after the material is intellectually rejected. It's as though, within these negative influences, there's a hidden virus whose invasion of our psyche goes unnoticed.

Additionally, we often relax our circumspection when encountering material that assigns the attributes of spiritual insight or religion to itself; we forget that every heinous crime that man is capable of has been perpetrated in the name of God. While violent cults may be clearly repellent, belief systems that masquerade as piety are far more insidious, for they corrupt by the silent entrainment of invisible attractor fields.

Here, it's best to heed the traditional wisdom that

tells us not to fear evil or fight it, but merely avoid it; yet in order to do so, one first has to have the capacity to recognize it. Socrates said, in effect, that without such capacity, youth (including the youth that continues to reside within every adult) is corrupted by low-energy attractor fields. Although Socrates was put to death for trying to teach this discernment, his entreaty remains: Obscurity is dispelled by augmenting the light of discernment, *not* by attacking the darkness.[1] The final issue, then, is the problem of how we may best cultivate and preserve the power of moral discretion.

Our journey of investigation has finally led us to the most critical realization of all: *Mankind lacks the capacity to recognize the difference between truth and falsehood.*

By humbly surrendering to this awareness, man may be forearmed. When we admit that we're gullible and easily seduced by the senses and deluded by glamour (including intellectual glamour), we have at least the beginning of discernment. Fortunately, in this world of duality, man has been given a consciousness that can instantly detect what's destructive—and signal it to his otherwise ignorant mind—by the grossly visible weakening of his body in the presence of the hostile stimuli. Wisdom can ultimately be reduced to the simple process of avoiding what makes you go weak—nothing else is really required.

Through frequent practice of this technique, spiritual blindness to truth and falsehood can be progressively replaced by a growing intuitive vision. Some lucky few seem born with this innate perceptivity; their lives remain clear and undamaged by negative entrainment. But for most of us, life hasn't been so easy; we've spent a great deal of it repairing the damage done by destructive attractors that act like hypnosis. Recovering from a single addiction can take up the majority of a lifetime—and the most common and insidious addiction is to denial, which "unenlightens" us through our intellectual vanity.

Contrary to its delusions of grandeur, the intellect not only lacks the ability to recognize falsehood, but also grossly lacks the necessary power to defend itself, even if it had the capacity for discernment. Is it irreverent, in light of history's enormous collection of works of intellectual speculation, to say that man's boasted capacity of reason lacks the critical faculty of discernment? The entire field of philosophy is merely evidence that man has struggled and failed for thousands of years to arrive at the simplest recognition of what's true and what's false, or the discourse would have reached some consensus long ago. And it's clear from common human conduct that even if the intellect could reliably arrive at this basic conclusion, *it still lacks the power to stop the effect of negative fields.* We remain unconscious of the causes of our afflictions while the intellect dreams up all kinds of plausible excuses, hypnotized by these same forces. Even when a person intellectually knows his behavior is self-destructive, this knowledge has no necessary deterrent effect whatsoever; intellectual recognition of our addictions has never given us the power to control them.

In scripture, we're told that man is afflicted by forces unseen.[2] In this century, we've learned that silent, invisible rays of energy are emitted by innocent-looking objects—the discoverers of radium paid for this realization with their lives. Roentgen x-rays are lethal; radioactive emissions and radon kill silently. The attractor energy fields that destroy us are equally invisible and no less powerful, but they're far more subtle.

When it's said that someone is "possessed," what's meant is that his consciousness has become dominated by negative attractor fields. By this definition, we can see that entire segments of society are so thoroughly "possessed" that they themselves are totally unconscious of their motives. Wisdom tells us that one worships either heaven or hell and will eventually become the servant of one or the other. Hell isn't a condition imposed by a judgmental God, but rather the inevitable consequence of one's own decisions—it's the final outcome of constantly choosing the negative and thus isolating oneself from love.

Enlightened beings have always described the general populace as being "trapped in a dream"; the majority of people are driven by unseen forces, and for a great deal of our lives, most of us are in despair over this fact. We pray to God to relieve us of the burden of our sins, and we look for relief through confession. Remorse seems woven into the fabric of life. How can salvation be possible, then, for those who have unwittingly become ensnared by such destructive influence?

In fact, even from a merely scientific viewpoint, salvation is indeed possible; in truth, it's guaranteed by the simple fact that the energy of a loving thought is enormously more powerful than that of a negative one. Therefore, the traditional solutions of love and prayer have a sound scientific basis; man has within his own essence the power of his own salvation.

Humanity is an "affliction" that we're all burdened with. We don't remember asking to be born, and we subsequently inherited a mind so limited that it's hardly capable of distinguishing what enhances life from what leads to death.[3] The entire struggle of life is in transcending this myopia. We can't enter into higher levels of existence until we advance in consciousness to the point where we overcome duality and are no longer earthbound. Perhaps it's because of our collective will to transcend that we've earned the capacity to finally discover an inborn compass to lead us out of the darkness of ignorance. We needed something very simple, which could bypass those traps of the wily intellect that we've paid such an enormous price for. This compass merely says yes or no—it tells us that what's aligned with heaven makes us go strong and what's aligned with hell makes us go weak.

The ubiquitous human ego is actually not an "I" at all; it's merely an "it." Seeing through this illusion reveals an endless Cosmic Joke, where the human tragedy itself is part of the comedy. The irony of human experience is in how fiercely the ego fights to preserve the illusion of a separate, individual "I"—even though this is not only a metaphysical impossibility but the wellspring of all suffering. Human reason exhausts itself ceaselessly to explain the inexplicable. Explanation itself is high comedy, as preposterous as trying to see the back of one's own head, but the vanity of the ego is boundless, and it becomes even more overblown by this very attempt to make sense of nonsense. The mind, in its identity with the ego, cannot, by definition, comprehend reality; if it could, it would instantly dissolve itself upon recognizing its own illusory nature. It's only beyond the paradox of mind transcending ego that what *Is* stands forth, self-evident and dazzling in its infinite Absoluteness. And then all of these words are useless.

But perhaps from compassion for each other's blindness, we can learn to forgive ourselves, and peace can then be our assured future. Our purpose on Earth may remain obscure, but the road ahead is clear. With the consciousness level of humanity finally above 200, we may expect great transformations throughout human culture, as mankind becomes more responsible for its knowledge, and thus its deeds. We've become fully accountable, whether we like it or not. We're at the point in the evolution of our collective awareness where we may even assume stewardship of consciousness itself. Humanity is no longer resigned to passively paying the price of ignorance, or its communal consciousness wouldn't have risen to its new level. From this time forth, man may choose to no longer be enslaved by darkness; his destiny can then be certain.

Gloria in Excelsis Deo.

APPENDIX A

Calibrated Levels of Truth of the Chapters

Chapter 1	780	Chapter 13	870
Chapter 2	830	Chapter 14	870
Chapter 3	750	Chapter 15	730
Chapter 4	770	Chapter 16	760
Chapter 5	740	Chapter 17	770
Chapter 6	710	Chapter 18	770
Chapter 7	740	Chapter 19	830
Chapter 8	820	Chapter 20	890
Chapter 9	800	Chapter 21	870
Chapter 10	780	Chapter 22	860
Chapter 11	770	Chapter 23	880
Chapter 12	800	Chapter 24	860

APPENDIX B

Details of Kinesiologic Testing

Scientific validity depends upon replicability. To ensure reliable duplication of results, the kinesiologic testing technique used for all of the research cited in this book is described in detail below. It's essentially the same method developed by Dr. John Diamond in his pioneering work, *Behavioral Kinesiology*.

Step 1

Two people are required (see note). To determine the suitability of a test subject, the tester presses down quickly with two fingers on the wrist of the horizontally extended arm of the subject, simultaneously telling them to "resist" (against the downward pressure). A normal subject is able to resist the pressure and keep their arm extended parallel to the ground.

Occasionally, there are people who are unable to keep their arm extended when *any* downward pressure is applied due to previous contact with weakening energy fields or negative health conditions; these aren't suitable test subjects. Some of these subjects can recover by thumping themselves over the thymus gland (at the top of the breastbone) in a "one-two-three" rhythm, while they smile and think of someone they love. They'll then "go strong" and respond normally, but the "fix" may last for only four hours and this "thymus thump" will then have to be repeated.

(**Note:** Some people are able to get good results just by themselves by making an "O" ring with their thumb and forefinger. When the results are "true," the "O" is strong and it's difficult to pull the thumb and forefinger apart; a "no" makes them relatively weak and easy to separate. If an important decision is to be made, it's best to verify the answer by the 2-person method described above.)

Step 2

Keep the testing situation impersonal—refrain from smiling or making personal comments; keep the environment free of noise, background music, or distractions such as pets or intrusive children. Remove metal objects, such as eyeglass frames, from the test subject's body midline. Also remove watches or jewelry (including necklaces). Be aware that aberrant stimuli, such as a tester's perfume or aftershave lotion, may affect the test results. To improve concentration, have the test subject close their eyes.

Step 3

If subjects repeatedly go weak, evaluate the examiner's voice. The voice that makes others go weak disqualifies its owner as a tester under ordinary conditions.

Step 4

Do a trial run with the prospective subject. Ask the candidate to think of someone they love, then press down with two fingers on the wrist of the arm extended out to the side, parallel to the ground. A normal subject will go quite strong and be able to resist firmly. Next, have the party think of someone they hate, fear, or have a resentment toward. (Aldof Hitler will alternatively work.) A normal subject will go very weak and be unable to resist downward pressure on their wrist. Run through a few more contrasting pairs of stimuli to establish consistency of response and to develop a rapport between tester and subject. Some sample ideological, visual, and auditory stimuli with predictable responses are:

Test Weak	Test Strong
Hate	Love
Swastika	American flag
Joseph Stalin	Mahatma Gandhi
Gangster rap music	Classical music

(Also see Chapter 7.)

Step 5

After establishing that the test subject reacts reliably and is in a normal state, proceed with the topic under investigation by making declarative statements. Questions should always be posed as a declaration of fact; it's useless to ask questions about the future, as the test results will have no reliability. Always preface the investigation with the statement, "I have permission to make inquiry into _____ (the specific topic)." (Y/N?) The line of questioning itself can be checked by stating, "This is the correct form for the question." (Y/N?) The statement— such as "The accused committed the burglary." (Y/N?)— may be made by either the questioner or the test subject. Each time a question is stated, the test subject is told to resist and the tester presses down quickly with two fingers on the test subject's extended wrist.

In our research, we frequently used teams of test subjects. For example, 20, 30, or up to 1,000 people were divided into two-person teams who took turns as tester and test subject. The entire group was asked the same question at the same time, or was divided into subgroups for independent research projects. In a group of 100 people (50 two-person teams), perhaps one or two will have difficulty in obtaining the same results as the others. They can be taken aside to do the "thymus thump" (described on page 296), which will return their responses to normal, and they can then rejoin the group.

Using the above method, test results are 100 percent replicable over the course of time so that *any group of people anywhere* will always produce the same results; for example, the image of Adolf Hitler will make everybody go weak, even if they've never heard of him or think that he's a great national hero.

Step 6

The test can also be performed by holding test objects next to the solar plexus of the test subjects. They'll be found to go weak in response to artificial sweetener, pesticides, or even a picture of Hitler concealed in a manila envelope. They'll go strong in response to nutritious food, beneficial medicines and nutrients, a concealed picture of Abraham Lincoln, and so on.

Step 7

Test results can be verified to be independent of the test subject's knowledge, opinions, belief systems, or attitudes. For example, an image of Nelson Mandela will make all test subjects go strong, even racists who resent him. The music of Bach makes everyone go strong, even if they don't personally like it, just as heavy metal music makes all subjects go weak, even if they personally prefer it.

This confirmability of results has been observed during the last 20 years by thousands of clinicians using kinesiology in their everyday clinical practices or for research. The results, in fact, are more consistent than conventional diagnostic methods used in traditional medicine (that is, a weak heart never tests strong with kinesiology, but may give an erroneous normal EKG tracing—this is a well-known fact).

Videotapes

Video demonstrations of the various subjects and techniques described herein are available from:

Veritas Publishing
P.O. Box 3516
West Sedona, AZ 86340
Fax: (928) 282-4789

NOTES

(See **Bibliography** for publication data.)

Foreword

1. American Heritage Dictionary, Houghton Mifflin, 1987.
2. See Goodheart, 1976.
3. See Diamond, 1979.
4. See Kendall, 1971.
5. Diamond, op. cit.

Introduction

1. See Maharshi, 1958.
2. See Kosslyn and Anderson, 1993.
3. See Ruelle, 1980, for a definitive discussion.
4. See Maharshi, op. cit., 118–126.

1. Critical Advances in Knowledge

1. See Goodheart, 1976.
2. See Peat, 1988.
3. See Briggs and Peat, 1989.
4. See Walther, 1976.
5. See Lorenz, 1963.
6. See Mandelbrot, 1977.

7. Geoffrey Chew originated the Bootstrap/S-Matrix Theory and is quoted in Fritjof Capra's *The Tao of Physics* as saying that by extension, the bootstrap approach may lead to the unprecedented necessity of including the study of human consciousness explicitly in future theories of matter (1975).

8. See Bohm, 1987.

9. As Ken Wilber has pointed out, any theory of reality must include and coincide with the perennial philosophy and an ontological order of being: (1) matter; (2) biology; (3) psychology; (4) subtle/saintly; (5) sage; (6) ultimate (beyond consciousness). This is discussed in Wilber's *The Holographic Paradigm*, p. 159.

10. See Maharshi, 1958.

11. See Hawkins, 1992.

12. See Gleick, 1987.

13. The essentials of chaos theory are clearly explained by James Gleick in *Chaos: Making a New Science,* and by John Briggs and F. David Peat in *Turbulent Mirror.*

14. See Capra, 1975.

15. Bohm's universe is explained well by Bohm himself in an interview in *The Holographic Paradigm,* edited by Ken Wilber, 1982.

16. This state of pure awareness is Level 6 of Wilber's hierarchy, and is described in detail by Maharshi, Huang Po, and Nisargadatta Maharaj in the excellent English translations of their works cited in the Bibliography.

17. This was validated by Ramesh Balsekar who, after years of being Nisargadatta Maharaj's translator, arrived at the same state of consciousness, demonstrated during interviews (1987) and in the series of six books cited in the Bibliography.

18. See Hoffman, 1992.

19. See Li and Spiegel, 1992.

20. Ibid.

21. See Hoffman, 1992.

22. See Gleick, 1987.

23. This phenomenon, called "iteration," was discussed in 1960 by Edward Lorenz in his historic computer analysis of weather data.

24. The correlation between the work of David Bohm, Karl Pribam, Rupert Sheldrake, and Ilya Prigogine was discussed

throughout the *Brain/Mind Bulletin*, Vol. IV, 1979. (*Brain/Mind Bulletin*, P.O. Box 42211, Los Angeles, CA 90042).

25. Nobelist Sir John Eccles states that the energy of mind excites the brain to response; this is expressed in his address to the Convention of the Parapsychology Association in Utrecht, Netherlands, 1976.

2. *History and Methodology*

1. See Hawkins, *The Villa Lectures*, 1987.
2. See Kendall, Kendall, and Wadsworth, 1971.
3. See Goodheart, 1976.
4. See Mann, 1974.
5. See Walther, 1976.
6. See Diamond, 1979.
7. See Hawkins and Pauling, 1973.
8. This desynchronization was demonstrated by John Diamond at the Academy of Preventative Medicine, 1973.
9. Kinesiologic demonstrations often result in paradigm shock for people who have an investment in strict materialism. One such observer, a research psychiatrist, responded by first trying to prove that the demonstration was a fake. When he failed to do so, he walked away, saying, "Even if it's true, I don't believe it."
10. These procedures were developed over a period of several years, during regular weekly testing sessions at the Institute for Advanced Theoretical Research, Sedona, AZ, 1983–1993.
11. Hawkins, public lectures, Sedona, AZ, 1984–1989.
12. This is well documented in the field of neurolinguistic programming.
13. Diamond, lectures at the Academy of Preventative Medicine, 1978.
14. Research protocol, Institute of Advanced Theoretical Research, 1992.
15. This has been repeatedly demonstrated in public and is adequately described in Diamond's book *Your Body Doesn't Lie*.
16. The perennial philosophy is an extract of the spiritual truth of all religions and reflects expanding awareness on a scale

progressing from matter to protoplasm, animal life, emotional responsiveness, capacity for thought, abstract thought, archetypal awareness, higher mind, saintly love and bliss, nonduality (the sage), and ultimate pure awareness. As Ken Wilber has pointed out, these strata appear universally—any theory of reality must comprehend these axioms of existence.

3: Test Results and Interpretation

1. See Eadie, p. 114.

4: Levels of Human Consciousness

1. See James, 1929.
2. Personal experience of the author.

5: Social Levels of Consciousness

1. The level of consciousness of mankind as a whole remained at 190 for many centuries and then suddenly jumped to its present level of 204 after the Harmonic Convergence of the late 1980s. Did the rise in consciousness bring about the Harmonic Convergence? Did the Harmonic Convergence bring about the increase in the level? Or, did a powerful, unseen "implicate order" attractor field bring about both phenomena?

6: New Horizons in Research

1. See Hawkins, 1988.
2. God is both transcendent (traditional religion) and immanent (the experiential truth of the mystic).
3. *Arizona Republic,* December 20, 1993.
4. Fedarko, *Time,* December 13, 1993.
5. See Josephson, 1959, p. 20.
6. The fact-based movie that tells the entire story and its consequences was called *Barbarians at the Gate* and was shown on network TV in 1993.
7. This is a traditional observation of clinicians, confirmed by the author's clinical experience over decades.

7: Everyday Critical Point Analysis

1. See Appendix A.
2. See Brunton, 1984.

8: The Source of Power

1. This was a special area of research reported by Diamond in *Behavioral Kinesiology*, 1979.
2. Discussed at length in Weber's *Holographic Paradigm and Other Paradoxes*, 1982.
3. Bohm, D., *Brain/Mind Bulletin*, 10:10, May 27, 1985.
4. See Sheldrake, 1981.
5. Sheldrake called for a more public approach to the scientific research. In response, prizes were awarded in the U.S. ($10,000) and Britain (£250) for confirmatory tests of the hypothesis. A Morse code experiment supported the theory, and was reported by Mahlberg in *Brain/Mind Bulletin*, 10:12, July 8, 1985.
6. The mutual dependence and interpenetration of all things is observable as one leaves duality. Oneness is central to all of the major religions and spiritual systems as the ultimate reality underlying and within all forms.
7. See Land and Jarman, 1992.

9: Power Patterns in Human Attitudes

1. See Bohm, 1982.
2. See Sheldrake, 1981.
3. "Test Supports Sheldrake Theory," *Brain/Mind Bulletin*, 8:15, September 12, 1983.

10: Power in Politics

1. See Rudolph and Rudolph, 1983.
2. See Mehta, 1982.
3. See Fischer, 1982.
4. See Loczay, 1972.
5. Ibid.
6. See *Newsweek*, May 9, 1994.

7. "Crusade in Europe," *March of Time Video Series, 1939*; also Lash, 1976.

8. See Tucker, 1990.

9. This interaction between the idealism of Communism and the realities of ongoing labor wars was well presented in the PBS series *The Great Depression,* 1993.

10. Stewardship as a primary leadership role has received considerable emphasis in recent sociopolitical dialogue.

11. See Cuomo, *Lincoln,* 1990.

12. See Fischer, op. cit.

11: Power in the Marketplace

1. See Trimble, 1990.

2. In this classic analysis of business principles, Peters and Waterman identified the sources of power as *principles* rather than business policies and procedures, management practices, or technology.

12: Power and Sports

1. *The Big Blue* (starring Rosanna Arquette and Jean-Marc Benn), directed by Luc Besson, produced by Studio le Clare, Paris, 1985.

2. The mottoes of Goshin-Kan (classical Okinawan karate) are: (1) Strive for good moral character; (2) keep an honest and sincere way; (3) persevere; (4) maintain a respectful attitude; (5) restrain the physical by spiritual attainment; and (6) cultivate and preserve life and avoid its destruction.

3. Personal karate instruction of the author by Shihan Dennis Rao, 1986.

4. Personal instruction by Master Seiyu Oyata, 1986.

13: Social Power and the Human Spirit

1. *Spirit* is defined in the *Living Webster Encyclopedic Dictionary of the English Language* (English Language Institute of America, Chicago, 1971) as: "Latin *spiritus:* breath, air, life essence, soul;

the incorporeal principle of life, the vital principle of man, conscious being as opposed to matter; vigor, courage, aliveness; character, the divine aspect of the Trinity; the principle behind action; general meaning, active principle; dominant tendency."

2. The definition of *spirit* as a concept has always presented a difficult challenge to the human intellect; a full comprehension of its significance seems beyond the capacity of the left brain (which, like a digital computer, defines how one thing differs from another). *Spirit* is a holistic term best grasped by the right brain (which, like an analog computer, deals with wholes and essences). The lengthy philosophical discussions that have wrestled with the idea of spirit or soul through the centuries testify to the inability of the intellect alone to deal with essence. The paradox of these philosophical debates is that any discussion at all regarding meaning utilizes essence as the very stuff of its discourse. Thus, even a discussion that rejects known ideas/essence/spirit does so on the presumption of the existence of truth as the basis of the argument. If there's no such thing as reality-based spirit/essence/truth, then there is no premise for any argument against their existence either, as no argument would have a reality base. In modern times, we could say that the concept of spirit refers to Bohm's implicate order, just as the concept of the corporeal refers to the explicate order.

3. What's unique about the basic premise of the U.S. government—and the source of its power—is the concept that it derives its authority by consent of the governed, who are equal by virtue of the divinity of their Creator ("one nation under God". . .).

4. A calibrated comparison between the original spiritual foundations of the world's great religions and their subsequent formal expressions is presented in Chapter 23—there's a notably wide disparity between the two readings.

5. The preamble to every AA meeting states: "Alcoholics Anonymous is a fellowship of men and women who share their experience, strength, and hope with each other that they may share their common problem and help others to recover from alcoholism. The only requirement for membership is a desire to stop drinking. There are no dues or fees for AA membership; we are self-supporting through our own contributions. AA is not allied with any sect,

denomination, politics, organization, or institution; does not wish to engage in any controversy; neither endorses nor opposes any causes. Our primary purpose is to stay sober and help other alcoholics to achieve sobriety." (Alcoholics Anonymous, P.O. Box 459, Grand Central Station, New York, NY, 1941, 1993.)

6. See *Twelve Steps and Twelve Traditions*, 1952.

7. See Chapter 11 in *Alcoholics Anonymous*, 1955.

8. See Bill W., 1988; *Selected Letters of C.G. Jung, 1909–1961*.

9. Ibid.

10. See "Bill's Story" in *Alcoholics Anonymous*, 1955, 1–17.

11. Ibid., 171–182.

12. See *Life's 100 Most Important Americans of the 20th Century*, 66.

14: Power in the Arts

1. Liner notes to *Tabula Rasa*, ECM Records, 1984.

15: Genius and the Power of Creativity

1. See Dilts, 1992.

2. Frank Lloyd Wright stated that "the Artist's perception science later verifies." (See Wright, R.L., 1949.)

3. See Galaman, 1992.

4. See Loehle, 1990.

5. See Heilbron, 1992; also Churchill, 1949.

17: Physical Health and Power

1. See Hawkins and Pauling, 1973.

2. See Tkacz and Hawkins, 1981.

3. See Hawkins, 1989.

4. See Hawkins, 1991.

18: Wellness and the Disease Process

1. See Walther, 1976.

2. See Mann, 1974.

3. See Diamond, 1979.

4. See Briggs and Peat, 1989.
5. See Redington and Reidband.
6. This is emphasized in the basic book of AA, *Alcoholics Anonymous*, 1955.
7. See Bill W., *The Language of the Heart*, 1988.
8. See *AA Comes of Age*, 1957, and *AA Today*, 1960.
9. See *Twelve Steps and Twelve Traditions*, 1953.
10. See *AA Comes of Age*, 1957.

19: The Database of Consciousness

1. See Jung, 1979.
2. Ibid. The implication of synchronicity is that two events aren't causally connected in reality but are perceived so by the observer because they're meaningful. As one's consciousness advances into the high 500s, everything begins to happen by synchronicity, and the events of life unfold in perfect order and harmony with precise timing. See also Insinna, 1994.
3. See Maharshi, 1958; Maharaj, 1973; Huang Po, 1958; and Belsekar, 1987–1991.

20: The Evolution of Consciousness

1. See Eadie, 1992.
2. In an interesting coincidence, after this chapter was written, "a 75-year-old man with a tobacco-stained white beard . . . [who] . . . would not describe himself as homeless, [said] only that he was without a home temporarily while 'he waited for a friend.'" This man set up an impromptu camp on public land adjacent to the highway in a community neighboring the author's. During his month's residence there, Cyrus (as he identified himself) was the center of a minor controversy. Some citizens said he was an eyesore and clamored for his removal, and the sheriff's department viewed him with suspicion and threatened to arrest him for trespassing. Others found him a harmless novelty or applauded his individualism; at least one local resident "offered him lodging, which he thought about, he said." He refused to request help from social-service organizations, "saying, 'I don't need any and don't want any,' but he did accept

kindness from individuals. People came by bringing him food, particularly sandwiches, he said." (*Red Rock News,* Sedona, Arizona, November 27, 1993.) On the day of the deadline given him by sheriff's deputies, Cyrus mysteriously disappeared.

3. See Maharaj, 1973.

21: The Study of Pure Consciousness

1. See Descartes.
2. See section on "Poverty" in *Kaplan & Sadock's Comprehensive Textbook of Psychiatry,* 2000.
3. See Maharshi, 1952; Maharaj, 1982.
4. Ibid.
5. See Maharaj, 1973.
6. See James, 1929.
7. Personal experience of the author.
8. See Maharaj, op. cit.; Huang Po, op. cit.; Maharshi, 1952; and Balsekar, 1987–1991.
9. See Maharaj, op. cit.; Huang Po, op. cit.; Balsekar, op. cit.
10. See *Brain/Mind Bulletin,* op. cit.
11. See Chapter 15, "Genius and the Power of Creativity."
12. See Kuhn, 1970.
13. See Kübler-Ross, 1993.
14. See Kripper, 1974.
15. Ibid.
16. See *AA Comes of Age.*
17. Bill W., 1988.
18. See Chapter 1, "Bill's Story," in *Alcoholics Anonymous,* 1952.
19. See *Twelve Steps and Twelve Traditions.*

22: Spiritual Struggle

1. See Maharshi, 1958; Huang Po, 1958; Maharaj, 1973; Balsekar, 1990.
2. See Balsekar, 1989.
3. See Walsh, 1985.
4. See Maharshi, 1958.

5. "Anguish of the Soul" is a theme throughout classic Christian literature. See Peers, 1958; Blackney, 1942; French, 1965; Walsh, 1985.

6. See Krippner, 1974.

7. See Diamond, J., *Lectures on Behavioral Kinesiology*, NY, 1972.

8. Sedona Villa of Camelback Hospital treated more than 100 cocaine addicts a year for a five-year period (1981–1986). None of the patients who continued to listen to heavy metal rock music recovered (follow-up survey, 1986).

9. Addicts who leave 12-step programs relapse (clinical observation of the author).

10. See Maharshi, 1958.

11. See "St. Francis of Assisi," in *Butler's Lives of the Saints,* 1985, 314–320.

12. See *A Course in Miracles,* 1975.

13. See Capra, 1976.

23: The Search for Truth

1. Christianity's fall from a calibrated 930 to 498 must be recognized as the greatest single catastrophe in the history of Western religion. Here we can see the origin of the spiritual divorce from the actual teachings of Jesus Christ that allowed the later atrocities of the Crusades and the Inquisition. The historic decline of Christianity centers around the inclusion of the negative or relatively weak books of the Old Testament, and the Book of Revelations in the New Testament, in the canon of Christian scripture. What, really, does the "eye-for-an-eye" ethic of the prophets have to do with Christ's appeal for universal love and forgiveness? The question has rightly been asked: Why, if Jesus came to teach the Old Testament, should he have bothered coming at all?

More to the point, as in the case of Islam, the everyday practice of Christianity is most conspicuously tainted by militant fundamentalist groups that define themselves by their hates and hawk agendas, which are primarily based on depriving others of their freedoms. It may well be this burden of vitriolic negativity that keeps current

Christianity below the level of Love. It's interesting that these so-called Christians rarely quote Christ. Their repertoire of passionate arguments and self-justification is drawn almost entirely from the Old Testament; when they say "scripture," that's usually what they mean.

Had Christianity, in valuing moral behavior, kept exclusively to the tenets of the New Testament, one wonders what the world would be like today.

2. Author's clinical experience.

3. Freud remained below the critical level of 500 because of his denial of man's spirituality, whereas Carl Jung, who affirmed the spiritual nature of man, calibrates at a much higher 560.

24: Resolution

1. Socrates taught that man's purpose is to dedicate his life to the enlightenment of his soul (the light) rather than the pursuit of materialism and the senses (which leads to darkness). See Plato's *Republic*, op. cit.

2. *Epistle of Paul to the Ephesians,* 6:12. "For your conflict is not only with flesh and blood, but also with the angels, and with powers seen and unseen, with the rulers of the world of darkness, one with the evil spirits under the heavens." Holy Bible, Trans. George Lamsa, (Philadelphia: A.J. Holmes Co., 1957).

3. This is often stated as a starting point from which to eventually arrive at a realization of our true nature, by teachers such as Nisargadatta Maharaj (in *I Am That,* 1973).

◎ ◎ ◎

GLOSSARY

Chaos theory: The science of *process* as opposed to *state*. This theory originates in the discovery of patterns within a condition of unpredictability. The view it proposes discerns global possibilities rather than local events—and entails a topologic system using patterns and shapes to visualize the intrinsic form of a complex system that, though locally unpredictable, is globally stable. Chaos theory recognizes the capacity of a complex system to simultaneously give rise to both turbulence *and* coherence.

In the late 1800s, Jules-Henri Poincaré noted that Newtonian physics was mathematically accurate—*if* the interaction studied was between two bodies only. The addition of a third element made Newton's equations unreliable, and only approximations could be obtained. This nonlinearity implied that any system over time could, by feedback and repetition, become unpredictable. In the journal article titled "Deterministic Nonperiodic Flow" (1963), E. N. Lorenz provided a new paradigm of science—which James Yorke had famously termed "chaos theory." Chaos theory encompasses such subjects as period doubling, iteration, fractals, and bifurcation, and recognizes that within finite space, there's an infinite number of dimensions. The first meeting on chaos was in 1977, at the New York Academy of Science; and in 1986, the academy had its first meeting on chaos theory in medicine and biology.

Context: The total field of observation predicated by a point of view. Context includes any significant facts that qualify the meaning of a statement or event. For instance, data is meaningless unless its context is defined. To "take out of context" is to distort the significance of a statement by failing to identify contributory accessory conditions that would qualify the inference of meaning. (This is a common trial strategy—an attorney will try to distort a witness's testimony by suppressing the inclusion of qualifying statements that would alter the implications of the testimony, demanding that the witness answer only "yes or no.")

Creation: A continuous process without beginning or end, through which the manifest universe of form and matter is produced by repetition, starting from three points. In Sanskrit, the three aspects of origination of all that can be experienced are called *Rajas, Tamas,* and *Satva.* These are symbolized by the Hindu deities *Shiva, Vishnu,* and *Brahma.* In Christianity, these are represented by the Trinity (*God, Jesus Christ,* and *the Holy Ghost*).

Duality: The world of form, which is characterized by seeming separation of objects (reflected in conceptual dichotomies such as "this/that," "here/there," "then/now," or "you/me"). This perception of limitation is produced by the senses because of the restriction implicit in a fixed point of view. Science has finally gone beyond the artificial dichotomy of observer and observed characteristic of 17th-century Cartesian duality, and now assumes that they're one and the same. The universe has no center, but is continually expanding equally and simultaneously from every point. Bell's Theorem helped to demonstrate that this is a universe of simultaneity—rather than Newtonian cause and effect over distance in an artificial time frame. Both time and space themselves are merely the measurable products of a higher implicit order.

Energy field: A range set by parameters off the phase space of an attractor field—whose pattern operates within the larger energy field of consciousness and is observable by characteristic effects in human behavior. The power of energy fields is calibrated much like voltage in an electrical system or the power of magnetic or gravitational fields.

Entrainment: A phenomenon illustrated by the principle of "mode locking." For example, when a number of clocks are placed close together, their pendulums will eventually synchronize. In human biology, this is manifested when groups of women who work or live together progressively synchronize their menstrual cycles. It's similar to the phenomenon of a tuning fork beginning to vibrate at the rate of an adjacent fork; it's because of this process that troops tend to break cadence when they cross a bridge.

Fractal: Fractal patterns are characterized by irregularity and infinite length, and strange attractors are composed of fractal curves. A classic example is the attempt to determine the length of the coastline of Britain: If one adds lengths using smaller and smaller scales of measurement, it turns out to be infinitely long. *Fractal* implies an infinite length in a finite area.

Hologram: A three-dimensional projection into space of the image of an object, created by projecting laser light so that half of the beam is directed to the object and then onto a photographic plate, which receives the other half of the beam directly. This creates an interference pattern on the plate so that a laser beam projected through the plate recreates the image of the object in three dimensions. It's of interest that every fragment of the photographic plate is capable of reproducing the entire image of the whole. In a holographic universe, everything is connected to everything else.

Iteration: Repetition. Nonlinear iteration is present in innumerable systems—because of this repetition, a very slight change in the initial condition will eventually produce a pattern dissimilar from the original. In a growth equation, the output of the prior iteration becomes the input for the next series. For example, if a computer calculates to 16 decimal places, the last digit is the rounding off of the 17th. This infinitesimal error, magnified through many iterations, results in substantial distortion of the original data and makes prediction impossible. (Thus, a slight change in a repetitious thought pattern can bring about major effects.)

Left-brain: Referring to thought sequenced in the linear style, which is commonly described as "logic" or "reason." Processing of data in a sequence A➤B➤C; comparable to a digital computer.

Linear: Following a logical progression in the manner of Newtonian physics and, therefore, solvable by traditional mathematics through the use of differential equations.

M-fields: Morphogenetic fields, which are equivalent to attractor patterns. In the hypothesis presented by Rupert Sheldrake, morphogenetic fields are part of the *theory of formative causation*—that energy fields of form evolve and reinforce each other.

Neural network: The interlocking patterns of interacting neurons within the nervous system.

Neurotransmitters: Brain chemicals (hormones and the like) that regulate neuronal transmission throughout the nervous system. Very slight chemical changes can result in major subjective and objective alterations in emotion, thought, or behavior. This is the prime area of current research in psychiatry.

Nonduality: Historically, all observers who have reached a consciousness level over 600 have described this reality, which is now suggested by advanced scientific theory. When the limitation of a fixed location of perception is transcended, there's no longer an illusion of separation, nor of space and time as we know them. All things exist simultaneously in the unmanifest, enfolded, implicit universe, expressing itself as the manifest, unfolded, explicit perception of form. In reality, these forms have no intrinsic, independent existence but are the product of perception (that is, man is merely experiencing the content of his own mind). On the level of nonduality, there's observing but no observer, as subject and object are one. You-and-I becomes the One Self experiencing all as divine. At level 700, it can only be said that "All Is"— the state is one of Being-ness; all is consciousness (life, infinite, God) and has no parts or a beginning or end. The physical body is a manifestation of the One Self who, in experiencing this dimension, had temporarily forgotten its reality, thus permitting the illusion of a three-dimensional world. The body is merely a means of communication; to identify one's self with the body as "I" is the fate of the unenlightened, who then erroneously deduce that they're mortal and subject to death. Death itself is an illusion, based on the false identification with the body as "I." In nonduality, consciousness experiences itself as both manifest and unmanifest, yet there's no experiencer. In this Reality, the only thing that has a beginning and an end is the act of perception itself. In the illusory world, we're like the fool who believes that things come into existence when he opens his eyes and cease to exist when he closes them.

Nonlinear: Unpredictably irregular in time, "noisy," nonperiodic, and unpredictable. The term also describes the mathematics of chaotic signals, including the statistical analysis of time series for deterministic nonlinear systems. *Nonlinear* means diffuse or chaotic; not in accordance with probabilistic logical theory or mathematics; not solvable by differential equations. This is the subject of the new science of chaos theory, which has given rise to an entirely new, non-Newtonian mathematics.

Oxymoronic: An expression of complexity or ambiguity in deceptively simple, apparently contradictory terms. The resolution of contradiction by juxtaposition and contrast—as in "cold fire" or "wise fool." Oxymoronic styles reflect the essence of paradox, and paradox itself arises from the contrast between different levels of abstraction, occasioned by the presentation of concepts from different contexts and points of view.

Paradigm: The dimensions of a context or field, as limited by parameters that inherently predict one's perception of reality. A paradigm is generally a definition of one's perception of reality according to its limitations.

Phase space: A map that affords the condensation of time-space data into a pattern in multiple dimensions. A Poincaré map is the graphic depiction of a slice through a multidimensional pattern that demonstrates the underlying attractor.

Right-brain: Generally meaning "holistic"; enabling such functions as evaluation, intuition, and comprehension of significance, meaning, and inference. Nonlinear; operating from patterns and relationships rather than through the logical sequences of Newtonian causality.

The right brain is assumed to deal with wholes rather than parts. Like an analog computer, it deals with processes and is generally capable of operating without the necessity of time reference. Right-brain perception detects essence within a complex field of data that might not otherwise lend itself to meaningful cognitive analysis—such general phenomena as "falling in love" or creativity. (The terms "left-brain" and "right-brain" originated in reference to different styles of perception that were once thought to be localized to certain cerebral areas, but as Karl Pribam has shown, the brain acts holographically rather than by precise anatomic localization.)

Scientific: The method of inquiry into nature specifically designed to derive predictable laws of physical properties. Modern scientific theory began in the 16th century with René Descartes's *Discourse on Method*, followed by Francis Bacon's *Inductive Inquiry*, and Isaac Newton's *Principia*. John Locke first used the term *scientific* and proposed that certainty about the interaction of physical events was based on data arrived at by physical sensation. These concepts resulted in a model of a mechanical, predictive universe, but this view was upset by a modern quantum theory, which states that at the subatomic level, the laws of chance replace deterministic laws.

History has noted that science doesn't advance by an extension of established theories, but instead takes leaps by a shift of paradigm. The inference is that science is merely a reflection of a point of view, and there's no real separation between observer and observed. Relativity theory further states that matter equals energy, depending on one's point of reference. David Bohm's later *Holographic Model* predicates an explicit order based on an implicit order. Form becomes the consequence of inference, space and time are nonlocalized, and there is no "here" or "there" (the nonlocality of quantum wholeness). The universe thus described contains an infinite number of dimensions and higher-dimension realities.

Stochastic: Random, unpredictable, nonlinear, erratic, "noisy," chaotic.

Strange attractor: A term coined by David Ruelle and Floris Takens in 1971, in a theory that stated that three independent motions are all that's necessary to produce the entire complexity of nonlinear patterns of the universe. A strange attractor is a pattern within a phase space. The pattern is traced by the dynamic points in time of a dynamic system. The central point of an attractor field is analogous to the center of an orbit. Attractors are fractal and therefore of infinite length. The graphics of attractors are depicted by taking a cross section of a Poincaré map. The topographical shaping of phase space creates an attractor such as a torus, which is shaped like a folded donut.

Universe: There may be seen to be an infinite number of dimensions to our universe. The familiar three-dimensional universe of conventional consensus is only one, and is merely an illusion created by our senses. The space between planetary bodies isn't empty, but filled with a sea of energy; the potential energy in one square inch can be said to be as great as that of the whole mass of the physical universe. Bohm has proposed the model of enfolded/unfolded states of being—with an explicit order and an implicit order of reality, comparable to the manifest/unmanifest states of reality that have been described for centuries by those who have achieved enlightenment and experienced nonduality.

In the causality model:

the A→B→C is the unfolded, explicit, manifest, discernible universe of form. The ABC is the enfolded, implicit, unmanifest potential beyond which is the formless, infinite matrix of both form and nonform—which is omnipotent, omniscient, and omnipresent.

BIBLIOGRAPHY

Abraham, R., and Shaw, C., *Dynamics: The Geometry of Behavior,* Vols. I–III. Santa Cruz, California: Aerial Press, 1984.

Amoroso, R., "Consciousness: A Radical Definition." *Toward a Scientific Basis for Consciousness; an Interdisciplinary Conference.* University of Arizona, Health Sciences Center, Tucson, Arizona, April 12–17, 1994.

Anonymous, *AA Today.* New York: Cornwall Press. 1960.

Anonymous, *A Course in Miracles.* Huntington Station, New York: Foundation for Inner Peace, Coleman-Graphics. 1975.

Anonymous, *Alcoholics Anonymous.* New York: Alcoholics Anonymous Publishing, Inc. 1955.

Anonymous, *Alcoholics Anonymous Comes of Age: A Brief History of AA.* New York: Alcoholics Anonymous Publishing, Inc. 1957.

Anonymous, *Twelve Steps and Twelve Traditions.* New York: Alcoholics Anonymous Publishing, Inc. 1953.

The Anti-Stalin Campaign and International Commission: A Selection of Documents. New York: Columbia University (Russian Institute). 1956.

Balsekar, R. S., *A Duet of One: The Ashtavatra Gita Dialogue.* Redondo Beach, California: Advaita Press. 1989.

———, *Experiencing the Teaching.* Redondo Beach, California: Advaita Press. 1988.

———, *Exploration into the Eternal.* Durham, North Carolina: Acorn Press. 1989.

———, *The Final Truth.* Redondo Beach, California: Advaita Press. 1989.

———, *From Consciousness to Consciousness.* Redondo Beach, California: Advaita Press. 1989.

———, *Personal Interviews.* Redondo Beach, California: Advaita Press. 1987.

———, *Pointers from Nisagargadatta Maharaj.* Durham, North Carolina: Acorn Press. 1990.

Barzon, J., "The Paradoxes of Creativity." *The American Scholar.* No. 50, pp. 337–351. Summer 1989.

Bendat, J. S., and Pearson, A. G., *Measurement and Analysis of Random Data.* New York: John Wiley and Sons. 1966.

Beringa, M., "The Mind Revealed." *Science.* No. 249, pp. 156–158. August 24, 1990.

Bill W., *The Language of the Heart.* New York: Cornwall Press. 1988.

Blakney, R. B. (trans.), *Meister Eckhart.* New York: Harper & Row. 1942.

Bohm., D., *Quantum Theory.* New York: Prentice-Hall. 1980.

———, *Wholeness and the Implicate Order.* London: Routledge & Kegan Paul. 1980.

———, and Peat, F. D., *Science, Order, and Creativity.* New York: Bantam Books. 1987.

———, Hiley, B., and Kaloyerous, P. N., "An Ontological Basis for Quantum Theory." *Phys. Reports.* No. 144:6, p. 323.

Briggs, J., *Fractals: The Patterns of Chaos.* New York: Simon & Schuster. 1993.

———, and Peat, F.D. *Looking Glass Universe.* New York: Simon & Schuster. 1984.

———, and Peat, F.D., *Turbulent Mirror: An Illustrated Guide to Chaos Theory and the Science of Wholeness.* New York: Harper & Row. 1989.

Brinkley, D., *Saved by the Light.* New York: Villard Books. 1994.

Bruner, J. S., and Posteman, L., "On the Perception of Incongruity: A Paradigm." *Journal of Personality.* No. 18, pp. 206. 1949.

Brunton, P., *A Search in Secret India.* Los Angeles: Weiser. 1984.

Butz, M., *Psychological Reports.* No. 17, pp. 827–843 and 1043–1063. 1993.

Capra, F., *The Tao of Physics: An Exploration of the Parallels Between Modern Physics and Eastern Mysticism.* New York: Bantam. 1976.

——, *The Turning Point: Science, Society, and the Rising Culture.* New York: Bantam. 1982.

Chalmers, D., "On Explaining Consciousness Scientifically: Choices and Challenges." *Toward a Scientific Basis for Consciousness; an Interdisciplinary Conference.* University of Arizona, Health Sciences Center, Tucson, Arizona, April 12–17, 1994.

Chew, G. F., "Bootstrap: A Scientific Idea." *Science.* No. 161. May 23, 1968.

——, "Hadron Bootstrap: Triumph or Frustration?" *Physics Today.* October 23, 1970.

——, "Impasse for the Elementary Particle Content." In *The Great Ideas Today.* Chicago: Encyclopedia Brittanica. 1974.

Churchill, W. S., *Blood, Sweat, and Tears.* New York: G. P. Putnam and Sons. 1941.

Combs, A., "Consciousness as a System Near the Edge of Chaos." *Toward a Scientific Basis for Consciousness; an Interdisciplinary Conference.* University of Arizona, Health Sciences Center, Tucson, Arizona, April 12–17, 1994.

Crick, C., and Koch, "The Problem of Consciousness." *Scientific American.* No. 267, pp. 152–159. September 1992.

Crusade in Europe. 1939: Marching Time. Collectors Videos.

Cuomo, M., *Lincoln on Democracy.* New York: Harper Collins. 1990.

Deikman, A. J., "The Role of Intention and Self as Determinants of Consciousness: A FunctionalApproach to a Spiritual Experience." *Toward a Scientific Basis for Consciousness; an Interdisciplinary Conference.* University of Arizona, Health Sciences Center, Tucson, Arizona, April 12–17, 1994.

Descartes, R., in *Great Books of the Western World,* Vol. 31. Chicago: Encyclopedia Brittanica. 1952.

Diamond, J., *Behavioral Kinesiology.* New York: Harper & Row. 1979.

————, *Your Body Doesn't Lie*. New York: Warner Books. 1979.

Dilts, R., "Strategies of Genius." *Success*. No. 39. October 26–27, 1992.

Dunn, J. (ed.), *Prior to Consciousness: Talks with Nisargadatta Maharj*. Durham, North Carolina: Acorn Press. 1985.

————, *Seeds of Consciousness*. New York: Grove Press. 1982.

Eadie, B. J., *Embraced by the Light*. Placerville, California: Gold Leaf Press. 1992.

Eccles, J., *Evolution of the Brain: Creation of the Self*. Edinburgh, Scotland: Routledge. 1989.

————, *The Human Psyche: The Gifford Lectures, University of Edinburgh, 1977–78*. Edinburgh, Scotland: Routledge. 1984.

———— (ed.), *Mind and Brain: The Many Faceted Problems*. New York: Paragon House. 1986.

————, and Robinson, D. N., *The Wonder of Being Human: Our Brain and Our Mind*. New York: Free Press. 1984.

Fedarko, K., "Escobar's Dead End." *Time*. No. 142:25, pp. 46–47. December 13, 1993.

Feigenbaum, N.J., "Universal Behavior in Nonlinear Systems." *Los Alamos Science*. No. 1, pp. 4–29. 1981.

Fischer, L., *Gandhi: His Life as a Message for the World*. New York: New American Library. 1982.

Freeman, W. J., and Skarda, C. A., "Spatial EEG Patterns: Nonlinear Dynamics and Perception." *Brain Res. Review*. No. 10, p. 147. 1985.

French, R. M. (trans.), *The Way of A Pilgrim*. New York: Seabury Press. 1965.

Galin, D., "The Structure of Subjective Experience." *Toward a Scientific Basis for Consciousness; an Interdisciplinary Conference*. University of Arizona, Health Sciences Center, Tucson, Arizona, April 12–17, 1994.

Gardner, H., *The Mind's New Science*. New York: Basic Books. 1985.

Gilbert, M., *The Complete Churchill Videos*. BBC. 1993.

Glass, L., and MacKay, M. W., "Pathological Conditions Resulting from Instabilities in Physiological Control Systems." *Ann. NY. Acad. Sci*. No. 316, p. 214. 1979.

Gleick, J., *Chaos: Making a New Science*. New York: Viking Penguin. 1987.

Godman, D. (ed.), *Be As You Are: The Teachings of Ramana Maharshi*. Boston: Arkana. 1985.

Golaman, D., et al., "The Art of Creativity." *Psychology Today,* No. 25, pp. 40–47. March/April 1992.

Goldman, A., "Philosophy of Mind: Defining Consciousness." *Toward a Scientific Basis for Consciousness; an Interdisciplinary Conference.* University of Arizona, Health Sciences Center, Tucson, Arizona, April 12–17, 1994.

Goodheart, G., *Applied Kinesiology,* 12th ed. Detroit: Privately Published. 1976.

Hardy, C., "Meaning as Interface Between Mind and Matter." *Toward a Scientific Basis for Consciousness; an Interdisciplinary Conference.* University of Arizona, Health Sciences Center, Tucson, Arizona, April 12–17, 1994.

Harman, W., "A Comparison of Three Approaches to Reconciling Science and Consciousness." *Toward a Scientific Basis for Consciousness; an Interdisciplinary Conference.* University of Arizona, Health Sciences Center, Tucson, Arizona, April 12–17, 1994.

Hawkins, D. R., *12 Lectures on: Stress; Weight Reduction; Alcoholism; Illness; Health; Depression; Spiritual First Aid; Pain and Suffering; Sex; Worry, Fear and Anxiety; The Aging Process; Handling Major Crises.* Farmingdale, New York: Coleman Graphics. 1986.

———, "Consciousness and Addiction," in Kiley, L., Burton, S. (eds.), *Beyond Addiction.* San Mateo, California: Brookridge Institute. 1987.

———, *Consciousness and Addiction: The Way Out.* The Villa Lectures. Farmingdale, New York: Coleman Graphics. 1988.

———, "Expanding Love: Beauty, Silence and Joy." *Call of the Canyon,* Vol. II. Sedona, Arizona. 1983.

———, "Love, Peace and Beautitude." *Call of the Canyon,* Vol. I. Sedona, Arizona. 1982.

———, *A Map of Consciousness* (video). Sedona, Arizona: Institute for Advanced Theoretical Research. 1993.

———, "Orthomolecular Psychiatry." *International Encyclopedia of Psychiatry, Psychoanalysis and Psychiatry.* 1979.

———, *The Sedona Series Lectures: A Map of Consciousness; Death and Dying; Hypertension and Heart Disease; AIDS; Cancer; Alcoholism and Drug Addiction; Consciousness and Addiction; Healing Relationships.* Sedona, Arizona: The Research Institute. 1987.

————, "Successful Prevention of Tardive Dyskinesia." *Journal of Orthmolecular Medicine.* Vol. 4, No. 1. 1989.

————, "Successful Prevention of Tardive Dyskinesia: A 20-Year Study of 64,000 Patients." *Journal of Orthomolecular Psychiatry.* January 1991.

————, and Pauling, L., *Orthomolecular Psychiatry.* San Francisco: W.H. Freeman and Company. 1973.

Heilbron, J. L., "Creativity and Big Science." *Physics Today.* No. 45, pp. 42–47. November 1992.

Henon, J., "A Two-Dimensional Mapping with a Strange Attractor." *Com. Math Physics.* No. 50, pp. 69–77. 1976.

Hoffman, R. E., "Attractor Neuro Networks and Psychotic Disorders." *Psychiatric Annals.* No. 22:3, pp. 119–124. 1992.

Hofstadter, D. R., *Metalogical Themes: Questing for the Essence of Mind and Pattern.* Toronto, Canada: Bantam Books. 1985.

Huang Po (John Blofield, trans.), *The Zen Teaching of Huang Po: On Transmission of the Mind.* New York: Grove Press. 1958.

Insinna, E., "Synchronicity Regularities in Quantum Systems." *Toward a Scientific Basis for Consciousness; an Interdisciplinary Conference.* University of Arizona, Health Sciences Center, Tucson, Arizona, April 12–17, 1994.

James, W., *The Varieties of Religious Experience.* New York: Random House. 1929.

Josephson, M., *Edison.* New York: McGraw Hill. 1959.

Jung, C. G., *Collected Works.* Princeton, New Jersey: Princeton University Press. 1979.

———— (R. F. Hull, trans.), *Synchronicity as a Causal Connecting Principle.* Bollington Series, Vol. 20. Princeton, New Jersey: Princeton University Press. 1973.

Kelly, V. C., "Affect and Intimacy." *Psychiatric Annals.* No. 23:10, pp. 556–566. October, 1993.

Kendall, H., Kendall, F., Wadsworth, G., *Muscles: Testing and Function.* Baltimore: Williams and Wilkins. 1971.

Kosslyn, S., and Anderson, R. (eds.), *Frontiers in Cognitive Neuroscience.* Cambridge, Massachusetts: MIT Press. 1993.

Krippner, S., *Western Hemisphere Conference on Kirlian Photography.* Garden City, New York. 1974.

Kübler-Ross, E., *On Life after Death.* New York: Celestial Arts. 1991.

————, *Questions and Answers on Death and Dying.* New York: Macmillan. 1993.

Kuhn, T., *The Structure of Scientific Revolutions*. Chicago: University of Chicago Press. 1970.

Laczey, E., *Gandhi: A Man for Humanity*. New York: Hawthorne. 1972.

Lamparski, R., *Lamparski's Hidden Hollywood*. New York: Simon & Schuster. 1981.

Lamsa, G. (trans.), *Holy Bible from Ancient Eastern Manuscripts*. Philadelphia: A.J. Holmes Co. 1957.

Land, G., Jarman, B., *Breakpoint and Beyond*. New York: Harper Business. 1992.

Lee, T. D., *Particle Physics and Introduction to Field Theory*. Switzerland: Harwood Academic Pubs. 1981.

Li, E., and Spiegel, D., "A Neuro Network Model of Associative Disorders." *Psychiatric Annals*. No. 22:3, pp. 144–145. 1992.

Libet, B., *Brain 106*. Pgs. 623–642. University of California at San Francisco Physiology Dept. 1984.

"Life's 100 Most Important Americans of the 20th Century." *Life*. No. 13:12. Fall, 1990.

"Lincoln, Abraham." In *The New Encyclopedia Brittanica*, 15th Ed. Chicago: Encyclopedia Brittanica. 1984.

Loehle, C., "A Guide to Increase Creativity in Research." *Bioscience*. No. 40, pp. 123–129. February 1990.

Lorenz, E. N., "Deterministic Nonperiodic Flow." *Journal of Atmospheric Science*. No. 20, pp. 130–141. 1963.

———, "Predictability: Does the Flap of a Butterfly's Wings Set off a Tornado in Texas?" *American Association for the Advancement of Science*. December 29, 1979.

———, "The Problem of Deducting the Climate from the Governing Equations." *Tellus*. No.16, pp. 1–11. 1964.

Losh, J. P., *Roosevelt and Churchill*. New York: W. W. Norton. 1976.

Lowinsky, E. A., "Musical Genius: Evolution and Origins of a Concept." *Musical Quarterly*. No. 50, pp. 321–340 and 476–495. 1964.

Maharaj, N., *I Am That*, Vols. I and II. Bombay, India: Cetana. 1973.

Maharshi, R., *Talks with Sri Ramana Maharshi*, Vols. I-III. Madras, India: Jupiter Press. 1958.

——— (foreword by Carl Jung), *The Spiritual Teachings of Ramana Maharshi*. Boulder, Colorado: Shambhala. 1972.

Mandelbrodt, G., *The Fractal Geometry of Nature*. New York: W. H. Freeman and Co. 1977.

Mandell, A. J., "From Molecular Biologic Simplification to More Realistic Central Nervous System Dynamics." In Cavenar, et al. (eds.), *Psychiatry: Psychological Foundations of Clinical Psychiatry*. New York: Lippincott. 1985.

Mann, F., *The Meridians of Acupuncture*. London, England: William Heinemann Medical Books Limited. 1974.

Maslow, A. H., *The Farther Reaches of Human Nature*. New York: Viking. 1971.

McAlear, N., "On Creativity." *Omni*. No. 11, pp. 42–44. April 1989.

Mehta, V., *Mahatma Gandhi and His Apostles*. New York: Penguin Books. 1982.

"Mind's Chaotic Periods May Lead to Higher Order." *Brain/Mind Bulletin*. No. 18, p. 12.

Monroe, R., *Journeys Out of the Body*. New York: Anchor/Doubleday. 1971.

"Musical Composition." In *The New Encyclopedia Brittanica*, 15th Edition. Chicago: Encyclopedia Brittanica. 1984.

Nathanson, D. L., "About Einstein" and "Understanding Einstein." *Psychiatric Annals*. No. 23:10, pp. 543–555. October 1993.

Nome, B., *Personal Interviews*. Santa Cruz, California. 1988.

"Nonlinear Analysis Reveals Link Between Heart and Mind." *Brain/Mind Bulletin*. No. 18:12, September 1993.

Peat, F. D., *Artificial Intelligence*. New York: Baen. 1988.

———, "Time, Structure and Objectivity in Quantum Theory." *Foundation of Physics*. December 1988.

Peers, E.A. (trans.), *St. John of the Cross: Ascent of Mount Carmel*. New York: Doubleday. 1958.

Penrose, R., "Quantum Coherence and Consciousness." *Toward a Scientific Basis for Consciousness; an Interdisciplinary Conference*. University of Arizona, Health Sciences Center, Tucson, Arizona, April 12–17, 1994.

Peters, T. J., and Waterman, R. H., *In Search of Excellence*. New York: Warner Books. 1982.

Plato, *The Republic*. In *Great Books of the Western World*. Vol.7. Chicago: Encyclopedia Brittanica, 1952.

Prigogine, I., and Stengers, I., *Order Out of Chaos: Man's New Dialogue with Nature*. Toronto, Canada: Bantam Books. 1984.

Raspberry, W., "Rap Music Shares Same Qualities as Nicotine: Dangerous, Addictive." *The Arizona Republic.* July 4, 1994.

Ray, M., and Rinzler, A. (eds.), *The New Paradigm in Business: Emerging Strategies for Leadership and Organizational Change.* New York: Tarcher/Perigee. 1993.

Redington, D., and Reidbond, S., *Journal of Nervous and Mental Disease.* No. 180, pgs. 649–665; No. 181, pgs. 428–435. 1993.

Ring, K., *Heading Toward Omega.* New York: William Morrow. 1984.

Rosband, S. N., *Chaotic Dynamics of Nonlinear Systems.* New York: John Wiley and Sons. 1990.

Rudolph, S. H., and Rudolph, L. I., *Gandhi: The Traditional Roots of Charisma.* Chicago: University of Chicago Press. 1983.

Ruelle, D., *Chaotic Evolution and Strange Attractors: The Statistical Analysis of Time Series from Deterministic Nonlinear Systems.* New York: Cambridge University Press. 1989.

———, "Strange Attractors." *Mathematical Intelligence.* No. 2, pp. 126–137. 1980.

Schaffer, W. M, and Kot, M., "Do Strange Attractors Govern Ecological Systems?" *Bioscience.* No. 35, p. 349. 1985.

Scott, A., "Hierarchical Organization in the Brain—Emergence of Consciousness." *Toward a Scientific Basis for Consciousness; an Interdisciplinary Conference.* University of Arizona, Health Sciences Center, Tucson, Arizona, April 12–17, 1994.

Sheldrake, R., *A New Science of Life.* London, England: Victoria Works. 1981.

———, Essay in *New Scientist.* No. 90, pp. 749 and 766–768. June 18, 1981.

———, "Formative Causation." Interview in *Brain/Mind Bulletin.* No. 6, p. 13. August 3, 1981.

Simonton, D. K., "What Produces Scientific Genius?" *USA Today.* No. 117, June 11, 1988.

Smale, S., *The Mathematics of Time: Essays on Dynamical Systems.* New York: Springer-Verlag. 1980.

Stewart, H. B., and Thompson, J. M., *Nonlinear Dynamics and Chaos.* New York: John Wiley & Sons. 1986.

Stone, A. M. "Implications of Affect Theory for the Practice of Cognitive Therapy." *Psychiatric Annals.* No. 23:10, pp. 577–583. 1993.

Tcaz, C., and Hawkins, D., "A Preventative Measure for Tardive Dyskinesia." *Journal of Orthomolecular Psychiatry*. No. 10, pp. 120–123. 1981.

Trimble, V., *Sam Walton*. New York: Dutton. 1990.

Tritton, D., "Chaos in the Swing of a Pendulum." *New Scientist*. July 24, 1986.

Tucker, R. C., *Stalin in Power*. New York: W. W. Norton. 1990.

Tuckwell, H. C., *Introduction to Theoretical Neurology: Nonlinear and Stochastic Theories*. New York: Cambridge University Press. 1988.

Varvoglis, M., "Nonlocality on a Human Scale: PSI and Consciousness Research." *Toward a Scientific Basis for Consciousness; an Interdisciplinary Conference*. University of Arizona, Health Sciences Center, Tucson, Arizona, April 12–17, 1994.

Walsh, M. (ed.), *Butler's Lives of the Saints*. New York: Harper & Row. 1985.

Walther, D., *Applied Kinesiology*. Pueblo, Colorado: Systems DC. 1976.

Weisburd, S., "Neural Nets Catch the ABCs of DNA." *Science News*. August 1, 1987.

"What is Consciousness?" Interviews with C. Koch, T. Winograd, and H. P. Moravat. In *Discover*. No. 13, pp. 95–98.

Wilber, K. (ed.), *The Holographic Paradigm and Other Paradoxes: Exploring the Leading Edge of Science*. Boston: Shambhala. 1982.

———, Engler, J., and Brown, D. P., *Transformations of Consciousness*. Boston: Shambhala. 1986.

Winfree, A., "Is It Impossible to 'Measure' Consciousness?" *Toward a Scientific Basis for Consciousness; an Interdisciplinary Conference*. University of Arizona, Health Sciences Center, Tucson, Arizona, April 12–17, 1994.

Wing, R. L., *The Tao of Power: An Introduction to the Tao Te Ching of Lao Tsu*. Garden City, New York: Doubleday. 1986.

Wright, R. L., *Genius and the Mediocracy*. New York: Drell, Sloan, and Pierce. 1949.

Yorke, J. A., and Tien-Yien, L., "Period Three Implies Chaos." *American Math Monthly*. No. 82, pp. 985–992. 1975.

Zukav, G., *The Dancing Wu-Li Masters: An Overview of the New Physics*. New York: Bantam. 1982.

INDEX

A

Abraham, 273
Academy of Preventive
    Medicine, 57
Acceptance, level of, 87
acupuncture, 64, 210
acupuncture meridians,
    56, 216–217
addiction, 81, 90,
    103–109, 265, 289
addictive substance, 104
advertising, 80, and desire,
    81
AIDS, 216
Alcoholics Anonymous,
    137, 181ff, 219, 259,
    264
allergies, 58, 111
ambiguity (in testing), 117
American Revolution, 151
anabolic stimuli, 30
Anger, level of, 82
anguish of the soul, 263
anti-drug programs, 109
Apathy, level of, 78
applied kinesiology, 2, 57
architecture, 55, 93, 100,
    192–193

art, 31, 55, 93, 100,
    189–191
artificial high, 106
artificial intelligence, 41,
    45, 51, 136
artificial sweetener, 3, 4,
    59, 212
astrology, 228
athletics, 171ff
attractor fields, 31, 42, 52,
    53, 102, 115, 145,
    161, 261
attractors, 29, 42
avatar, 94, 261, 282
awareness, 21, 28, 247

B

Bannister, R., 137, 172
behavioral kinesiology, 3,
    33, 58, 65
Bell's Theorem, 136
Bhagavad Gita, 14, 275
Big Blue, The, 173
Bill W., 137, 185–186,
    219, 259, 264
binary response, 6
biochemical pathway, 59

birth level of consciousness, 101
bliss, state of, 19, 92
Bohm, D., 50, 136, 250
Bohr, N., 48
brain function, 51, 59
Briggs, J., 141
British Empire, 72–73, 152
Buddha, 13, 94, 261, 273, 275
Buddhism, 273
business analysis, 121

C

Calcutta, 79
calibrated scale of truth, 6,
    30–31
calibration, 6–7, 30, 36–37, 52,
    55, 60ff, 75, 102, 115
Camelback Hospital, 265
capital punishment, 78, 280
Capra, F., 256
catabolic stimuli, 30
causality, 26, 27, 46, 49–50, 72,
    89, 139, 166, 205, 228,
    244
chakras, 263
channelers, 126
chaos, 42, 114, 191
chaos theory, 31, 33, 41, 51–52,
    138ff
chiropractic, 210
choice (and evolution), 102
Christianity, 272–273
Christmas Carol, A, 129
Churchill, W., 153, 156
clinical addiction, 104

closure, 32, 145
collective level of unconscious-
    ness, 85, 128
communism, 152, 154, 199
computer games, 278
conference on consciousness
    (April 1994), 254–255
consciousness, 26, 29, 43, 53
Constitution, U.S., 120, 131,
    156, 158, 180
constraint satisfaction systems,
    51
Council of Nicea, 272
counterbalance, 95, 282
Courage, level of, 70, 84
Course in Miracles, A, 267, 273
crime, 25, 103
critical level, 84, 95
critical point analysis, 45,
    48–49, 115ff

D

declarative statement, 61
denial, 83, 186, 246, 289
depression, 59, 79, 134, 278
Descartes, R., 99, 250, 268, 281
Desire, level of, 81
desynchronization, 60, 276
Diamond, J., 3–5, 29–30, 58,
    60, 64–65, 264
disease process, 42, 215ff
diseases (chronic or progres-
    sive), 78
distribution of levels of
    consciousness, 236

divine grace, level of, 94
divinity, 7, 54, 92, 93–94, 261
divorce, 72, 211
double-blind studies, 123

E

Earhart, Amelia, 119
Ebby (Edwin T.), 184–185
Eccles, J., 54
Edison, T., 109
ego, 54, 83, 204, 291
Einstein, A., 48, 89, 99, 136,
    196, 268, 281, Theory of
    Relativity, 136
emergency emotions, 210
emotional stimuli, 3
Empire State Building, 136, 139,
    229–230
energy fields, 31, 45, 51, 53,
    75ff
enfolded universe, 136, 139,
    195, 250
enlightenment, 7, 37, 52, 65,
    70, 93–94, 129, 233, 254,
    259, 265, 287
Enlightenment, level of, 93
entrainment, 245, 262, 264
epistemology, 28, 33, 111ff
evolution of consciousness, 26,
    51, 71, 91ff, 96, 101, 114,
    235ff, 292
explicate order, 50

F

false negative response, 64
Fear, level of, 80
field of dominance, 48
fractal, 42
Freud, S., 76, 89, 99, 123, 268,
    281
fundamentalism, 112, 273, 274

G

Gandhi, M., 73, 132, 152, 157
Gettysburg Address, 156–157
Goodheart, G., 2, 29, 56–57
Gorbachev, M., 116, 154, 156,
    198
Great Teachers, 93, 141, 255
Grief, level of, 79–80
Guilt, level of, 77–78

H

healing, 73, 91
heavy metal, 5, 124, 265
Heisenberg, W., 48
high state, 104–107
Hinduism, 273
Hitler, A., 61, 153
holistic practitioners, 58, 60,
    258
holographic universe, 50, 54,
    239
Huang Po, 13

I

implicate order, 50
India, 72, 125
infinite peace, 94, 106
innocence of consciousness, 247
intellectual stimuli, 3
International College of Applied
    Kinesiology, 57, 111
IQ, 201
irregular response, 63
Islam, 274

J

James, W., 185, 253, 257
Joy, level of, 91–92
Judaism, 273–274
Jung, C., 5, 184, 191, 220, 227,
    259

K

Kabbalah, the, 274
Kendall, H., 3
kinesiology (muscle testing), 2,
    29, 41–42, 43, 56ff, 111,
    116, 251
Kirlian photography, 258
Koko, 280
Koran, the, 274
Krishna, 94, 273, 275
Kübler-Ross, E., 258

L

Lamsa translation (New Testa-
    ment), 272
left-brain, 32, 33, 53, 135, 139,
    164, 269
Lenin, V., 116
Lincoln, A., 61, 157
logarithmic progression, 75, 102
logical empiricism, 135
Lorenz, E., 46
Lost Horizon, 105
Love, level of, 89–91
low self-esteem, 76
LSD, 105

M

M-fields, 136–137, 148, 256
magnetic field, 48
Maharaja, N., 14
Maharshi, R., 14
Mandela, N., 152
Mann, F., 57
map of consciousness, 7, 67ff
market analysis, 110, 121
martial arts, 174, 177
Maslow, A., 257
materials research, 109
Mayol, J., 173
Meister Eckhart, 273
Michelangelo, 190
mind, 44, 54, 248
Mohammed, 274
Morales, P., 174
moralism, 281

Moses, 273–274
Moss, T., 258
Mother Teresa, 79, 126
mudra, 94
mystics, 7,138, 230

N

near-death experience, 92, 105,
   148, 258
negative influence, 70, 84
neural networks, 51
neurophysiologic modeling, 51
Neutrality, level of, 85–86
Newton, I., 33, 42, 48, 99, 228,
   268
Nobel Prize, 89, 126, 154
nonlinear dynamics, 29, 33,
   41–43, 45, 51, 138ff, 236
numerical scale, 61, 65, 67ff
nutritional supplements, 2, 111

O

Olympics, 174ff
ontology, 33, 232
organic food, 63
Ornstein, R., 256

P

paradigm blindness, 257
paradoxical response, 64
parapsychology, 257

pattern recognition, 28, 32, 34
Pauling, L., 13, 59
Peace, level of, 92–93
perennial philosophy, 31, 65
phase space, 51
philosophy, 111ff
physical stimuli, 3
positive influence, 70, 84
positivism, 135
possession, 290
poverty, 78, 103, 252
Pribram, K., 54
Pride, level of, 82–83
product development, 109–110
progression of consciousness,
   100ff, 285
psychiatry, 11, 43, 59, 257
psychics, 126
psychological stimuli, 38
psychopharmacology, 43
psychosomatic disease, 77
public office, 118, 238
pure states, 76, 104

Q

quantum mechanics, 41
quantum nonlocality, 123
questioning process, 117

R

Reason, level of, 88–89
reflexology, 210
replicability, 56, 58

reprogramming, 105
responsibility for others, 87, 92
right-brain, 32, 138, 191
RJR Nabisco Holdings Corp.,
    109
Rowland, H., 184–185, 220,
    259

S

Saint Francis of Assisi, 266
saints, 7, 14, 91, 262
salvation of humanity, 70, 114,
    290
samadhi, 105
Satanism, 276ff
self-help groups, 71, 91, 181ff,
    210, 211, 259, 260,
    263–264
sexual abuse, 75, 277, repressed
    childhood memories of, 123
Shame, level of, 76–77
Shangri-La, 105
Sheldrake, R., 54, 137
Silkworth, W., 185
Socrates, 288
South Africa, 152
spiritual blindness, 280, 288
spiritual evolution, 106, 268
spiritual teachers, 71, 92, 125,
    256, 269
spiritus mundi, 5
spontaneous cure, 218ff
Stalin, J., 116, 153, 154
Stewart, I., 256
strange attractors, 47, 52

stress, 72, 211
Sufi dancers, 174
suicide, 76, 78, 134, 242
Supreme Court, U.S., 89, 98

T

tardive dyskinesia, 213
theology, 111ff, 232
theoretical physics, 31, 41, 48,
    136, 148, 245, 285
Third Reich, 141
thymic dominance, 64
thymus thump, 64
Tiebout, H., 219
Torah, the, 274
Trimble, V., 162
Trotsky, L., 116
turbulence, 33, 217
TV, 81, 97, 278
type A personality, 215

U

unconditional love, 71, 90–91,
    177, 193, 223, 262
unfolded universe, 136, 250
United Nations, 128
United States Marine Corps, 82
University of Arizona, 255

V

victim (role), 72, 77, 87, 221,
    238

Vietnam War, 236
vitamin C, 59, 119, 212

W

Wal-Mart, 162–163, 164
Walther, D., 57
Walton, S., 162
war, 28, 83, 154, 169
welfare emotions, 210
white supremacism, 287
Willingness, level of, 86–87

X

x-rays, 136, 187, 289

Z

Zen, 196, 238, 273
Zohar, the, 274

OTHER HAY HOUSE TITLES
OF RELATED INTEREST

Books

Absolute Happiness: The Way to a Life of Complete Fulfillment,
by Michael Domeyko Rowland

*The Body "Knows": How to Tune In to Your Body and Improve
Your Health,* by Caroline Sutherland, Medical Intuitive

Infinite Self: 33 Steps to Reclaiming Your Inner Power,
by Stuart Wilde

The Reconnection: Heal Others, Heal Yourself, by Dr. Eric Pearl

Sanctuary: The Path to Consciousness,
by Stephen Lewis and Evan Slawson

Audios

The Conscious Universe, by Deepak Chopra, M.D.

The Expectant Universe, by James Redfield (with Michael Toms)

Science and Soul: The Survival of Consciousness After Death, by
Gary Schwartz, Ph.D., and Deepak Chopra, M.D.

There Is a Spiritual Solution to Every Problem (book, 6-tape set,
6-CD set. or video), by Dr. Wayne W. Dyer

All of the above are available at your local bookstore,
or may be ordered through Hay House, Inc.:

(800) 654-5126 or (760) 431-7695
(800) 650-5115 (fax) or (760) 431-6948 (fax)
www.hayhouse.com

ABOUT THE AUTHOR

David R. Hawkins, M.D., Ph.D., has practiced psychiatry since 1952, and is a life member of the American Psychiatric Association. A widely respected therapist and lecturer, his national television appearances include *The MacNeil/Lehrer News Hour*, *The Barbara Walters Show*, and the *Today* show. He has published numerous scientific papers and videotapes, and co-authored the book *Orthomolecular Psychiatry* with Nobelist Linus Pauling. His diverse background as a researcher and teacher is noted in his biographical listing in *Who's Who in America*.

Dr. Hawkins currently divides his time between his practice, books in progress, and direction of The Institute for Advanced Theoretical Research in rural Arizona.

✝ ✝ ✝

The author was Knighted for this work by the Danish Crown. Officiated October 1996 by Crown Prince Valdemor into the Sovereign order of St. John of Jerusalem (established in the year A.D. 1070).

✝ ✝ ✝

For additional materials, literature, lecture schedule, or videos, contact:

The Institute for Advanced
Spiritual Research
P.O. Box 3516
West Sedona, AZ 86340
Phone: (928) 282-8722
Fax: (928) 282-4789
www.veritaspub.com

Sign up via the Hay House USA Website to receive the Hay House online newsletter and stay informed about what's going on with your favorite authors. You'll receive bimonthly announcements about: Discounts and Offers, Special Events, Product Highlights, Free Excerpts, Giveaways, and more!

◉ ◎ ◉

We hope you enjoyed this Hay House book.
If you would like to receive a free catalog featuring
additional Hay House books and products, or if you
would like information about the Hay Foundation,
please contact:

Hay House, Inc.
P.O. Box 5100
Carlsbad, CA 92018-5100

(760) 431-7695 or (800) 654-5126
(760) 431-6948 (fax) or (800) 650-5115 (fax)
www.hayhouse.com

✤ ✤ ✤

Published and distributed in Australia by:
Hay House Australia, Ltd., 18/36 Ralph St., Alexandria NSW
2015 • *Phone:* 612-9669-4299 • *Fax:* 612-9669-4144
www.hayhouse.com.au

Published and Distributed in the United Kingdom by:
Hay House UK, Ltd. • Unit 202, Canalot Studios
222 Kensal Rd., London W10 5BN
Phone: 44-20-8962-1230 • *Fax:* 44-20-8962-1239
www.hayhouse.co.uk

Distributed in Canada by:
Raincoast • 9050 Shaughnessy St., Vancouver, B.C. V6P 6E5
Phone: (604) 323-7100 • *Fax:* (604) 323-2600

◉ ◎ ◉